CW00385677

The Lord Chamberlain's Blue Pencil

JOHN JOHNSTON

The Lord Chamberlain's Blue Pencil

Hodder & Stoughton
LONDON SYDNEY AUCKLAND TORONTO

British Library Cataloguing in Publication Data

Johnston, John
The Lord Chamberlain's blue pencil.
1. England. Theatre. Censorship, history
I. Title
792

ISBN 0-340-52529-0

First published in Great Britain 1990

Published by Hodder and Stoughton,
a division of Hodder and Stoughton Ltd,
Mill Road, Dunton Green, Sevenoaks, Kent TN13 2YA
Editorial Office: 47 Bedford Square, London WC1B 3DP

Photoset by Rowland Phototypesetting Ltd,
Bury St Edmunds, Suffolk
Printed in Great Britain by
St Edmundsbury Press Ltd, Bury St Edmunds, Suffolk

This book is dedicated
to the Lord Chamberlains
who wielded the blue pencil
and
to their Examiners of Plays

Contents

APPENDIXES

Illustrations in Text

Acknowledgements for the photographs:

The portraits of Viscount Sandhurst, the Duke of Atholl and the Earl of Cromer are copyright reserved and reproduced by gracious permission of Her Majesty the Queen. The portraits of the Earl of Clarendon, and of the Earl of Scarbrough are reproduced respectively by permission of the present Earls; and the picture of Lord Cobbold by permission of Hermione, Lady Cobbold.

Acknowledgements

I am particularly grateful to Her Majesty The Queen for allowing me to research in and quote from the records of the Lord Chamberlain's Office and to have access to certain material in the Royal Archives.

The present Lord Chamberlain, the Earl of Airlie, has given me much encouragement; and I have been glad of the help of Sir Eric Penn, my predecessor as Assistant Comptroller and then Comptroller, and of John Titman, Secretary, Lord Chamberlain's Office, in supplementing my memories of the censorship.

Geoffrey Dearmer (aged ninety-six) and Tim Harward, the surviving Examiners of Plays, have been a wonderful source of information, with clear memories of the past, and their eager and willing help I have very much appreciated. I am also grateful to Geoffrey Dearmer for allowing me to print his ode to 'Those poor damned plays' at the end of the book.

Both Elizabeth Cuthbert (former Registrar), Sheila de Bellaigue (present Registrar) and others patiently coped with many demands I made on the Royal Archives in Windsor Castle. Oliver Everett (Librarian) was tasked to 'censor' the manuscript and Bridget Wright (bibliographer in the Royal Library) gave me much valuable help.

The late Lord Cobbold, during his time as Lord Chamberlain, brought the censorship to a satisfactory conclusion. Lord Airlie, the present Lord Chamberlain, said to me recently, referring to the censorship, 'If it hadn't been for Kim I would be in treacle.'

A few weeks before his death in 1987, Kim Cobbold wrote in answer to a letter of mine, 'Of course I will give you any help I can over your book.' His widow, Hermione, took on his offer and generously gave me, and allowed me to reproduce, a valuable memorandum which Lord Cobbold had written for his own family.

The present Earls of Cromer, Clarendon and Scarbrough have also given me helpful information about their forebears. Mrs Jean Anderson, the Duke of Atholl's archivist, provided me with some information about the 8th Duke who was Lord Chamberlain in 1922. I am, indeed, most grateful to them all.

I am glad to acknowledge the assistance I have received from the Home Office and the Crown Prosecution Service.

Michael Borrie, the Manuscripts Librarian of the British Library, has been particularly helpful. The Library now has in its possession the original scripts of all plays submitted for licence since 1900, and will in due course be receiving the correspondence relating to these plays.

I owe a debt of thanks to Kay Hutchings, Librarian at the Garrick Club, for giving me access to that library; to Enid Foster, Head Librarian of the British Theatre Association; and to Dr David Menhennett of the House of Commons Library.

I wrote to all the surviving members of the 1966–7 Joint Committee on Theatre Censorship and I acknowledge their help; also the assistance given me by Lord Jenkins of Hillhead, who, as Home Secretary at the time, played a key role in bringing about the 1968 Theatres Act.

I am grateful to Sir Julian Paget for his initial encouragement; and during the writing of the book I had most interesting discussions and/or correspondence with John Arden, Michael Codron, Lucy Fleming, William Gaskill, Lord (Bernard) Miles and Timothy West. I am indebted to all of them for their contributions.

As for the publication of the book, my thanks go to Michael Shaw, my agent; to Ion Trewin and John Bright-Holmes of Hodder and Stoughton who pointed me in the right direction; and to the late J. C. Trewin, whose encyclopaedic knowledge of the theatre saved me from a number of pitfalls.

I owe a debt of thanks, too, to Sukie Hay and Anne Harris who had the unenviable task of interpreting my handwriting and committing it to the word processor, a machine I shied away from using.

This book could not have been written without the exceptional assistance I have had from Mary Fisher, the play readers' clerk in the Lord Chamberlain's Office, 1960–68, who, as my researcher, spent endless hours in the cellars of St James's Palace foraging amongst the records of the Lord Chamberlain's Office and invariably surfacing with just the right document.

I would like to acknowledge the permission to use various quotations from Bernard Shaw's letters and articles granted by the Society of Authors on behalf of the Bernard Shaw Estate.

The Prince of Wales and his Household, who now occupy the premises that were once those of the Lord Chamberlain's Office, generously allowed me the use of a room at St James's Palace in which I was able to work undisturbed.

Finally, my thanks to my wife are incalculable for, despite her ill-health, she has encouraged me to stick to the task.

None of these people who have helped me bears responsibility, which is, of course, mine, for the facts and the opinions given in the text.

I should add, that, since most of my written evidence has come from the files of the Lord Chamberlain's Office, I have not presented a formal bibliography. I have, though, had recourse to many books to help give added background to the story, and these I have mentioned at the appropriate point in the text.

Author's Preface

In 1987, shortly before I was to retire as Comptroller of the Lord Chamberlain's Office, Michael Shaw of Curtis Brown suggested that a book telling the story of the Lord Chamberlain as censor of plays should be written before the Lord Chamberlain's theatre records were made available to the public. I welcomed this idea, but it was never my intention to write a formal, definitive or comprehensive book on the subject. Two such have already been published, namely L. W. Connolly's *Censorship of English Drama 1737–1824* and J. R. Stephens' *Censorship of English Drama 1824–1901*; and there are several others which are mentioned in the text.

The book does draw, however, on original source material as well as on my own experiences. Except for the playscripts, which are now in the British Library, all other material relating to the Lord Chamberlain's role as the censor of plays (including correspondence relating to plays) is included in the records of the Lord Chamberlain's Office which, from 1900, have been housed in St James's Palace and have never been opened for historical or other research. I have been allowed to research this archive for the greater part of the book which is devoted to the period since 1900.

Although I have attempted to show how the censorship came into being, I am more concerned with how the system worked over the years and with the powers of the Lord Chamberlain as 'the nation's conscience', especially when, in the later twentieth century, attitudes changed, and the problems became larger, more complex and more diverse. I have not, however, set out to argue for or against the censorship. Some authors have chosen the latter course, but it seems to me, having worked on the inside, that it is very easy to overstate the case against the censorship.

Parliament's requirement of the Lord Chamberlain was twofold. Not only was he the censor of plays but it was his duty to license the London theatres and a few others as well, such as the Theatre Royal, Windsor. Except for passing references, I have excluded this latter duty from the story.

From its infancy this book has been named 'The Blue Pencil'. But how did a blue pencil come to be associated with censorship? I am grateful to Frank Muir and Philip Howard for telling me that it was in use in the late nineteenth century. For example, in the *New York Herald* of 1888: 'The editor of the Century Magazine blue pencils magazine articles by the bushel'.

Rudyard Kipling in *Many Inventions* (1893) wrote, 'The blue pencil plunged remorselessly through the script'. And in the *Daily News* in 1899 there appears: 'The actor will have a better chance after the blue pencil has eliminated the unnecessary verbiage in the dialogue'.

In an obituary of E. F. S. Pigott, an Examiner of Plays, in 1895 there is a reference to his 'kindly blue pencil'; and Clement Scott (drama critic, 1841–1904) used the same phrase in 1892 when he wrote,

> The laws of decency and order must be administered by someone, and it is far better to check before than to correct after. The preliminary stroke of the kindly blue pencil in a tentative play or sketch is better than the spreading of objectionable matter. Hundreds of ears may be poisoned before the remedy is found.

And, of course, in the two world wars service letters sent home were censored, for security reasons, with a blue pencil. No doubt too there are still some people who can recall how the late Jack Warner extracted a lot of fun from 'the blue pencil' in the Second World War radio show *Garrison Theatre*.

The Theatres Act 1843 required only one copy of a new play to be submitted to the Lord Chamberlain. However, many theatre managers used to send two copies, asking for one to be returned showing, where necessary, any cuts required by the Lord Chamberlain. These deletions were invariably made with a blue pencil by Ruth Webster, who was the play readers' clerk from 1918–60; but I feel sure there were blue pencils in regular use in the Lord Chamberlain's Office well before then.

Prologue

On the first Friday in July, 1964, I was in Germany saying goodbye to a battalion of Grenadiers, which I had commanded for two years. I was leaving the Army.

The following Monday I was back in England and spending my first day in the Lord Chamberlain's Office, St James's Palace, London. It was quite a change.

I was there to succeed Lieutenant-Colonel Eric Penn as the Assistant Comptroller for he had been appointed Comptroller in place of Brigadier Sir Norman Gwatkin who was retiring.

During the next four weeks I was involved in a state visit to London of the President of the Sudan, and attended on duty three garden parties and two investitures at Buckingham Palace, learning my new job. The Lord Chamberlain's Office, or LCO as it is referred to, is one of the departments of the Queen's Household, and is responsible for such ceremonial occasions; but I soon found that it was concerned with other duties of a diverse nature which included arranging royal weddings and funerals, administering the royal palaces and the Royal Collection, awarding royal warrants, and even looking after the Queen's swans.

These duties are carried out for the Queen. In 1964 the LCO had one other function with which I became personally involved – the licensing of plays and theatres. This was a public duty carried out by authority of Parliament. I discovered that we were administering the Theatres Act of 1843 which required the Lord Chamberlain to license a new play before it could be publicly performed on the stage.

When I joined the Lord Chamberlain's Office I found that a new play sent in was immediately given to one of the

Examiners of Plays (usually referred to by us as play readers). It was the reader's job to read the play, write a synopsis of the story, and to draw attention to any possibly doubtful or offensive scenes, language or 'business'. Finally, he was to recommend whether or not the play should be licensed. My task, as Assistant Comptroller, was to endorse – or otherwise – the play reader's recommendation before passing it to the Lord Chamberlain himself, whose responsibility it was to give or withhold a licence.

I always read the reader's synopsis as well as those play scripts which the readers asked me to examine, and others where I considered that a second opinion might be helpful to the Lord Chamberlain. The scripts which presented no problems – and these were the majority – were first initialled by me and then by the Lord Chamberlain and a licence was issued (see page 67). In those texts where attention had been drawn to certain language or 'business' I would mark the passages – 'leave', 'cut' or 'alter' as appropriate – and the Lord Chamberlain would concur or otherwise.

With plays where the reader called for considerable alterations the Lord Chamberlain would read the scripts himself and frequently discuss them with me and the reader. After that I would convey the Lord Chamberlain's decision to the applicant in a letter which usually read:

> I am desired by the Lord Chamberlain to inform you that he regrets he must disallow . . . those parts detailed in the annexure to this letter. An undertaking that these disallowances will be observed must be submitted before a licence for the play can be issued.
>
> Should you wish to make any substitutions these should be submitted to the Lord Chamberlain before they can be included in the manuscript.

In most cases the applicant would agree to the cuts or provide acceptable substitutions. Alternatively, it was open to the manager of the theatre, or the producer or director of the play, to come and discuss these points with us, and often the author would come too. I always welcomed and enjoyed these talks as they gave me a better insight into plays and playwrights; and they were remarkably friendly occasions. On our side we made every effort to reach an agreement; on their side they were often able to adapt their work to meet the Lord Chamberlain's requirements. There was a good deal of give and take.

The Lord Chamberlain's decision, as stated in the Theatres Act 1843, was in all cases final; however, he regarded himself as the licensor of plays rather than as a censor, and he considered it his duty to allow all plays submitted to him unless there seemed to be clear and unmistakable reasons to disallow them. As Lord Cobbold (the last Lord Chamberlain to administer the 1843 Act) put it when he was interviewed by J. W. Lambert of the *Sunday Times* in April 1965, his bias was

> always to give a licence unless there is very strong ground for objection. My personal objective is to try to assess the norm of educated, adult opinion and if possible to keep just a touch ahead of it.

The licensing of a script as prescribed by the 1843 Act appeared to be the only practicable and economic method of control. Examination of plays in production would have been an impossibly broad task. By comparison censorship of the screen seems much more straightforward, for the Theatres Act gave the Lord Chamberlain no authority to attach any conditions to a licence, such as allowing it only to be performed by a particular company or, as in the cinema, only to be seen by a particular audience. Nor did it protect the author, producer, manager or actor from possible charges of libel or slander.

From time to time I, or others from the LCO, would go and see a play officially. This could be at the request of the theatre manager, or because of a letter of complaint from a member of the public, and sometimes this resulted in our sending a reminder that the script *as licensed* must be adhered to in performance. Often, too, I would go out of personal interest and hoping to confirm our belief that a correct decision had been made! There were some rare occasions when the help of the police and the Director of Public Prosecutions and his staff had to be called upon, and these I will describe later in this book which aims to show how successive Lord Chamberlains – mainly during the present century – administered the Theatres Act of 1843 until it was superseded by the Act of 1968.

This latter Act brought the work of the Lord Chamberlain's Office in supervising the theatre to a close by blue-pencilling, so to speak, the Lord Chamberlain's blue pencil. Since 1968 the theatre has been free of any form of censorship other than the laws of the land common to us all.

But why was it, I asked whcn I became part of this team, that the Lord Chamberlain, who is head of the Sovereign's Household, was the licensor of plays? Why did drama have to be singled out for this apparently autocratic treatment? How and why did it all start?

Chapter One

Curtain Up on the Censorship

To begin with, the censorship, such as it was, was exercised by the Master of the Revels, an officer of the King's Court under the control of the Lord Chamberlain. He was first appointed by Henry VII (1485–1509) to supervise the players, singers and jugglers who provided amusements for the Court, and to ensure that they performed in an orderly manner and gave no offence to the King.

Under Henry VII, the Master of the Revels was only a minor official, but in the succeeding, more stabilised reign of Henry VIII, who enjoyed entertainments and wrote music himself, celebrations featured more prominently at Court and by 1524 the office of Master of the Revels had become important enough for a Yeoman of the Revels to be appointed to serve under him. As time went on, the work expanded further.

In 1549, after the Duke of Somerset, Lord Protector during Edward VI's reign, was overthrown, plays and interludes (short pieces played between the acts of a long play) were prohibited throughout the realm for three months, as they were seen to be seditious. Three years later a special licence of the Privy Council was declared necessary for any dramatic performance.

At the start of their reigns, Mary and Elizabeth both issued proclamations asserting their control of plays; and in 1559 Mayors and Justices of the Peace were commanded to ensure that no plays with a religious or political theme be performed. This was later amended to allow for such plays so long as there was not critical content. Queen Elizabeth and the Lord Chamberlain (and individual peers like the Earl of Leicester) had their own companies of players who went on tour just as did the Queen and the Court.

St James's Palace – which housed the Lord Chamberlain's Office from *c*. 1760 until 1988 – in a coloured engraving (1817) by Charles Wild (1781–1835). Published in *The History of the Royal Residences*, by W. H. Pyne (1819)

The responsibilities of the Master of the Revels as censor and licensor were initially confined to the Court, but in 1581 Elizabeth authorised Edmund Tilney, the holder of the post, to be responsible for the performance of plays anywhere. He was then allowed to earn fees for approving manuscripts, but his principal function does not appear to have been in any way to act as a public guardian of morals. His job was to protect royal interests.

James I carried the protection of royal interests a stage further by having an Act of Parliament passed to control the stage: 'To restrain the abuses of players . . . for preventing and avoiding of the great abuse of the Holy Name of God in Stage Plays, Enterludes, May-Games, Shews, and such like.'

By the time Sir Henry Herbert was appointed by Charles I, the Master of the Revels was claiming the right through the Royal Prerogative to license every kind of public entertainment throughout the land. For example, the King had a company of young actors known as the Cockpit Actors and certain plays belonging to them were not allowed to be performed by other companies. When, in 1640, they put on a play which the Master of the Revels had not licensed they 'were restrained from doing so in the future'.

During the Commonwealth, in 1648, all royal patents and licences from the Master of the Revels were declared abolished and playhouses in or near London were pulled down. A few performances of plays were given in secret, but an actor caught performing was punished. However, with the Restoration the theatre came into its own again. In 1660 Charles II issued patents to Thomas Killigrew and William D'Avenant to build and manage theatres and to license their own plays. Killigrew built the Theatre Royal, Drury Lane, and his company, known as The King's Men, performed both at Court and in the theatre. D'Avenant built the Haymarket Theatre. Both these theatres became known as the Patent Theatres. There was argument between the Master of the Revels (still Sir Henry Herbert), who sought fees for performances of plays at these theatres, and Killigrew and D'Avenant who refused to pay such fees as they had patents to license their own plays. This resulted in the powers of censorship virtually passing from the Master of the Revels to Thomas Killigrew.

The few plays that were prohibited in the reigns of Charles II and James II were not banned for moral reasons, but for political or religious ones, or, as in 1665, when during the Great Plague, Charles II made an order to stop plays being performed in order to prevent public gatherings.

Curiously it was Thomas Killigrew who was appointed to succeed Herbert as Master of the Revels on his death in 1673. Killigrew died ten years later and was succeeded by two of his sons in turn. In 1709 the managers of both Patent Theatres were warned that all their plays were to be relicensed by the Master of the Revels, then Thomas Killigrew the younger.

In 1696 it was recorded that 'All Plays [were] to be sent to the Master of the Revels to be licensed and his fees paid under penalty of silence'; and in 1699 William III issued a 'Notice to the Master of the Revels not to license any Play containing expressions contrary to Good Manners and should the Comedians presume to act anything he has struck out, notice is to be given to the Lord Chamberlain'. This was a sign that the Lord Chamberlain was taking greater control, especially of religious and political issues which continued to be his main concern. His powers derived, of course, from the Royal Prerogative – that is, by right of the sovereign and subject to no restriction.

Enter Walpole, stage right

After the Revolution of 1688 the delicate balance between the Whigs and the Tories led to an increase in the number of political pamphlets and plays. During Sir Robert Walpole's premiership, which began in 1720, the system of government by which he maintained control of Parliament was constantly attacked from the stage. John Gay's *The Beggar's Opera* (1728) was a thinly concealed onslaught on Walpole, suggesting that his dealings with public money were indistinguishable from those of highwaymen and thieves, while Henry Fielding's *The Historic Register for the Year 1736* particularly infuriated Walpole as a character called Quidam (meaning, a certain somebody) appeared to be a caricature of himself.

Walpole had become so unpopular a Prime Minister that a number of the opposition playwrights even enjoyed royal patronage. He therefore hurried through Parliament the Stage Licensing Act of 1737 which, for the first time, gave the Lord Chamberlain a statutory function. The Act required that all new plays, and additions to old plays, were to be submitted to the Lord Chamberlain at least fourteen days before the first performance, stating where that performance was to take place. It gave the Lord Chamberlain power to license and to withhold a licence, and theatre managers stood to lose £50 *and* their theatre licence if they defied His Lordship. Furthermore the Lord Chamberlain did not have to give a reason for withholding a licence, nor was there any appeal against his decision.

Incidentally, the term 'legitimate theatre' derives from this Act of 1737 where it says that plays could 'legitimately' only be staged in the Patent Theatres and not in the illegitimate playhouses springing up in London.

One man who bitterly opposed the Act was Lord Chesterfield who, in a stirring speech in the House of Lords, said:

> Do not let us subject them [authors] to the arbitrary will and pleasure of any one man. A power lodged in the hands of one single man, to judge and determine, without any limitation, without any control or appeal, is a sort of power unknown to our laws, inconsistent with our constitution. It is a higher, a more absolute power than we trust even to the King himself; and, therefore, I must think, we ought not to vest any such power in his Majesty's Lord Chamberlain.

Stemming from the Act was the appointment of an Examiner of Plays, whose function was similar to that once exercised by the Master of the Revels. The Act gave no guidance, however, to the Lord Chamberlain or his Examiner as to what they should or should not allow on the stage. As a result they made up their own rules as they went along. One such area was political censorship and another was satirical attacks on prominent people, as part of which mimicry on the stage was specifically outlawed.

For a couple of years after the Act was passed Walpole

continued to be the subject of personal and political lampoons. However, by the time he resigned in 1742 the censorship was becoming established and in the next fifty years little political censorship needed to be exercised. Even the press became almost silent on the subject, although there were complaints that the Lord Chamberlain was not being strict enough in matters of morality and language.

High society scandals were often used in a disguised way by playwrights, but the higher the society the greater the protection was likely to be given by the Lord Chamberlain. In the play *She Would Be A Duchess*, the story was told of one Elizabeth Gunning which involved the family of a former Lord Chamberlain, the fourth Duke of Marlborough, and this play was refused a licence. Elizabeth Gunning, born in Ireland, came to London in 1751 with the intention of going on the stage. She made quite an impact on London society and married, first, the Duke of Hamilton and, second, the future Duke of Argyll.

A Lord Chamberlain who took a real interest in the theatre was the Marquess of Hertford (1766–83). He read a large number of playscripts and would seek the advice of such men as Horace Walpole. When an Examiner recommended that a licence be refused his advice was usually accepted by the Lord Chamberlain, but a notable exception was Sheridan's *The School for Scandal* (1777) when Lord Hertford overruled the puritanical advice of Edward Capell, the Deputy Examiner.

In 1790 the managers of Covent Garden and Drury Lane theatres petitioned King George III for permission to open more theatres. The number had been reduced to two by Act of Parliament in the previous reign because so many licentious farces were being put on. Meanwhile the population had grown, and the surviving theatres had become, in the managers' opinion, almost too respectable. Part of the petition read:

> from hence tis Evident 'twas the licentious use and abuse of the Stage that was the real Cause of the Restraint by wh only Two Theatres were from that time permitted, and those under ye immediate Inspection of the Ld Chamberlain, whose licence must give sanction to every piece before

> it can appear: this restriction has totally suppressed every abuse nay it has even banished every indelicacy . . . – the Stage at this day is so Chaste, that it is become a School of Morality.

During the later years of George III's life, when he was mentally ill, the Lord Chamberlain let it be known to theatre managers that it would be in poor taste to put on Shakespeare's *King Lear*. The two marriages of the Prince of Wales, later George IV, caused a good deal of scandal and had the Examiners of Plays looking with special care at any scripts that featured bigamy or divorce.

By the early 1800s, in fact, public opinion had become so keen on moral propriety in plays that the Lord Chamberlain had little censoring to do. One exception, which was banned because of its bawdy language, was Shelley's *The Cenci*.

In 1832 a Select Committee on Dramatic Literature met under the chairmanship of Edward Bulwer-Lytton (later Baron Lytton). The Committee suggested no changes to the current system of theatre censorship (i.e., it recommended that censorship should continue and that the Lord Chamberlain should continue to be censor), yet only a few years were to elapse before a change *was* made.

Theatres Act, 1843

In 1843 the government, headed by Sir Robert Peel, passed in Parliament a new Theatres Act. Its full title was the Theatres Act of 1843 (6 & 7 Vict., C.A.P. 68), and it repealed all previous acts relating to the control of the stage, and consolidated the law on the whole subject, including the Stage Licensing Act of 1737. In fact, it did little more than confirm the Lord Chamberlain's censorship powers although it did give him greater authority over the licensing of theatres.

The 1843 Act – which applied to England, Scotland and Wales but not to Northern Ireland – contains twenty-five sections of which the most important is Section 12. This required, as had the 1737 Act, that one copy of every new stage play, or of an alteration to an old play, intended to be produced or 'acted for hire' at any theatre in Great Britain, should be sent to the Lord Chamberlain, but now at least *seven* days before the first performance. Acting for hire was defined in Section 16, amongst other provisions, as when 'any money or other reward shall be taken or charged directly or indirectly'.

Section 14 gave the Lord Chamberlain power to forbid any old play or a licensed play 'whenever he shall be of opinion that it is fitting for the preservation of good manners, decorum, or of the public peace so to do'. Section 15 made it an offence to present a play before it received a licence or a play that was refused a licence. The penalty was a fine of up to £50 and the possibility of the theatre being deprived of its licence.

Section 23 defined 'a stage play' as 'every tragedy, comedy, farce, opera, burletta, interlude, melodrama, pantomime or other entertainment of the stage'. Therefore any stage entertainment with a plot or continuity of action required a licence. Ballet was excluded; and so were such acts as jugglers, circuses and comedian cross-talk patter acts with no dramatic content.

Section 13 made it lawful for the Lord Chamberlain to charge a fee for the examination of a play, the amount not to exceed two guineas. In practice, during the whole period when the Act was in force – right up to 1968 – one guinea was charged for examining a one-act play and two guineas for a play with two or more acts.

The Act gave no legal cause for requiring the Lord Chamberlain to defend or explain his decisions. The decision of the Lord Chamberlain in all cases was final and there was no provision for appeals.

No more than the 1737 Act did the new Act specify any guidelines for the Lord Chamberlain as to what he should or should not allow. He was expected to use his own judgement, although sometimes he would seek the advice of others. He treated all plays on their merits and judged them according to the social and moral conditions of the time. It was not until 1909 that the Lord Chamberlain, in reaching his decisions, was required to take note of the recommendations of the Joint Select Committee set up that year which, for the first time, tried to define these criteria.

So pre-censorship was to continue, that is, a licence was

given to a script, not to a production. It was the only practical method of supervision. Once a play was licensed it could be staged by anybody, and the Lord Chamberlain would only intervene if there was evidence that a production of the play was failing to adhere to the licensed script – and 'the script' meant, of course, not just the dialogue, but all the stage directions and 'business'.

Chapter Two

The Victorian and Edwardian Years

Queen Victoria was always fond of dramatics and enjoyed having plays staged at Windsor Castle. She used to write letters in her own hand in the third person, and in one dated 7 December 1859 to Sir Charles Phipps, Keeper of the Privy Purse, she said:

> The Queen must ask Sir C. Phipps *not* to settle definitively about the *Plays* for Windsor. On reflection she thinks the 3rd Act of 'The Unequal Match'* *too* offensive on account of the ridicule it throws on German life – the soldiers of a small German Country . . . and to *have* at Court. Any foreign Prince might arrive and we should have suddenly to alter the *Play*. Can Sir C think of any other for Miss Sedgwick? Then again she does not feel sure of the 'House or the Home'* – she should like a few days reflection for this last.

She did reflect and wrote again to the Keeper on 13 December:

> Would Sir C. Phipps desire a copy of 'House or the Home' to be sent. We think 'The Hunchback' might do instead of 'An Unequal Match'. Miss Sedgwick acts Julia admirably – and if there are any objectionable passages or scenes, surely they might be omitted?

Amy Sedgwick had acted in *The Unequal Match* (Queen Victoria saw a performance at the Haymarket Theatre in

*Both plays were written by Tom Taylor (1817–80).

1858), *The Hunchback* and many other plays. She also gave recitals for Queen Victoria at Osborne in 1865 and 1883.

The Prince of Wales (later Edward VII) was also keen on theatre. The Annual Report of the Lord Chamberlain's Office of 1873 mentions that the Prince complained that a burlesque called *The Happy Land* by F. Tomline (W. S. Gilbert), at the Court Theatre, brought Her Majesty's Ministers into contempt. The prompt copy of the script, it was found, varied considerably from the one which was licensed. The Lord Chamberlain, Viscount Sidney, withdrew the play licence, thereby closing the Court Theatre for one night, but later relicensed it.

On seeing a performance of *The Gaiety Girl* in 1893 the Prince objected to the character of the parson, even though the part had been rewritten and the objectionable portions cut out at the suggestion of E. F. S. Pigott, the Examiner of Plays. Lord Carrington, the Lord Chamberlain, concluded a note he wrote to Queen Victoria's Private Secretary by saying:

> but no doubt great liberties have been taken by Monkhouse, who plays the part, and it had better be cut out altogether and the character turned into a Squire or a Doctor.

Lord Carrington went to see the play himself and arranged with the manager for the parson to be taken out and the part rewritten. The Examiner, Pigott, was told to allow no more clergymen in burlesques. The Lord Chamberlain reported this to the Queen's Private Secretary and expressed the hope that the Prince of Wales would be satisfied. *The Gaiety Girl* ran for 413 performances on its first production and was revived in 1899.

In 1896 the Prince objected to *Michael and his Lost Angel*, by the distinguished dramatist Henry Arthur Jones, as it was prejudicial to the Church. However, it was a financial failure and was withdrawn independently of the royal disapproval.

As king after 1901 Edward's advice was sought by the Lord Chamberlain, the Earl of Clarendon, about a play which portrayed the marriage of Prince George of Wales (afterwards George III) with Hannah Lightfoot. His Majesty commanded that the play should not be allowed as the subject-matter was objectionable.

In 1907 the Lord Chamberlain, Viscount Althorp, hesitated to license *Votes for Women* because it dealt with the women's suffragette movement. On the advice of Lord Knollys (the King's Private Secretary) the matter was not submitted to the King because, as he told the Lord Chamberlain, he was sure His Majesty would offer no objection on grounds of the subject.

Several Select Committees on the theatre sat in the House of Commons during the second half of the nineteenth century. Those in 1853 and 1866 reported in favour and admiration of the censorship. The Comptroller was called as a witness by the first of these committees; and at the second he, the Lord Chamberlain and the Examiner of Plays all gave evidence. Between the two committees the Home Secretary, Sir Cornwall Lewis, in 1860 and 1861 proposed a Bill to define more widely the meaning of a 'stage play'. He suggested the phrase: 'as including every Tragedy, Comedy, Farce, Opera, *Operetta*, Burletta, *Burlesque*, Interlude, Melodrama, Pantomime, *Dialogue (if spoken as well as sung)*, *Drawing Room Entertainment*, *Vaudeville* or any theatrical entertainment whatever, or any part or parts thereof' (the words in italics are not included in Section 23 of the 1843 Act). As the definition was thought to be too stringent compared to the one in the Act, the Bill each time was withdrawn.

In 1884, and again in 1889, an unsuccessful attempt was made in Parliament to place all London theatres under the jurisdiction of the London County Council. The Lord Chamberlain asked the Queen's advice but, whereas she raised no objection, she made it plain that she would not approve any change in the system of the censorship of plays. In the event the Bill was not carried through. When the attempt was repeated in 1891 the actors and managers forwarded a memorandum of protest.

In 1892 a further Select Committee sat, at which the Comptroller and the Examiner of Plays gave evidence, and this committee recommended that the Lord Chamberlain should retain his censorship duties. In 1899 Samuel Smith MP thought the Lord Chamberlain was being too liberal and suggested that the London County Council should take over his censorship role. The Home Secretary supported the view of the 1892 Select Committee. Over this period there were a number of attacks on the current system of licensing plays, but the government made no changes.

In 1901, when the Lord Chamberlain was the Earl of Clarendon, he received a deputation of theatre managers who expressed the hope that the London County Council would not become the licensing authority for theatres, as had been proposed in Parliament a few years previously. They felt that if Parliament agreed to this, the licensing of stage plays would soon follow. The result, in their view, would be disastrous to dramatic art, besides interfering with the prerogative of the sovereign under whose guidance the Lord Chamberlain had hitherto acted as Dramatic Censor.

In the 1850s and 1860s an average of 200 plays a year were licensed. In the 1870s and 1880s this figure rose slightly to 250 per year, but after 1890 it shot up to 400 a year and in the first decade of this century over 500 plays a year were licensed. The number of plays which were refused a licence averaged about one per year in the second half of the last century and about two or three per year in the first decade of the twentieth century. In percentage terms this is considerably less than one per cent. Were the Lord Chamberlains being too lenient, or was the reason simply that the sort of plays that could not be licensed were very few? The majority of these latter, it seems, were foreign-language plays, and in 1860 it was recorded, 'No English Play was rejected, nor has any one been liable to serious objection on moral or political grounds'.

Ibsen's *Ghosts* was one notable play which the Lord Chamberlain, the Earl of Lathom, refused to license in 1891. This surprised John Palmer who, in his book *The Future of the Theatre* (1913), suggested this was:

> a comparatively harmless play from a Censor's point of view compared with *A Doll's House* . . . [which] is Ibsen's

Loyal addresses from actors and theatre managers: (opposite) to Queen Victoria in 1887; (above) to King Edward VII on his coronation in 1902

TO THE QUEEN'S
MOST EXCELLENT MAJESTY.

We the ACTORS and MANAGERS of the UNITED KINGDOM tender to Your Majesty our truest congratulations on the Attainment of the FIFTIETH YEAR of your Reign. We your faithful Servants rejoice that the Period of your Illustrious Government has been so prolonged, and we pray that it may long continue. The Manifold Blessings of Peace have been showered on the Land through your Righteous Dealing with your People and with other Peoples, and under your Gracious Protection all the Arts have flourished. For us who follow the Stage as a Calling a New Era has come. With the remainder of your Subjects, we rejoice at the Blessings which have followed in your Footsteps, and as Actors we are proud to be "the Abstract and Brief Chronicles of your Time."

invitation to ninety-nine Englishwomen out of a hundred to abandon the beds and boards of their husbands.

When *Ghosts* was performed privately at the Royal Theatre, the Lord Chamberlain, Lord Carrington, did not intervene but the licensee stopped the play (because it had not been licensed) and promised that no unlicensed play would be performed in his theatre again.

In 1902 the Lord Chamberlain, the Earl of Clarendon, refused to license *Monna Vanna* by Maurice Maeterlinck, adapted by Alfred Sutro, because, so it appears, the Examiner, G. A. Redford, took exception to a stage direction that the heroine, Monna Vanna, in order to save the lives of her fellow citizens, agrees to the request of the victorious general to go to his tent at night 'nude under her mantle'. Are we not all nude under our clothes?

La Dame aux Camélias by Alexandre Dumas *fils* was not allowed a licence for many years but in 1881 one was given which, according to the Annual Report, 'drew remonstrances from Lord Shaftesbury and others'.

Whitechapel Murder, an unlicensed play, was performed in two provincial theatres in 1876 and the Lord Chamberlain, the Marquess of Hertford, stopped these performances. The Earl of Kenmare had to take similar action in Blackburn in 1883 over *The Invincibles*, a play which had not been submitted for licence since, being of a political nature, it probably would not have been approved. Another unlicensed play, *Deenning*, was performed at Liverpool in 1892. The theatre manager was fined and his theatre licence withdrawn. The play was about a man of that name who in real life had committed a series of crimes for which he was convicted and hanged.

On the other hand, an important change was made by Viscount Sidney as Lord Chamberlain, in 1865. Whereas in the past new ballets had not been submitted for a play licence, Sidney decided that in future they did require one, even though the definition of a stage play in the 1843 Act did not include a ballet. Whether, in fact, this action had any legality is doubtful, and certainly, in later years, ballet was thought to be outside the jurisdiction of the Lord Chamberlain.

A reaction to this came in a splendid letter that appeared in *Punch* in February 1868 addressed to the Earl of Bradford as Lord Chamberlain and signed 'Foozle':

> No modest woman will be able to take her daughters to the theatre . . . the indecent exposure of poor wretched ballet girls who are compelled to submit to such indignities for the sake of an engagement. My Lord Chamberlain, you are not doing your duty. Should Her Gracious Majesty again honour the theatres with her presence she will certainly give Your Lordship a wigging.

The LCO Annual Reports of these years record complaints being received about a number of plays. In 1893 the Turkish Ambassador objected to the Foreign Office about a mention of the Sultan of Turkey and his harem in a burlesque *Don Juan*, by J. T. Tanner, as a result of which the manager of the Gaiety Theatre was ordered to remove this offending material. In 1899 several letters were received about Sir Arthur Pinero's *The Gay Lord Quex* as being 'prejudicial to morals' and the Lord Chamberlain was urged by the Member of Parliament, Samuel Smith, to receive a deputation. This the Lord Chamberlain declined to do, saying that the matter had already been settled by the issue of his official licence. The play has been revived four times since, most recently in 1975 under John Gielgud's direction, with Judi Dench.

At the turn of the century Bernard Shaw was beginning his long career as the foremost dramatist of the day, and very soon he was encountering the blue pencil of the Lord Chamberlain.

The third play he wrote, in 1894, was *Mrs Warren's Profession*. This was published in *Plays Pleasant and Unpleasant* in 1898, the same year as he submitted it for a licence. The Examiner who read it was G. A. Redford and he refused a licence without even referring it to the Lord Chamberlain, the Earl of Lathom. It was a controversial play, not because of its style – which was in fact quite traditional – but simply because the role that Mrs Warren 'professed' was that of a prostitute, and Redford refused a licence on that score alone. She had been a prostitute in her youth and, as she grew older, became a successful proprietor of brothels in cities on the Continent with a wealthy clientele. The play, however, was not set in a brothel but in the country cottage of Mrs Warren's daughter, Vivie, at Haslemere in Surrey.

In his biography of Shaw, Michael Holroyd writes:

> London was honeycombed with houses of assignation illegally maintained through police bribery: but only on the Continent had the brothel become an established social institution operating under Government licence. The more superior of these brothels were run as clubs, and they offered shrewd businessmen such as Sir George Croft [a character in the play] opportunities of forming profitable syndicates.

There was no means for Shaw to appeal against the refusal of a licence. However, on 5 January 1902 the play was performed privately at the New Lyric Club for the members of the Stage Society, with which Shaw was later closely associated as a member of its council.

In his Preface to a special edition of the play on this occasion, Shaw wrote that the play,

> was written to draw attention to the truth that prostitution is caused, not by female depravity and male licentiousness, but simply by underpaying, undervaluing, and overworking women so shamefully that the poorest of them are forced to resort to prostitution to keep body and soul together . . . It is true that in *Mrs Warren's Profession* Society – and not any individual – is the villain of the piece . . .

In his book *Shaw In His Time* Ivor Brown defended the Lord Chamberlain's stand on the play:

> The patrons of the fashionable London theatres were well aware of the Mrs Warrens and their professional activities . . . But what was gossiped about and even gloated over was not to be exposed on the stage. The Censor was there to

> prevent such unmannerly candour and veracity and his discipline was not resented by the public which expected sex in plays to be either a demonstration of menaced but triumphant purity in melodrama or a bubble of champagne in comedy. If the Censor stopped the vinegary comments of a Socialist Puritan he was regarded as earning his keep by silencing one of the tiresome trouble-makers.

In truth, the play did not shock those who saw it and it was performed many times in London and abroad. But a licence was still not granted and Shaw was greatly upset. He complained that his play had been stigmatised by the Lord Chamberlain, who 'by Act of Parliament has despotic and even super-monarchical power over our theatres'.

The plot of the play is summarised by Shaw in a letter he wrote to Janet Achurch who, he hoped, would play the daughter, Vivie:

> I have made the daughter the heroine and the mother a most deplorable old rip. The great scene will be the crushing of the mother by the daughter. I retain the old roué, but keep him constrained by a continued doubt as to whether the heroine may not be his daughter. The young lover's father, an outrageous clergyman is in the same perplexity, he also being an old flame of the mother's . . . The mother, uncertain who the girl's father is, keeps all the old men at bay by telling each one that he is the parent.

In 1897 a member raised a question in the House of Commons as to why the play *Nelson's Enchantress* by R. Horne had been licensed and asked for its withdrawal from the Avenue Theatre in Shaftesbury Avenue. At the Home Secretary's request the Lord Chamberlain, the Earl of Lathom, sent him a memorandum to the effect that this play was founded on historical incidents at the beginning of the century, that there was nothing in it to justify the refusal of a licence and that, for these reasons, he did not propose to interfere in any way with its performance. Queen Victoria also expressed concern and was given the same answer by the Lord Chamberlain who added that in the play Nelson was not exposed to ridicule.

In 1900 a reader of *The Times* wrote complaining of the general immoral tendency of *Mr and Mrs Daventry* and later in the year a similar protest was made by the Church Army. In his reply the Lord Chamberlain, the Earl of Clarendon, regretted that the play had been licensed, probably because Redford, the Examiner, had not consulted him.

In 1904 the Earl of Clarendon received a complaint, this time about Pinero's play *A Wife Without A Smile* at Wyndham's Theatre in which a doll suspended from the ceiling was agitated in a suggestive manner. The Lord Chamberlain went to see the play and 'was of the opinion that although the doll incident might be indelicately construed, it might also be regarded as a childish accessory'. The Bishop of London, however, as Chairman of the Public Morality Council, asked the Lord Chamberlain to alter the doll incident 'to relieve London of what many felt to be a degrading spectacle'. The Lord Chamberlain then took the drastic step of withdrawing the play.

In 1907 Prince Fushimi of Japan paid a visit to Britain as the guest of King Edward VII. The Savoy Theatre had planned to put on at that time Gilbert and Sullivan's popular comic opera *The Mikado* (licensed in 1885), but some Japanese officials told the Lord Chamberlain (Viscount Althorp) that they objected to this. Althorp decided to forbid the production for the time being, as it ridiculed the Emperor of Japan, and this decision was communicated to the manager of the Savoy Theatre.

Helen D'Oyly Carte replied to the Lord Chamberlain expressing her disappointment and ended her letter:

> I shall respectfully bow to such decision: but in that case I would ask you to favour me with a communication . . . the substance of which I may send to the London press so as to explain that the withdrawal of the opera is caused by circumstances of an imperative nature which are wholly beyond my control.

The explanation was sent; and the Lord Chamberlain informed the King who also banned *Mikado* music being played at places to be visited by the Japanese Prince.

Mrs D'Oyly Carte, for some reason believing that the ban applied only to London, decided to mount a production with her own company in Sheffield. Granted an interview with Viscount Althorp, she maintained that the Lord Chamberlain's prohibition applied only to the Savoy Theatre and not elsewhere. Althorp stated that if there was a misunderstanding on her part there was none on his, and, with reluctance, Mrs D'Oyly Carte called off the Sheffield production.

Meanwhile questions were being asked in Parliament, but the Lord Chamberlain's decision received the support of both the Home and Foreign Secretaries. However the Home Secretary, in a letter in his own hand dated 7 May, took the Lord Chamberlain to task by suggesting he should have consulted the Home Office before prohibiting a production:

> The particular case of *The Mikado* is not likely to recur but there are other possibilities, and it is best to profit by experience. The present difficulty arises mainly from the fact that your order was not specifically communicated to those concerned in a manner in which it could not subsequently produce misunderstandings . . . In administering the Act of 1843 or indeed any Act, it is essential to follow both the letter and the spirit very closely . . .
>
> I venture therefore to suggest that when you decide to take action which *may* rouse feeling and opposition, it would be for our joint interest that your Dept. should communicate beforehand with the Home Office, so that we might be able to advise you as to the best procedure under the law . . . But *when* there is danger, it is necessary to frame the order in precise legal terms, and to issue it formally with adequate notice to all whom it may concern.

The Lord Chamberlain accepted this rebuke and, in his reply, said, 'I entirely concur and I will certainly inform the Home Office whenever I have to take any drastic action with regard to the Act which regulates my powers.'

The Lord Chamberlain's prohibition was confirmed in writing to Mrs D'Oyly Carte but he told her he was prepared to consider a revised version of the opera, which could embrace a change of locale and characters and also a change of title. He told her privately that the Japanese had said they could not thank the Lord Chamberlain enough for his action in withdrawing the licence as they felt so strongly about the semi-divinity of The Mikado. There is a note in the LCO file which reads:

> The Japanese ambassador had not liked to make any public protest as he did not wish to interfere; but as the question has become public property he wishes it to be known that the comic opera had hurt the susceptibilities of himself and the Japanese nation and that he is grateful for the action which the Lord Chamberlain has taken.

In a later interview to the press the Japanese ambassador said:

> To say the Japanese are offended by *The Mikado* would be using too strong a term. They do not like it just as I suppose the English would not care to see King Edward made a laughing stock of.

Mrs D'Oyly Carte decided to take up the Lord Chamberlain's offer and approached W. S. Gilbert about a revised script. This prompted the celebrated librettist to write firmly to Viscount Althorp in a letter dated 11 June:

> To all intents and purposes I am accused of having written a libretto which, for whatever reason, is so conspicuously unfit for public performance that your Lordship has considered yourself justified in taking the unprecedented course of suppressing it unconditionally after a most prosperous career of twenty-two years . . .
>
> As I understand, I am now informed that if I will consent to make certain specified alterations in the title and the text, the ban that has been placed upon the libretto will be removed . . .
>
> I must point out to your Lordship that my consent to this course of action would involve, by inference, an admission on my part that my play has gravely sinned against good taste; and this, with all respect, I must decline to do . . .

Gilbert finished the letter by reminding the Lord Chamberlain that he had been ignored throughout this affair. The ban had been placed without any explanation being made to him.

As a result of this, and of the pressures being put on the Lord Chamberlain from various sources (including the Home Office) and further questions being asked in the House, Althorp decided to relent and, on 15 June, both Mrs D'Oyly Carte and Mr Gilbert received the following letter from the Assistant Comptroller:

> The Lord Chamberlain desires me to inform you that, having taken the matter into his careful consideration, he has felt justified in deciding, in the circumstances now obtaining, to withdraw his prohibition of the public performance of *The Mikado*.

By this time Prince Fushimi's visit had ended and the Japanese did not protest.

Chapter Three

Examiners of Plays, 1737–1930

The Examiners of Plays were the linchpin of the dramatic censorship and played a central role in its story.

When the Licensing Act of 1737 was passed, the function of censoring plays was performed by an official variously known as 'Licensor of the Stage' and 'Inspector or Examiner of Plays'. In effect the Examiner took over the duties of the Master of the Revels, and the first official to be appointed by the Lord Chamberlain, the Duke of Grafton, in 1738 was William Chetwynd, a former Comptroller of the Revels. His salary was £400 p.a., no small sum in those days. A Deputy was also appointed, one Thomas Odell, a playwright and theatre manager, who was succeeded in 1749 by Edward Capell, a Shakespearean editor. Although they were salaried, both were allowed to charge reading fees, but the authority to do so was not formally accorded until the Act of 1843!

Chetwynd died in 1778 but Capell, who was an enthusiastic but perhaps rather over-zealous deputy, was passed over in favour of John Larpent. Capell retired, or died, in 1781.

Larpent (Examiner, 1778–1824) was a Methodist and had served in the Foreign Office and in George III's Household as a Gentleman Usher and Groom. His wife also read a number of the plays.

Inevitably the Examiner tended to become more of a controversial figure than the Lord Chamberlain who had many other responsibilities. On the whole, however, Examiners and theatre managers seemed to have got on reasonably well together and there was give and take between them. In some respects theatre managers were the first link in the censorship chain for they were known to alter some texts themselves and, in so doing, saved the Examiner quite a lot of work. There was little interference then by Examiners to check that a script as licensed was being adhered to.

No provision had been made in the 1737 Act as to what should happen to a script after it had been submitted. It was probably in order for it to be retained in the Lord Chamberlain's Office, although this was not legally allowed until 1912. It was certainly not permissible for an Examiner to take possession of them. John Larpent reckoned, however, the scripts were his to keep and at the time of his death he had over two thousand in his possession. They were sold by his widow, and in 1917 came into the possession of the Huntington Library in California.

Larpent was succeeded by George Colman, known as 'Colman the Younger' to distinguish him from his dramatist father. Born in 1762, he had a chequered career. He was considered a good dramatist and had written twenty-five plays. He had been a theatre manager, but not a very good one, being reckless and extravagant and constantly involved in lawsuits. He also served in the Yeomen of the Guard. Whereas some of his plays had been considered licentious, once he became the Examiner he applied, almost like a poacher turned gamekeeper, a stricter censorship than ever his predecessor had.

As Clement Scott wrote in *The Drama of Yesterday and Today*, Colman 'had peculiar views as to profanity or irreverence expressed in stage dialogue'. He considered the application of the phrase 'My angel' to a beautiful woman or an adored wife to be 'profane' and cut out the unholy words accordingly. When he was asked why he cut out 'angel' as applied to a woman, he replied:

> Because it *is* a woman, I grant, but it is a celestial woman. It is an allusion to the scriptural angels which are celestial bodies.
>
> The words 'Oh, Lud!' or 'Oh, La!' he deemed irreverent, and out they went, in defiance of the old dramatists. When asked why he had cut out 'Damme!' which he had used so often in his own plays, he replied: 'At that time I was a careless, immoral author. I am now the Examiner of

Plays. I did my business as an author at that time, and I do my business as an Examiner now.'

Colman reckoned that the Lord Chamberlain could only dismiss him if he misbehaved himself, and that the job of Examiner was his for life. Indeed he died in office in 1836. On his death the Lord Chamberlain asked the Colman family to return the scripts examined by him to the Lord Chamberlain's Office, for which they were given £100.

The next Examiner's tenure of office was short-lived. Charles Kemble, who had retired as an actor-manager in 1832 because of increasing deafness, was appointed in 1836 and resigned in 1840 in favour of his son John Mitchell Kemble, an historian and philologist. This did not prevent Charles Kemble reading Shakespeare's *Cymbeline* before Queen Victoria on 24 April 1844 and, on 16 February 1846, he read *Antigone* before Her Majesty and the Prince Consort, accompanied by choir and orchestra.

John Kemble wrote in his register in December 1856:

> In spite of the past increase in the population of London there is no increased prosperity for theatrical adventure . . . The upshot is that the state of the theatres at this time is a wretched one . . . it must be remembered that Covent Garden and the Pavilion Theatre have both been burned down this year.

Kemble died the following year (1857) and was succeeded by William Bodham Donne, also a scholar and an antiquary, who for a considerable time had been Kemble's deputy. Donne's salary was £320 p.a. He was responsible for the theatrical performances at Windsor from 1859–61, and letters survive from him to Sir Charles Phipps. About one play he wrote, in 1859:

> All went on behind the curtain excellently, and I feel sure that everyone with whom I came in contact was well pleased . . . As this has been the first appearance of the Sadlers Wells Company at Windsor Castle I will add that a more quiet and well behaved *troupe* cannot be.

Donne sometimes found it necessary to make alterations to the licensed script because of the nature of the occasion. In a letter the following year he wrote:

> At present Mr Harris has only two dramas in his repertoire which could be acted before the Court. *Puss* which I proposed in one of my schemes submitted to the Prince, but which would not fit with any of the selected programmes, and *Home Truths*, which is a less amusing version of *The House or Home* . . . Widdicombe is not an actor to bring to Windsor, for though in his way a genius, he is of the genus 'Jack Pudding'.

At the time of Donne's appointment the Lord Chamberlain decided to enlarge the duties of the Examiner and involve him in the inspection of theatres with regard to safety and comfort. There is an entry in the Annual Report of the Lord Chamberlain's Office of 1857:

> The Lord Chamberlain decided that for the future the Examiner of Plays should reside in London so as to ensure access to his opinion, that he should attend at the office at least once a week to examine the Play Bills and where necessary that he should attend personally at the theatres to see that alterations in Plays made by the Lord Chamberlain are actually carried out.

In August 1868, just before going on ten days' leave, Donne wrote to the Comptroller, 'I have no plays in hand; and wish to preserve what is left of me by a little change.' Perhaps he was hinting that he was overworked!

Donne resigned in 1874 and died in 1882. He was succeeded by E. F. S. Pigott, selected from a number of candidates in 1874. When Pigott died in 1895 the press paid tribute to his work as an Examiner, referring to his 'determination to persist in the path that seemed right to him' as well as to his 'kindly blue pencil'. Shaw took a different view, however, and wrote in the *Saturday Review*:

> The late Mr Pigott is declared on all hands to have been the

> best reader of plays we have ever had; and yet he was a walking compendium of vulgar insular prejudice, who, after wallowing all his life in the cheapest theatrical sentiment [he was a confirmed playgoer], had at last brought himself to a pitch of incompetence . . . He had French immorality on the brain; he had American indecency on the brain; he had the womanly woman on the brain; he had the Divorce Court on the brain; he had 'not before a mixed audience' on the brain; his official career in relation to the higher drama was one long folly and panic . . .
>
> It is a frightful thing to see the greatest thinkers, poets, and authors of modern Europe – men like Ibsen, Wagner, Tolstoi, and the leaders of our own literature – delivered helpless into the vulgar hands of such a noodle as this amiable old gentleman – this despised and incapable old official – most notoriously was.

It is difficult to find out much about Pigott, and perhaps it was bad luck that he made an opponent of Shaw. However in 1894 he did, as Examiner of Plays, issue a circular to the managers of music-halls in London, calling their attention to the performance of unlicensed plays and desiring them in future to submit them for licence. Only after this was the opinion of the Home Office sought as to whether, under the 1843 Act, the Lord Chamberlain could license a stage play to an unlicensed building. As their opinion was that he could not the Examiner was obliged to withdraw his circular.

Throughout the nineteenth century – indeed until 1924 – the Lord Chamberlain's appointment was a political one which changed with the government. In the later years of Queen Victoria's reign the government changed frequently and so there were many changes of Lord Chamberlain – she had fifteen Lord Chamberlains but, during the same period, there were only five Examiners of Plays. It is not surprising, therefore, if sometimes they left most of the decisions on play-licensing to the Examiners.

G. A. Redford was appointed to succeed Pigott in 1895. Although Bernard Shaw was no supporter of the censorship he wrote some kind words about Redford in a paper 'Our Theatre in the Nineties'. However in an article published in

LICENCES FOR REPRESENTATION.

Nº	Date.	Description and Title of Play.	Nº of Acts.	Manager of
450	190			

450

It having been represented to Me by the Examiner of All Theatrical Entertainments that a

does not in its general tendency contain any thing immoral or otherwise improper for the Stage I The Lord Chamberlain of **His Majesty's** *Household do by virtue of my Office and in pursuance of the Act of Parliament in that case provided Allow the Performance of the said*

at your with the exception of all Words and Passages which are specified by the Examiner in the endorsement of this License and without any further variations whatsoever.

Given under my hand this day of 190

Lord Chamberlain.

To The Manager of the

The Stage Licence in use before 1912

the *North American Review* in 1899 he was less complimentary:

> The Lord Chamberlain himself . . . has no time to keep any check on his subordinate, even if he could pretend to know anything more than he does about dramatic criticism and the foundation of morality. The result is that the Examiner of Plays, humble, untitled, middle-class though he be, is yet the most powerful man in England or America . . .
>
> It will be inferred that no pains are spared to secure the services of a very highly qualified and distinguished person to wield this astonishing power – say the holder of a University chair of Literature or Drama. The inference is erroneous. You are not allowed to sell stamps in an English post office without previously passing an examination, but you may become Examiner of Plays without necessarily knowing how to read or write. The post is held at present by one George Alexander Redford, said to have been a bank clerk, but not ascertained to have been anything except lucky enough to obtain a place at Court.

Shaw, to be fair, was not so much attacking the man or the post as the system. Towards the end of the article he wrote:

> Mr Redford cannot help himself: a Censorship cannot work in any other way, until a Censor can be found greater than the greatest dramatists. That being impossible, he is doomed still to put his hallmark on profligate farces and thinly sentimentalised tomcat love tales, and to shut the stage door against the great dramatic poets.

Shaw then goes on to ask what should be done to the Censorship:

> Nothing can be simpler. Abolish it, root and branch, throwing the whole legal responsibility for plays on the author and manager, precisely as the legal responsibility for a book is thrown on the author, the printer and the publisher.

Redford's salary was £300 p.a., less by £20 than that of his predecessor. Towards the end of his tenure he appeared to be usurping the Lord Chamberlain's authority and licensing plays without the knowledge of his superior.

One such case was a play called *The Devil* which was performed at the Adelphi Theatre in 1909 and received much unfavourable comment. It has a Faustian theme, in which the Devil's principal scheme (which triumphs as the curtain falls on the last act) is to bring together again the young artist, Maurice, and Helène Vaillant, who had been lovers in the past, despite her now being married to an elderly financier.

Redford wrote immediately, on 20 April, to Viscount Althorp, giving his own views of the play which he had read and then, apparently on his own authority, had sent the licence to the manager of the Adelphi. Lord Althorp replied the following day:

> I am afraid that some considerable comment is being made at my having licensed it at all. The Play seems to be not only coarse, but distinctly improper, and nearly indecent . . . It is unfortunate, to say the least of it, that nothing was known by me or Sir Douglas [Dawson] about this Play . . . Of course I hold myself responsible, though I could not easily say I know anything about the play.

Redford replied strongly in his defence on 22 April:

> It did not strike me, considering the theme, as any more risky than dozens of others, almost on all fours with it. I am sure it is not and I am equally confident that anyone of experience reading the play would be of the same opinion.

But he sells the pass by saying that he was always ready and anxious to *refer* any difficult or doubtful cases to the Lord Chamberlain and ends his letter, 'The Examiner can only exercise his trained judgement and experience to the best of his ability, and trust that the Lord Chamberlain *for whom he is acting* will approve his view.' The Lord Chamberlain sent his letter for Sir Douglas Dawson, the Comptroller, to see, commenting:

> It is an answer as far as it goes and he accepts the responsibility of licensing the play though I still consider myself responsible. A play founded on an immoral base . . . should not be licensed.

It is probable that this encouraged the Lord Chamberlain to set up an Advisory Board (see Chapter 5), not only to help him but to act as a check on the Examiner; and Redford's evidence to the 1909 Joint Select Committee was to come under particularly close scrutiny.

Charles Brookfield was appointed a joint Examiner with Redford in 1911, but they only worked together for a month before Redford resigned to become, until his death in 1916, the first President of the British Board of Film Censors.

Brookfield, fifty-five years old at the time, was an actor who had made his first professional appearance in 1879 and written a number of plays, but his time as an Examiner was to be short for he died in 1913. The Lord Chamberlain, Lord Sandhurst, wrote of him, 'I always maintained it was a very good appointment. His dramatic knowledge was very great. If he had had a fault he was a little over-critical, but it was a fault on the right side. He is a very distinct loss.'

Brookfield was succeeded by Ernest Bendall, who was just sixty-six. For thirty years he had been a clerk in the Paymaster-General's office, retiring in 1896, since when he had been a journalist. He was in turn drama critic of the London *Figaro*, the *Observer*, the *Daily Mail* and the *St James's Gazette*.

A year later, in 1914, George Street was appointed Joint Examiner, and, when Bendall died in 1920, he continued in office on his own until 1930. Born in 1867, Street had been a novelist, playwright and critic. He was chosen from thirty-five candidates and had many supporters, including Sir Herbert Tree. Five years later Sir Walter Raleigh, by then a member of the Advisory Board, wrote, 'I have a specially high esteem of Mr Street's good sense, literary taste and worldly wisdom.'

Soon after Street's appointment he was given the Lord Chamberlain's permission to write a letter to *The Times*, to clear up certain misunderstandings which arose about his job:

> Most of the newspaper comments on my recent appointment, kind and flattering to myself as they were, assumed that I had been made a censor of plays. That is not the case. My senior colleague, Mr Bendall, and I merely examine and report on plays for the information of the Lord Chamberlain . . . the granting or withholding of a licence is a function of the Lord Chamberlain.

However Lord Sandhurst, in a note to the Comptroller, remarked ruefully, 'I doubt from experience the public ever getting hold of the thing properly.'

Geoffrey Dearmer – who became an Examiner in 1936 when Street died and when Henry Game, who had been appointed in 1930, had taken over as Chief Examiner – told me that Street was a 'great man'. 'He did the whole thing by himself [he was the only Examiner between 1920 and 1930] although rather scattily. He loved reading plays.'

A fine example of Street's work came in 1923 when W. Somerset Maugham's play *Our Betters* was submitted for licence. His report is worth quoting in full for its own sake and to represent the care, thought and trouble taken by Street himself in particular, and by the Examiners of Plays in general in all their work:

> *Our Betters* is a fierce indictment of the views of English society and primarily a satire on some Americans who have made their way in it. It is outspoken, though not coarse in language, and extremely unpleasant and painful, though in form a comedy as the author calls it.
>
> It will serve the purpose of a report to deal with the characters and their relations and the principal event rather than to give a detailed narrative of the plot. The central figure is Pearl, a rich American married to Sir George Grayston, who never appears and is evidently a *mari complaisant*. She is an extraordinarily successful hostess (from the snob's point of view) and is assisted by the money of Arthur Fenwick, a very rich American, whose mistress she evidently is. Another rich American is the Duchesse de Surennes, who has divorced her husband and she is the mistress of a mercenary young blackguard, Tony Paxton.

Another is married to and separated from an Italian prince: she is virtuous. Thornton Clay is a pushing American, a shameless snob. The good element, apart from the Princess, consists of Bessie, Pearl's sister, a charming girl, newly arrived from America; Fleming Harvey, a decent American boy, and Bleane, a pleasant young English peer who wants to marry Bessie.

The great scene of the play is at the end of Act II, at Pearl's country house. Pearl and Tony have conceived a passion for one another. It is after dinner. They make an appointment in the summerhouse. The others play poker. The jealous Duchesse (guessing the appointment) sends Bleane to fetch her bag which she pretends to have left in the summerhouse. He returns and says it is not there. She asks Bessie to go. Bleane, much embarrassed, interposes and says she cannot – the door is locked. Bessie, sensing the truth, breaks down, humiliated. Pearl and Tony reappear and Pearl, realising that the truth is out, turns to Tony: 'You fool, I told you it was too risky.' The last act in a series of witty scenes, cynical to the last degree, shows Pearl re-establishing herself, making Fenwick forgive her and also the Duchesse by bringing down a famous dancing master for the latter's delectation, so that the party is not broken up and scandal is prevented. The vile Tony conciliates his Duchesse who promises to marry him. But Bessie, fearing she may become like her sister if she marries Bleane, goes home to America.

I believe there was some outcry over the play in New York, probably over the end of Act II, for it is not an attack on Americans in general, far from it, but only on some who live here, and Mr Maugham cannot of course mean that *all* Americans who marry titled foreigners are bad. From the censorship point of view two main points arise.

1. The two people being caught *in flagrante delicto* in Act II. Originally, as I gather from alterations in the text, Bessie discovered them, which would be much more unpleasant. As it is, it seems to me merely a case of a thing happening 'off' which has so happened in other plays. With this I join the general viciousness, immorality and sordidness of several of the characters, and about it all I think the

important point is that the effect is not sympathy with vice but intense scorn of it, not the less because it is made ridiculous as well as odious. If I am right in this it is the reverse of an immoral play.

2. This seems far more difficult to me. Pearl will suggest to many people Lady Cunard. That is pointed by her country house being called 'Feathers Nevill', as Lady Cunard used to live at Nevill Holt; that I should think is an accident. How far the identification goes others will know better than I. (The ringing up on p. 41, Act I, suggests her 'capturing' a statesman with musical tastes which may suggest somebody.) If it were only a question of social ambitions and success there would not be much in it: Lady Cunard is not the only successful hostess: I am not of course implying that it would be fair to her at all. But Pearl is represented as a callously vicious and mercenary person, and if any real person were obviously meant and so painted it is another thing altogether. I reserve this point as being less qualified than others, probably, to judge of it. With regard to the play as a whole I think it is clearly one which should be read by the Lord Chamberlain or the Advisory Board, and is certainly not a play for *la jeune fille* but as its effect is moral, a lashing of vice, though exaggerated in its presentation, and as there is nothing offensive verbally it is tentatively and with the reserve indicated

Recommended for Licence
(sd.) G. S. STREET

Chapter Four

The 1909 Joint Select Committee

On 27 October 1907 seventy-one authors wrote a letter of protest to *The Times*. The signatories included J. M. Barrie, Joseph Conrad, John Galsworthy, W. S. Gilbert, Laurence Housman, John Masefield and Bernard Shaw. They appealed also to the Prime Minister, Sir Henry Campbell-Bannerman, who agreed to receive a deputation.

A member of the deputation was Robert Harcourt, a recently elected Liberal MP, and it was probably he who was most influential in persuading the Prime Minister to appoint a Joint Select Committee in 1909. Its principal task was 'to inquire into the censorship of Stage Plays as constituted by the Theatres Act 1843, and into the operations of the Acts of Parliament relating to the licensing and regulation of theatres and places of public entertainment, and to report any alterations of the law or practice which may appear desirable.'

The Committee consisted of six peers and six commoners under the chairmanship of Herbert (later Viscount) Samuel, a Liberal lawyer. Robert Harcourt himself (1878–1962) was one of the members. Son of a one-time Leader of the House, he was educated at Eton and Cambridge and was a clerk in the Foreign Office until elected Liberal MP for Montrose Burghs in 1907. He also wrote two plays, *An Angel Unawares* and *A Question of Age*.

The Committee started its deliberations on 29 July 1909 and published its report of half a million words with commendable speed, just over three months later. It examined forty-nine witnesses including the Comptroller, Lord Chamberlain's Office (Sir Douglas Dawson), and the Examiner of Plays (G. A. Redford), but curiously did not call the Lord Chamberlain himself, Viscount Althorp. To quote from the report: 'We have had the advantage of hearing the opinions and suggestions of many representative dramatists, critics, managers of Theatres, and directors of music halls.'

The first witness to be called (at the first sitting on 29 July) was from the Home Office. He was W. P. Byrne, an Assistant Under-Secretary of State. He set the scene by giving the parliamentary history of the censorship and answered questions on the 1737 and 1843 Acts. He stated that the censorship in its origin was to protect the public against seditious plays and personal attacks and not for the purpose of protecting public morals. Questioned closely about the authority of the Examiner of Plays, he told the Committee that the report which led to the 1843 Act suggested that the censor (i.e., the Examiner of Plays) was subject to the Lord Chamberlain and should be removed if found not to be satisfactory. Both Acts, however, made the Lord Chamberlain the censor and judge of plays. Anyone employed by him was not the censor in any legal sense, being only his assistant.

Byrne went on to say that the 1843 Act did to some extent limit the previously held powers of the Lord Chamberlain. He quoted the definition of a stage play according to that Act, i.e., Section 14:

> The Lord Chamberlain may, whenever he shall be of opinion that it is fitting for the preservation of good manners, decorum or of the public peace so to do, forbid the acting or presenting of any Stage Play or part thereof . . .

He concluded his testimony with references to the Stage Society and private performances. He explained that the 1843 Act forbade the public productions or presentations of any unlicensed play; but if a bona fide society put on a performance not for hire or reward there was no requirement for that play to be licensed.

G. A. Redford (Examiner of Plays) was called next at the same sitting and his evidence covered two days. He said he had been a student of drama before his appointment as Examiner of Plays in 1895. In answer to what principles he used in 'licensing the plays that come before you' he replied, 'Simply bringing to bear an official point of view and keeping up a standard.' During the fourteen years of his examinership about 7,000 plays had been licensed and about 30 (less than one half per cent) had been refused a licence. He explained that Shakespeare's plays and Restoration dramas did not have to be submitted but that translations of early Greek plays did require a licence. Religious plays pointedly adapted from the Scriptures were not allowed.

Redford maintained that there were no instructions in writing as to the duties of the Examiner of Plays. He must have forgotten (or pretended to forget) the memorandum given to him on his appointment by the Lord Chamberlain, which spelt out precisely what the duties were (see Appendix C). A copy of this memorandum was later sent to the Committee by Sir Douglas Dawson, the Comptroller. Furthermore in 1900 (only five years after Redford's appointment), the Home Secretary requested the Lord Chamberlain to supervise more closely the duties of the Examiners.

Redford confessed that he decided most questions on his own authority but he did consult the Lord Chamberlain on questions of policy. He agreed that he would welcome some form of appeal against a decision of his or the Lord Chamberlain's, but he thought it would probably be unworkable. He was further forced to agree that he had no authority to license plays himself without reference to the Lord Chamberlain, although there were occasions when he had done so. He explained that he had to deal with theatre managers and not with authors, although he did have private and unofficial dealings with authors whom he knew.

It was to the sixth sitting on 6 August that Sir Douglas Dawson was called and examined. He began by saying that when the Examiner of Plays was in doubt about a play it was his duty to try and negotiate with the manager and then, if necessary, to refer the question to the Lord Chamberlain through the Comptroller. As recently as 29 June, Dawson, on the instructions of the Lord Chamberlain, had written a letter to Redford saying just that (see Appendix C). The letter was submitted in written evidence. Dawson also told the Committee that when Redford was appointed, his 'Letter of Service' (a copy of which was also submitted) recommended that he visit theatres frequently in order to see the plays which had been licensed. He stated that the Examiner refused a licence only with the authority of the Lord Chamberlain, but there undoubtedly were occasions when he had done this on his own authority. In answer to a question he said that the Lord Chamberlain 'takes into consideration the literary and artistic merit of the play'.

Sir Douglas made reference to the Advisory Board (see Chapter 5) and explained that it had not yet met as it was being held in abeyance pending the report of the Committee. He also handed in two further papers, a copy of a play licence and a memorandum on the Law and Practice regarding Restoration Plays.

Earlier that year a play *An Englishman's Home* by 'A Patriot' caused some controversy, its theme being the invasion of England by a foreign power. The author was in fact Major Guy du Maurier and the play, put on at Wyndham's Theatre on 27 January 1909, was directed by his younger brother Gerald du Maurier. Dawson was closely questioned about it and why it had been licensed. He explained that Mr Ashton Jonson, a prospective parliamentary candidate, had written a 'bothering letter' – before the play had opened – saying it was too evident that the invaders were Germans (the First World War was only five years away). The writer was told this was not the case, for 'if Germany or any other friendly power had been alluded to, the play would not have received His Lordship's licence'. However to be on the safe side, the Lord Chamberlain checked with the Foreign Secretary who saw no reason why the licence should be withdrawn.

The theatre manager was warned that the play must not be performed in any way that might suggest that Germany was the foreign power; he was also told by Dawson that 'the head-dress [of the invaders] should not be a helmet with a spike . . . and that the dress should be non-distinctive of any particular country . . . and no suggestion in the make-up or no moustache brushed up, as is the custom now so much in Germany'. Ashton Jonson attended the first night and wrote an 'I told you so' letter saying 'the names and make-up of the invaders were unmistakably German'. So Dawson went along to see it and replied:

> I never saw anything less German in my life than the dress, manners and general appearance of the invaders . . . With all my experience of continental armies, their uniforms, habits and customs I was totally unable to fit the Cap to any foreign power, European or otherwise.

Who was right – one wonders – Jonson or Dawson? What was certainly true was that the play stimulated Territorial Army recruitment. Guy du Maurier was killed in 1916.

On the other hand, a one-act burlesque *Chips*, a skit on *An Englishman's Home*, was not allowed by the Lord Chamberlain. Dawson was asked to explain why the Lord Chamberlain had licensed the play but not the skit, to which he replied that the skit would have given offence to a particular foreign power, which the original play would not have done.

Bernard Shaw was the sixth witness to be called. He had sent in a prepared statement which Mr Harcourt moved should be printed as an appendix to the report. The Committee voted five to four against the motion.

Shaw stated that three of his nineteen plays to date had not been licensed, one being *Mrs Warren's Profession*. He wanted the censorship abolished so that the drama and the author, as he put it, should both be brought under the law. He complained that the Examiner of Plays was licensing some plays which were revolting and disgusting and so conveying the impression, by giving them a licence, that they contained nothing objectionable.

Shaw suggested the Lord Chamberlain was employing some form of political censorship. In one play of his, *John Bull's Other Island*, a Liberal politician was held up to a little gentle ridicule and the play was licensed; in another play, *Press Cuttings*, a Conservative politician was treated the same way and the play was censored.

Although a number of authors testified in person – such as Barrie, Chesterton and Laurence Housman – many were not called but protested strongly in other ways. Arnold Bennett wrote:

> Immediately you begin to get near the things that really matter in a play, you begin to think about the censor, and it

> is all over with your play. I regard it as monstrous and grotesque and profoundly insulting, and to condescend to reason against a thing so obviously vicious humiliates me.

Other people spoke up for the censorship, the Home Secretary and the Speaker being among them.

The report is divided into three sections. The first, 'Origin of the present Controls over Theatres and Stage Plays', summarised the story up to 1843. The next section, entitled 'The Censorship', dealt with the situation as it was then, in 1909. Mention was made of three inquiries into the matter by Parliament since 1843 – in 1853, 1866 and 1892. Although the licensing of buildings had been the main subject of inquiry in 1866, it was reported 'that the Censorship of Plays has worked satisfactorily, and that it is not desirable that it should be discontinued'.

In this section of the report there is stated quite impartially the conflicting arguments of dramatists (supported by many men of letters and others such as the Bishop of Southwark) that there should be no special censorship of the drama, together with the views of those who wished to retain it, including managers, some actors and a considerable body of public opinion. The Committee considered that the existing laws regarding indecency, blasphemy and libel were not adequate for the control of drama and concluded that the public interest required theatrical performances should be regulated by special laws. The members reckoned from a business point of view that managers could not risk production of certain plays without some safeguard.

The third and most important section of the report was 'Proposals with respect to the Licensing of Plays'. The two most relevant were:

> 1. The Lord Chamberlain to remain the Licensor of Plays, and for this task not to be transferred to the Home Office; and that he should license any play submitted to him unless he considers that it may reasonably be held –
> (a) To be indecent;
> (b) To contain offensive personalities;

(c) To represent on the stage in an invidious manner a living person, or a person recently dead;
(d) To do violence to the sentiment of religious reverence;
(e) To be calculated to conduce to crime or vice;
(f) To be calculated to impair friendly relations with any Foreign Power;
(g) To be calculated to cause a breach of the peace.

2. It should be optional for a play to be submitted for a licence; and it should be legal to perform an unlicensed play, whether it had been submitted or not.

Amongst the other proposals was one that the office of Examiner of Plays should be continued, but that it was the Lord Chamberlain, and not the Examiner, who should be responsible for granting or withholding a licence. The Lord Chamberlain was also advised to proceed with the formation of a consultative committee. There was a recommendation that the seven-day minimum of submitting a play before production be extended back to fourteen days, as in the 1737 Act. With regard to plays with a religious theme, there was a proposal that these should be licensed provided they were not irreverent, but that those in which the Deity was represented should continue to be refused a licence. 'At the same time,' the report added, 'it will doubtless still be remembered that a play is not necessarily moral because its ultimate tendency claims to be moral. A right to a licence is not given to a play which presents vice in an alluring guise, by an ultimate, and perhaps perfunctory, condemnation of it.'

The Report proposed that the Director of Public Prosecutions, if of the opinion that the performance of an unlicensed play be indecent, should prosecute the manager – or the manager *and* author – and for the courts to impose penalties on them and prohibit performances for up to ten years; after which time the play must be licensed before further performances. Similarly, if the Attorney-General considered that an unlicensed play which had been performed offended on any of the seven grounds specified in the recommendation, a Committee of the Privy Council should have the power to prohibit performances of the play for up to ten years. It was recommended that the Director of Public

Prosecutions should be informed of plays refused a license and a copy of the script sent to him.

A further section of the Report dealt with 'The Licensing of Music-halls' but this was not the concern of the Lord Chamberlain.

Once the Joint Committee's report was published in November 1909 the question of the censorship occupied centre stage for a while and the arguments for and against it continued to be aired in Parliament, the press and in books. The Government, probably because there were other and more important matters to attend to, took no action and no legislation followed. The anti-censorship lobby continued to plead its case but the Lord Chamberlain had no alternative but to continue to administer the Theatres Act of 1843.

Chapter Five

'Refusing the Better and Licensing the Worse'

Although no legislation followed the report of the 1909 Committee, the Lord Chamberlain, Earl Spencer (as Viscount Althorp had now become), on his own initiative decided to follow up three of its recommendations.

First, he decided that he should license any play unless he considered it fell into one of the seven categories specified in the report (see pages 63–4). This was reflected in a new form of play licence, introduced in 1912. This revised licence, which was used thereafter, is illustrated opposite.

Second, a meeting was called in 1910 to discuss the recommendation that action should be taken against any unlicensed indecent play being performed. It was attended by the Clerk of the Privy Council, the Director of Public Prosecutions, a representative from the Home Office and the Comptroller, Lord Chamberlain's Office. The recommendation did not find favour, however, probably because it seemed impractical to implement, and the King gave approval that no such action be taken.

Third, Lord Spencer sought the King's approval to revive the Advisory Board which had been set up early in 1909 but had never met, pending the report of the 1909 Committee.

The Advisory Board was the brainchild of Sir Douglas Dawson, the Comptroller. Its purpose was to provide the Lord Chamberlain with extra advice over doubtful or difficult plays. Lord Spencer considered it important to appoint persons whose names carried weight and who would be content to give their services voluntarily, whilst leaving the final decision or veto to himself.

117

LORD CHAMBERLAIN'S OFFICE

I, the Lord Chamberlain of **The Queen's** *Household for the time being, do by virtue of my Office and in pursuance of powers given to me by the Act of Parliament for regulating Theatres, 6 & 7 Victoria, Cap. 68, Section 12. Allow the Performance of a new Stage Play, of which a copy has been submitted to me by you, being a ____________ in ___ Acts, entitled ____________*

____________ ____________

with the exception of all Words and Passages which are specified in the endorsement of this Licence and without any further variations whatsoever.

Given under my hand

this ______ day of ____________ 19__

Lord Chamberlain.

To The Manager of the ____________

____

T38.

The revised Stage Licence of 1912 remained in use until 1968

The original members chosen for the Advisory Board had been:

Sir John Hare, actor-manager
Sir Squire Bancroft, actor-manager
Mr Rufus Isaacs, KC, MP
Mr J. Comyns Carr, author
The Comptroller, Lord Chamberlain's Office (ex-officio)

When the Board was revived, Isaacs and Comyns Carr were replaced by Sir Edward Carson and S. O. (later Viscount) Buckmaster, both lawyers. In addition Walter Raleigh, Professor of English Literature at Oxford University, was appointed.

Lord Spencer proposed that the recommendations of the Board members should be kept private, but that their names – and the decision of the Lord Chamberlain regarding a play – should be made public. He had been assured by playwrights and other members of the theatrical profession that the existence of this Board would give renewed confidence to all concerned.

King Edward gave his approval but he wished the Lord Chamberlain to have the power of veto over the Board as otherwise it would abolish his right of censorship.

An early example of the Board's advice being sought was over a play called *The Abode of Love*, which had been refused a licence in 1905 and was resubmitted in 1913. The story concerns a rascally clergyman who is eager to possess the innocent Beryl. He abducts her by the aid of drugs to the 'Abode of Love', to become his 'ordained bride', where the hapless Beryl is thrashed and compelled to undergo a kind of burlesque bridal service. Although the heroine is freed before the curtain falls, the Examiner (Bendall) reported:

> This is a play almost as objectionable as its title . . . [it] is a crude and exaggerated study of lustful crime . . . This violent and foolish piece is so overdone in its attack upon vice that it would be likely to do much more harm than good: and it merely causes disgust instead of rousing the righteous indignation at which it presumably aims.

He did not recommend a licence. Although the Lord Chamberlain himself was strongly against the issue of a licence he clearly thought the play should be considered by the Board. All the members agreed with him and Sir Walter Raleigh (he had been knighted in 1911) wrote, 'This play is garbage – almost as bad as the thing it attacks, and a good deal sillier.' The author, Walter Saltoun, asked on what grounds the Lord Chamberlain had arrived at his decision and offered to make changes. Sir Douglas Dawson, who had originally minuted 'It makes me blush to think a gentleman should be called upon to license such rubbish', replied that 'Objection having been taken to the general plot and theme of the play, no amount of alteration would render it liable to be licensed'.

In 1910 Sir Thomas Beecham had decided to put on Richard Strauss's opera *Salome* at Covent Garden, but was surprised to learn that the Lord Chamberlain regarded the work as unfit for the British stage and had refused it a licence.

Beecham, as he related in his autobiography *A Mingled Chime*, sought the help of the Prime Minister, H. H. Asquith, who agreed to speak to Earl Spencer. As a result, Beecham was invited to St James's Palace and was told that the sacred character of John the Baptist could not appear on the stage. Doubtless due to Asquith's intervention, Spencer was eager to find a way around the problem; and so he suggested substituting 'a prophet' for John the Baptist and asking for certain alterations to the German text.

Beecham agreed and the alterations were made during rehearsal, to the bewilderment of the cast. However on the opening night, Salome, followed by the other singers, all of them carried away by the occasion, forgot the amended lines and lapsed into the 'banned' text. Beecham tried to get the orchestra to play louder to drown the words of the singers, but to no avail. He had visions of Covent Garden being threatened with the loss of its Letters Patent. The performance was given a great reception but afterwards Beecham froze as he saw the Lord Chamberlain approaching him; however, Earl Spencer was as enthusiastic in his praise as everyone else for he had assumed that the expurgated version had been sung.

Earl Spencer, after seven years as Lord Chamberlain, was

succeeded in 1912 by Lord (later Viscount) Sandhurst, a former Governor of Bombay.

As far as is known, the only occasion when a Lord Chamberlain was taken to court occurred that year, Lawrence Cowen applied for a summons against Lord Sandhurst for refusing to return to him the manuscript of his play *The Pity of It* which had been banned by the previous Lord Chamberlain. Lord Sandhurst maintained he was entitled to keep the scripts of all plays submitted for a licence and his counsel pointed out that the 1843 Theatres Act made no provision for returning scripts to authors or managers. Cowen's counsel, on the other hand, argued that there was nothing in the Act entitling the Lord Chamberlain to hold on to the scripts. The magistrate, taking the view that the Lord Chamberlain was only doing his duty, found in his favour and Cowen did not get his manuscript back. Thereafter, no doubt, dramatists took the precaution of making copies.

In 1912 the dramatic authors and others petitioned the King to abolish censorship. Not to be outdone, the Society of West End Theatre Managers and the Touring Managers' Association sent to His Majesty another petition requesting its retention! In a debate in the House of Lords the new Lord Chamberlain explained his position under the Theatres Act, which placed the dramatic censorship in his hands, and he described how the censorship duties were carried out in the Lord Chamberlain's Office.

In the following year (1913) Robert Harcourt MP, who had assisted the authors in their 1907 appeal to the Prime Minister, brought forward a motion in the House of Commons:

> That the attempt to maintain by means of antiquated legislation a legal distinction between a theatre and a music-hall, and to differentiate between productions called stage plays and other dramatic performances, is unworkable; that the system of licensing stage plays *before* production . . . by means of the perusal of a manuscript should be abolished; and that as regards stage exhibitions of whatever kind, reliance should be placed on subsequent control.

This was opposed by the Government but the motion was

agreed to without a division. Lord Sandhurst was told privately by the Home Office, however, that nothing would result from the carrying of the motion and that no legislation on the subject was intended.

With the outbreak of the First World War the following year arguments about the censorship were pushed into the background. During the war years serious drama on the London stage largely gave way to light entertainment. Even the Stage Society was unable to keep going as a pressure group, claiming that its fight against the censorship appeared to have attained its purpose.

One play in 1915 which, not unexpectedly, failed to gain a licence was *L'Horrible Experience*. G. S. Street, who read it, said that, in his opinion, 'the play was too dreadful and horrible for public presentation'. It contained a scene in which a doctor tried to resuscitate the corpse of his daughter, who had died in a motor accident, by making an incision (producing blood) and inserting an electric instrument into the heart. The 'corpse' puts up a hand, clutches the doctor's throat and strangles him.

In 1918 the Lord Chamberlain was asked to receive a deputation to discuss the censorship generally but, before agreeing, he sought the views of the Advisory Board. In a memorandum to its members he wrote:

> Lately a number of plays have been sent in for licence, which go very near the mark. That the tone of this kind of production is not moral there can be no question – making light of illicit love, cynical treatment of marriage vows and all the rest of it, comprise the greater part of the so-called plots.

He went on to question the possibility of checking the production of certain plays and confessed that, after six years as Lord Chamberlain, he found it difficult to draw a rigid line. He continued:

> In drama the whole question circles and comes back to questions of sex. If the drama is to go on I frankly do not see how the institution of Censor can proceed on lines different

> to those which now guide it, actuated by common sense, i.e. to differentiate between what may, to the ordinary mind, be really harmful, and matters which, though they go near the mark or even beyond it, cannot I believe be said to leave lasting impressions.

Mr Buckmaster seemed almost to prophesy the 1968 Theatres Act when he said in his reply:

> There is not so far as I know a single play now produced within my memory which would be stopped by the common law on the ground of obscenity or the corruption of morals. No doubt the distinction between books and drama is marked but none the less modern literature shows how standards vary. Take Arnold Bennett's last book *A Pretty Lady*; people criticise its art and its purpose but no one says it is unclean and yet the whole story is that of the life of a prostitute.

Towards the end of his letter he wrote:

> The truth is that your office must cater for all, it must stop all that is unclean, it must repress the thing that is gross, but to say that you must not laugh at anything connected with relations between men and women is more than you can safely do.

Sir Walter Raleigh replied at some length, giving credit to the Lord Chamberlain. He said that, as he read more plays referred to him, he was becoming:

> more of a sceptic on the useful possibilities of the Censorship . . . The Censor should be very reluctant to suggest verbal recommendations. Authors are sensitive about their works; and good authors are much more sensitive than bad authors . . . Indecency is not usually a matter of words. I have heard of a comic author who said he could recite 'Mary had a little lamb' in such a way as to make it a monument of obscenity, while pretending complete innocence . . . Another thing which makes censorship

> extraordinarily difficult is the difference of audiences. All plays are not for all people. This is not sufficiently recognised.

He said he would never refuse a licence to Bernard Shaw and continued:

> There remain the plays which should not be allowed anywhere. There are very few. Most of them would be condemned outright by the audiences, which is much more effective than condemnation by the Censor . . . What tried me most of all of the Censorship was the multitude of rubbishy, mildly lascivious plays which had to be licensed. I was not against them. But some plays to which a licence was refused were better than this licensed trash. So there was I, a kind of man of letters, refusing the better and licensing the worse.

Many people would agree with these sentiments. It is an admirable summary of the problems and difficulties of the censorship.

In 1921 the Lord Privy Seal was asked in the House if there was any consultative or advisory committee to assist the Lord Chamberlain in his duties as censor: and, if so, what was the composition of this committee and which of the members were regarded as representatives of the public interest? Lord Sandhurst replied: 'There is an Advisory Board in connection with the censorship of plays, which was first formed in 1909 and reconstituted the following year. The members of the Board are Lord Buckmaster, Mr H. Higgins, Sir Squire Bancroft and Sir Douglas Dawson. Lord Buckmaster is a very distinguished representative of the public interest.' (Mr Higgins, a solicitor, had joined the Board earlier in the year and Lord Sandhurst must have forgotten to mention Sir Walter Raleigh.)

When Lord Sandhurst died in office in 1921, he was succeeded by the 8th Duke of Atholl (then aged fifty) on 21 November, but his time as Lord Chamberlain lasted only one year. In October 1922 Lloyd George's coalition government

Viscount Sandhurst, Lord Chamberlain 1912–21; and his successor, the 8th Duke of Atholl, the last Lord Chamberlain to resign upon a change of government

fell and after the subsequent election there was a Conservative administration under Bonar Law. The Duke of Atholl offered his resignation, which was then still customary on a change of government, and, as there was some doubt about his loyalty to the Conservatives (which later proved incorrect), he was not reappointed, even though, in his year of office, he had shown himself a good and conscientious Lord Chamberlain as regards the theatre. On Bonar Law's recommendation King George V appointed the Earl of Cromer.

In the years immediately following the end of the war the Examiners seemed generally to take a more lenient – or more enlightened – view of their duties, no doubt reflecting consciously or unconsciously the changed climate of opinion which the war years had brought about. For example, Shelley's *The Cenci*, written one hundred years previously, and consistently refused a licence, was recommended for one in 1920 by G. S. Street, who reported:

> The subject of the play is of course distressing to the last degree. The gloomy and tragic study of Francesco Cenci's madness, culminating in the outrage of his daughter, Beatrice, done in mere devilry; his murder and the condemnation of Beatrice by the Pope – it is all one long horror. Nor as a matter of personal opinion do I think that Shelley's genius redeems the horror; there is little of his true poetry in the play. But it is a famous play by a great poet – it is universally read; it is throughout on a level of high tragedy . . . It is certainly, and strongly, 'Recommended for Licence' so far as I am concerned.

Lord Sandhurst agreed and awaited a submission for a particular production. This did not arrive until 1922 – for the New Theatre. His successor, the Duke of Atholl, then wrote:

> I am of the opinion that I should endorse the finding of my predecessor in office and pass the play. It is not as if a modern writer had invented the subject-matter, which in such a case would be disgusting. On the contrary the whole thing is a drama of real life that was acted long ago and Shelley's version of it may be looked upon as a

> reproduction watered down to enable it to appear upon the dramatic stage, but written in the style of the date of the occurrence, which helps to put it amongst the classics . . . I therefore pass the play.

The *Théâtre du Grand Guignol*, originating in France, had found its way to London in a modified form. Sybil Thorndike introduced a season of Grand Guignol at the Little Theatre in London from 1920–22. She herself, with her husband, Lewis Casson, and her brother, Russell Thorndike, acted in a number of these one-act plays, including *Terror* and *The Old Women*. Some caused quite a stir but the Lord Chamberlain allowed the plays on the grounds that no-one would go and see them without knowing what to expect.

By 1922 it had become apparent that a number of plays being put on in the provinces were either unlicensed or contained unlicensed material. The Lord Chamberlain approached the Home Secretary for help and he circulated the Chief Constables:

> Managers of Theatres should be in a position to produce, if required, either the Licence for the performance of a play or a written authority from the Lord Chamberlain that the play has been licensed, or changes made with his approval in a play previously licensed.

That same year Pinero's fable *The Enchanted Cottage* was performed in London, one act of which concluded with a tableau of a married couple in bed. The Duke of Atholl attended a performance and minuted:

> The scene was inanimate, i.e. a dream, and the bed scene was 'in the clouds' far away, and though not really desirable was 'cleanly' shown, with no intention of being offensive. Under the circumstances I thought it wiser to leave well alone – but it should not be treated as a precedent.

Between 1910 and 1922, 700 plays a year on average were licensed, the majority of which were light entertainments mainly for the benefit of soldiers on leave. The number that were refused a licence worked out at about four per year, a ratio of 175:1.

During this time Shaw's *Mrs Warren's Profession*, refused a licence in 1898, was resubmitted not once but three times – in 1911, 1914 and 1916, and each time a licence was refused. After it had met its fourth refusal Shaw wrote to Lord Sandhurst:

> The play has now been worn out on the American and Continental stages, and is, besides, so old-fashioned by this time that at one of the so-called private performances which took place in London a few years ago, Mr Granville-Barker and I could do nothing but laugh at its technique.

Bernard Shaw took the Lord Chamberlain to task for not having the play 'examined' again but Sandhurst replied that two readers had read the play in the past and that he himself was well acquainted with it. Shaw struck back:

> My contention is that *Mrs Warren's Profession* should be read carefully through by your whole staff, including Colonel Sir Douglas Dawson. My only fear is that it may end in the play being licensed, and my finding myself as a respectable elderly gentleman over sixty, credited with the recent production of a play written with a brutality extremely unbecoming to my age and serenity.

Shaw wrote this letter in 1916, during the war, and he went on:

> However, Mrs Warren is having the time of her life with our men in training and on leave from the front; and as the older I grow, the more inclined I am to believe that all plays whatsoever should be prohibited, I have nothing more to say, and am unaffectedly apologetic for having said so much.

In 1917 Edwin Heys, a producer/manager, seeking to drum up support to get a licence for the play, sent a petition to the Lord Chamberlain with the signatures of many important and influential people. The play was re-read, this time by E. A. Bendall who, with the support of all the members of the Lord Chamberlain's Advisory Board except for Sir Walter Raleigh, still did not recommend issuing a licence.

Four years later, in 1921, *Mrs Warren's Profession* was resubmitted yet again and a fresh reader, G. S. Street, reported:

> This play has been refused a licence more than once. The refusal was entirely justified at the time, but for reasons to be stated later I think on the whole a licence may now be granted . . . The chief reasons for its rejection have been the nature of Mrs Warren's business and the suggestion of incest . . . My reasons for reconsidering the refusal are: the play has been performed more than once by private societies in England and publicly in other countries. It has been freely circulated in book form. It has been extensively discussed for years. It is in fact very well known to a large public. Therefore in a way it is futile to prohibit its public performance . . . An audience will no longer be shocked as it would have been. A considerable number of people regard it as a valuable play on the side of morality . . . Certainly the play is deeply serious in intention . . . After very careful consideration I have changed my mind . . . So far as I am concerned the play is, though quite without enthusiasm, recommended for licence.

The Duke of Atholl felt, however, that he could not reverse a decision arrived at by his predecessors, arguing that 'life and wages now are much better than when the play was written and many people might think that the conditions then are the conditions now in social life'. The saga of this play and its licensing was to continue for a little longer yet.

Chapter Six

The Earl of Cromer, Lord Chamberlain 1922–38

Although the Duke of Atholl must have been disappointed not to continue as Lord Chamberlain in 1922, the Earl of Cromer's appointment was undoubtedly a good one. He brought a fresh look to the role of censor of plays and his judgements, with the hindsight of time, seemed perfectly sound for the 1920s and 1930s.

Lord Cromer had a deep love and knowledge of the theatre, and this included also French plays, for he was fluent in that language. During his sixteen-year-long tenure he wielded the blue pencil with a more enlightened outlook than any of his predecessors. He had comparatively little trouble with authors or management, as his son, the present Earl, explains:

> Whilst enforcing his duties as Censor [he] wanted to mitigate unnecessary rigidities and he introduced a custom, which was very much welcomed by the theatrical world, under which authors and producers were invited to come and discuss with the Lord Chamberlain and his staff passages in plays which offended against the written rules, with a view to seeing whether some compromise or alteration in wording could be adopted to eliminate the imposition of censorship. The dialogue between the Lord Chamberlain and the theatrical world was very much appreciated and helped greatly to find practical working solutions as problems arose.

The second Earl of Cromer was born in 1878 and, in the earlier part of the century, had been in the diplomatic service.

Later he was ADC to the Viceroy of India and then Equerry and Assistant Private Secretary to the King before being appointed Lord Chamberlain at the age of forty-four.

He was the first Lord Chamberlain who was not a political appointment. Whereas previously there had been a new Lord Chamberlain whenever there was a new Government, just before Ramsay MacDonald became the first Labour Prime Minister in January 1924, King George V obtained the agreement of all parties that the Great Officers of the Household (i.e. Lord Chamberlain, Lord Steward, and Master of the Horse), and certain other Court appointments, should in future be considered non-political. These appointments, as now, are made by the Sovereign with the agreement of the Prime Minister.

Since the office of Lord Chamberlain had now lost its political character, Lord Cromer decided to question the advisability of it continuing to have control over theatres and stage plays, for, as he used to say, it was becoming increasingly difficult for one man to control the tide of modern thought. It was now the case that the Lord Chamberlain himself, being 'a non-political officer and no longer a member of HM Government, is capable by misguided policy of involving the Crown, HM Government and the Office he holds in serious embarrassment'. He wrote on 16 December 1924 a letter to the Home Secretary, Sir William Joynson Hicks, stating this view and asking for his opinion. He said he felt it his duty to raise the question himself before it was raised in Parliament or elsewhere. Lord Cromer enclosed with his letter a confidential memorandum setting out the problem for the guidance of the Home Secretary and suggesting four alternative forms of censorship: the Lord Chamberlain himself (now no longer a member of the government), the Home Office, local councils, or a specially created Board of Authority. It is a well argued and forthright document (see Appendix D).

The Home Secretary replied by saying that the government did not wish to make a change:

> The fact of the LC's office becoming non-political does not seem to me to make any fundamental change in the exercise

> of his duties . . . to make any change now . . . would require legislation . . . it would be most inconvenient at the present time.

He went on to say he hoped that the Lord Chamberlain would continue to call upon the advice of the Home Office and the Law Officers on questions of policy.

Lord Cromer of course had to accept this decision, no doubt quite willingly. In his letter of 30 January 1925 to the Home Secretary he said:

> It will, I feel, be a matter of gratification to The King to know that the Government would certainly be reluctant to see any alteration in the existing system, which, in spite of the criticism that must necessarily be levelled from time to time against any system, seems to work quite well in practice.

Lord Cromer sent the correspondence for the King to see, expressing the view that, with no change in the situation, His Majesty need not have any apprehensions. In his covering memorandum he wrote:

> The truth is that the Censorship of Plays is so thorny a question that no-one is particularly anxious to take the responsibility out of the hands of the LC, and to tackle it themselves. This responsibility I am quite prepared to shoulder . . . If confidence continues to be placed in my doing my best to steer a middle course, His Majesty may rely on my continuing to act as I think right, however much my policy may at times be criticised, misrepresented or assailed by the Press and people who do not know the why and wherefore of any particular circumstances connected with stage plays.

From time to time the Public Morality Council would send deputations to the Lord Chamberlain when its members considered the censorship was becoming too lax. In 1924 one deputation pointed out that the current stage play licence no longer included the caution 'does not in its general tendency contain anything immoral or otherwise improper for the stage'. Lord Cromer explained that this was dropped in 1912 on the advice of the Home Office, it being considered obsolete in phraseology; but this had in no way affected the powers exercised by him under the 1843 Theatres Act. In 1929 another deputation complained about the general character and atmosphere of certain plays which might be considered immoral in tendency and contrary to religious teaching, and also about incidents in some current productions, particularly a revue called *Wake Up and Dream*.

Prosecutions under Section 15 of the Theatres Act involved forfeiture of the theatre's licence. This being so, magistrates often declined to record a conviction as they considered this penalty too severe. This rendered Section 15 practically inoperative. The matter was put right, at the instigation of Lord Cromer, by Parliament in 1925 inserting an appropriate clause in the Criminal Justice Bill.

The following year Lord Cromer made another change in the machinery of censorship. Previously only producers or managers could submit scripts of plays for licensing, but from then on authors were able to do so as well. However, the licence continued to be issued to the manager of the theatre where the play was first to be performed.

Also in 1926 the Lord Chamberlain decided to regularise private Sunday performances of plays by dramatic societies in those theatres licensed by him. A letter dated 23 June 1926 was sent to the licensees of these theatres. Two years later, in 1928, a deputation from the Society of West End Theatres asked whether *public* performances could be given on Sundays because the legitimate theatre was suffering as a result of the public being able to go to a cinema or a concert or a cabaret on Sundays. The Lord Chamberlain, having taken advice from the Home Office, replied that he was unable to allow this without legislation. Later, in 1934, the Fortune Theatre was prosecuted for putting on plays on Sundays which to all intents and purposes were public performances under the guise of a Society calling itself 'Experimental Theatre'.

One of the earlier plays to come Lord Cromer's way was *Our Betters* by W. Somerset Maugham, on which G. S. Street

The Earl of Cromer, appointed Lord Chamberlain in 1922

had reported in 1923 (see above, pages 55–57). It is a satire on American women who married into British titles. Maugham wrote the play in Rome in 1915 and it was first produced in New York in 1917. One of the characters, Tony Paxton, a gigolo, is modelled on Gerald Haxton, Maugham's secretary/companion/lover. Another character, Arthur Fenwick, may also have been meant to resemble Gordon Selfridge who founded the department store.

Street had 'tentatively and with the reserve indicated' recommended the play for licence. However most reviews of the New York production had expressed shock at the immorality of the play and its bad language. Ted Morgan, in his biography of Maugham, says that 'no English producer would touch it because the language was too shocking and because it made fun of Americans just when England was counting on America to enter the war', thus confirming Street's view. It ran for 112 performances.

Because of its theme – and certain criticisms of Americans – Lord Cromer sent the play to three members of the Advisory Board who saw no adequate reason for refusing a licence. One of them indeed, Lord Buckmaster, referring to the Act 2 climax, wrote, 'But it is not told indecently and I think the public will not be unduly shocked because a man and a woman are found locked in a summerhouse.'

So Lord Cromer gave it a licence with only one small endorsement: 'Licence issued on the understanding that the name of the country house "Feathers Nevill" is changed to "Grayston Towers".' (This, as Street had pointed out, was because Lady Cunard lived at 'Nevill Holt' which seemed to identify her with the part of Pearl.) During the summer months of 1923 *Our Betters* played to full houses at the Globe Theatre. A note in the programme read: 'Owing to various rumours which were circulated when the play was produced in America the author wishes to state that the characters in it are entirely imaginary'. There was some adverse press comment, including that of one critic who said that perhaps the Lord Chamberlain should now be called the 'No-Censor'.

Lord Cromer received a letter from Balmoral written by Lord Stamfordham, King George V's Private Secretary, on 18 September which stated that 'somebody had spoken to the

King about a play *Our Betters*: and if the report is true HM thinks it must be decidedly objectionable and he is inclined to wonder whether it was carefully considered by the censor'.

Lord Cromer wrote back on 21 September:

> Every LC is apt at times to be the butt of Press criticism and while, at present, some papers are saying I am unduly lax, others have been saying that I am ridiculously strict. There is no pleasing everyone successfully, and my own line is that so long as I take what I consider to be the right and common-sense view of things, I remain uninfluenced by newspaper blame or praise.

He went on to describe the theme of the play, how he himself was uncertain about licensing it but, on the advice of the Advisory Board did so. He said he could quite understand that many Americans might not like the play and that someone should have spoken to the King. He offered to send all the papers for the King to see, 'but they are rather lengthy'. He concluded his letter: 'However I would ask you to assure the King that the most careful consideration was given to this play, as indeed it is given to all plays that come before my Department before they are licensed, as the drama is a thing in which I take a great personal interest.'

Lord Stamfordham replied by return on 23 September:

> I showed [your letter] to the King, who desires me to say that he did not wish to find fault with what your department had done in the matter of the play *Our Betters*; nor was His Majesty aware that the piece had been produced in America, which of course affects the King's adverse criticism. Moreover, as three of the Advisory Committee, including a very important opinion like Lord Buckmaster's, recommended the sanctioning of the play, you could not have insisted upon censoring it.

Following this Lord Cromer wrote a note to Sir Douglas Dawson saying that personally he would have preferred to have banned the play as he knew it would give rise to feeling.

The play had, in fact, first been submitted in 1917, but

privately to Lord Sandhurst, Lord Chamberlain at the time. He had given it to Bendall to read who recommended a licence, but Lord Sandhurst was concerned about the Act 2 scene and asked the author to rewrite it. This gave cause for some people to think the play had been banned at first and that Lord Cromer had passed a play turned down by his predecessor. As the author did make some alteration to that scene, this was not true.

Our Betters ran for 548 performances at the Globe Theatre in 1923 and 1924, and a film was made of it in 1933. It was revived in 1946 at the Playhouse Theatre when, according to James Agate, the drama critic, the play stood up well and audiences twenty years on were less shocked: 'The young people of today think that "goings on" are what summer-houses are for,' Agate wrote.

In 1924 Lord Cromer at first refused to license Noël Coward's play *The Vortex* because of its theme of a nymphomaniac mother chasing after young men of a similar age to her drug-addicted son. Street, who read the play, recommended a licence although he had some misgivings about Act III in which the son upbraids the mother for the immoral conduct of her life.

Lord Cromer decided to seek the opinions of the Advisory Board. Only Dawson supported the Lord Chamberlain. Higgins, Buckmaster and Bancroft all backed the Examiner's recommendation for a licence. Lord Cromer, still in doubt, sent the play for King George V to read. His Majesty thought the play 'disgusting but unfortunately cannot be prohibited', wrote Lord Stamfordham. A note in the file in Lord Cromer's hand reads: 'The majority of the Advisory Board being in favour of a licence being issued for this play, I should not feel justified in refusing to allow its performance . . . I am reluctantly prepared to issue a Licence.'

Noël Coward went to see Lord Cromer at St James's Palace just before the play was due to open at the Everyman Theatre, Hampstead, in November 1924. As he relates in his autobiography:

> I was having a spirited duel with the Lord Chamberlain . . . and it was only after a long-drawn-out argument, during

which I must say, he was charming and sympathetic, that I persuaded him the play was little more than a moral tract. With a whimsical and rather weary smile he finally granted the licence.

The Vortex was a success – Noël Coward himself playing the lead and directing. It helped to establish his reputation as an actor, dramatist and director, and went on to play at the Royalty Theatre in Dean Street.

In 1924 Lord Cromer wrote to several people saying that he was anxious to add a lady to the Advisory Board as he felt that women should have opportunities of representation. Various names were suggested at the time but it was not until a few years later that the first woman was appointed, namely Lady Violet Bonham-Carter (later Baroness Asquith of Yarnbury), the celebrated Liberal and daughter of H. H. Asquith.

Sir Squire Bancroft resigned from the Advisory Board in 1926 and his place was taken by Sir Johnston Forbes-Robertson, the former actor-manager. In 1931 Sir Douglas Dawson wrote to the Lord Chamberlain saying that, as he was now rarely in London and out of touch with the theatre, he felt he should resign from the Board: 'It is a wrench to me after all these years, especially as I always looked on the Advisory Board as my child.' Lord Cromer accepted his resignation with reluctance and replied, 'As you were the creator of the Advisory Board, let me tell you how more than grateful I am to you for having brought this into existence'.

Professor Allardyce Nicoll, a professor of English Literature at London University, was selected to succeed Dawson, only to resign three years later on accepting an appointment at Harvard University. In 1934 Lord David Cecil, Professor of English Literature at Oxford University, and Professor Winifred Culls, a physiologist, joined the Board and soon afterwards so did Sir Ian Malcolm, a former MP and diplomat. By 1936 Sir Johnston Forbes-Robertson was no longer being sent plays owing to his advanced age of eighty-three. Viscount Ullswater, a former Speaker of the House of Commons, had been appointed by then and so too had Cyril

Maude, a retired actor-manager who had recently, on Street's death, applied to replace him as an Examiner of Plays.

In 1936 Sir Ian Malcolm wrote to Lord Cromer asking in what ways he wanted the Advisory Board to help him, to which Lord Cromer replied:

> As to the guidance I seek from members, it is more in the form of wishing to know whether they individually would be in favour of a play being licensed or not . . . With the march of time the views of what can, or cannot, be presented on the stage are bound to alter, although stage performances must of necessity lag somewhat behind the books of our most advanced novelists. Consequently, what I really look to my Advisory Board to give me is a commonsense view of how to deal with any particular play that comes before them.

Another play to give Lord Cromer cause for concern was *Six Characters in Search of an Author* by the Italian dramatist, Luigi Pirandello. Various versions in translation were submitted between 1922 and 1925 and the Examiner, Street, recommended a licence. However Cromer (as had his predecessor) disagreed, because there was incest in the story, and the play was banned. Lord Cromer wrote in 1925 a comprehensive minute in his own hand giving his reasons:

> The works of Pirandello are just now the fashion. He is acclaimed as the most famous living Italian, if not European, dramatist . . . I fail to see why all these considerations should influence impartial judgement in the consideration of this particular play.
>
> . . . No amount of supposed unreality of the characters, played as they must be by living people, can disguise the objectionable fact that a step-father goes to a brothel: that he nearly has intercourse with his step-daughter; that he is fortunately saved from this repulsive act by his maltreated wife . . .
>
> The Press tell us that this country will be the laughing stock of Europe if this play is not allowed to be performed.
>
> In Italian it was probably not fully understood by most

> English audiences, but when its full significance is brought home in English I cannot help feeling that most people would disapprove of its performance being permitted.

Nigel Playfair, the Licensee of the Lyric Theatre, Hammersmith, was one of those who submitted a version of the play and he, understandably, put forward a contrary plea:

> I know the general opinion is that it was refused a licence on the grounds that it deals with the subject of incest, but this is surely not the case: even if the relationship between a step-father and step-daughter can be called incestuous, not only does no intercourse actually take place, but there is no question of it taking place when the relationship is established.

He had the approval of the reader but not of Lord Cromer!

Another play refused a licence early in Lord Cromer's term of office was *Uplift*, later altered to *L'Ecole des Cocottes*, despite pressure being brought to bear on him by Sir George Arthur (soldier and author) and Gladys Cooper (actress). It tells the story of Ginette who, under the tuition of a professor of deportment, moves upwards in the social scale from one lover to another. The play, adapted into English by H. M. Harwood, was put on by the Play Actors' Society at the Princes Theatre in December 1925. It was finally performed at The Playhouse in September 1928 under the title *Excelsior*. In his report Street (who this time did *not* recommend a licence) wrote:

> It is an amusing play; much of the satirical dialogue is good. Played in French by French players it would not be objected to here; far less decent plays have been allowed when played in French. But in English I feel it would not do. The career of a cocotte rising higher and higher, and passing from lover to lover . . . would shock people too much. (I have not blue-pencilled passages emphasising this sort of thing – such as Amelie wishing to know 'a gentleman who would like a friend, not too expensive' and so on – as the whole play is on the same lines.)

Shaw's *Mrs Warren's Profession* had first been submitted in 1898. Now, after twenty-six years and six separate submissions, it was at last given a licence by Lord Cromer. Approached in 1924 by Charles Macdona, who held the touring rights of all Shaw's plays, he reversed the decisions of his predecessors, and recorded this note in his own hand:

> I fully appreciate and respect the motives which prompted my predecessors to refuse a Licence. Times have however greatly changed since 1898 . . . in these days the mentality of the average adult audience would neither be shocked nor harmed by the presentation of this subject on the stage merely because it is unpleasant . . . it would therefore be absurd to go on refusing a licence to this play, ignoring the march of time and the change it brings about in public opinion over facing such questions openly.

In 1926, when the play was due to open at the Strand Theatre in London, the *Daily Telegraph* reported that it was going to contain several lines which did not appear in the original text. Shaw was furious and wrote to the Lord Chamberlain:

> I have just had my breakfast considerably upset by an insane statement in the papers . . . It is pure folly, quite unauthorised by me . . . I wish your powers extended to the summary execution of Theatre Press Agents. You could not license the epithets they deserve.

Lord Cromer replied disarmingly:

> I confess I am becoming accustomed to the ways of some Theatre Press Agents, who have to make a living, so I was not seriously disturbed by what I read in today's papers . . . I naturally have every confidence in your insisting upon Mr Macdona abiding by the text . . . To me it seems unlikely that any manager or actor would take liberties with your text or do things in your plays without authority as an author's position should be paramount in such matters.

One subject that is seldom mentioned in discussions of the censorship is, how does a Lord Chamberlain actually view a play? Lord Cromer's son has an amusing sidelight on this:

> As a child I was taken to the theatre a great deal and my father was always welcomed by the theatrical management. The only snag was that on the occasions that he went, more often than not he had the Royal Box put at his disposal, not as a status symbol but because, being more expensive, it was usually the last to be sold. The Royal Box at most London theatres is on the right-hand side of the auditorium at gallery level, close to the stage. The result was that any action that took place on the stage in the right-hand top corner could never be seen from the Royal Box and very often the direction of a play was tailored to take this into account. As a consequence of this I can claim to have seen the least interesting half of more plays than most of my contemporaries!

He also recalls being led out of a play when he was a small boy because his mother thought some action to be obscene. Consequently he has never forgotten the incident, nor the alleged obscenity!

In 1923 Dr Marie Stopes had written and submitted *Our Ostriches*, which was largely a propaganda vehicle for her views on birth control. Initially Lord Cromer hesitated to give the play a licence and asked Dr Stopes to come and see him. He recorded that he told her, 'The obvious attack on the Roman Catholics would offend susceptibility and must be altered'. This she agreed to do and he responded, 'In the circumstances I am prepared to pass it in spite of the criticism it will doubtless arouse' – and his forecast was right. A further revised version was submitted and licensed in 1930. Examiner Street wrote, '*Our Ostriches* was passed after some hesitation in 1923. It was received, as was expected, with disfavour by Catholics . . .'; and Lord Cromer commented: 'The sensation caused at the time of this play's first production is unlikely to be repeated now.'

Another play by Dr Stopes, *Vectia*, was, however, banned in 1924, much to the amazement of Dr Stopes. The theme was of a husband's impotence and the wish of his wife to have a baby, advocating the view that girls should be taught all about the facts of life before marriage. The Lord Chamberlain, having consulted the Advisory Board, considered this theme to be an undesirable one to portray on the stage.

John van Druten's play *Young Woodley* caused a stir when it was submitted in 1925. The story is set in a minor public school and deals with the calf-love of growing schoolboys – a prefect falls in love with his housemaster's wife. Street, who read the play, recommended it for licence but Lord Cromer was not so sure and sought the views of the Advisory Board. All members advised against a licence and so it was refused. In 1928, however, the play was produced by Basil Dean for private performance at The Three Hundred Club, an offshoot association of the Stage Society, run by Mrs Geoffrey Whitworth, and he invited the Lord Chamberlain to see it. Afterwards Lord Cromer sent the play to the President of the Board of Education whose view was that more harm might be done by the knowledge that a play about public schools had been suppressed than by giving it a licence.

Basil Dean described the closing stages of his 'flirtation with the Lord Chamberlain's Office' in his second volume of autobiography, *Mind's Eye*:

> Lord Cromer himself came to one of the Arts Theatre performances. I remember going to see him as the curtain fell upon acts one and two, and feeling hopeful as he nodded approvingly at me, but I kept away at the end lest I should overplay my hand. The next morning I received a call from the Lord Chamberlain's office – all was well! The only objection was to the remark of one of the schoolboys that he 'wouldn't mind being boots in a girls' school for a bit'. This was an oblique reference to the recent scandal at a famous school, where a German bootboy was reported to have deflowered a number of the pupils in a capacious boot cupboard . . . I mention my little tussle not only because the ban had attracted much adverse comment at home and in America, but also because lifting it was the first sign of the loosening of the Lord Chamberlain's grip on the English theatre.

A different sort of controversial play, *The Harem* by the Hungarian author Ernest Vajda, was submitted in 1925. Street reported:

> I think the main idea, a husband spending the night with his wife under the impression that she is committing adultery, is enough to ban the play. An additional reason is the fetid atmosphere of facile adultery and cheap cynicism about it which affects the whole play.

The Lord Chamberlain was invited to attend a private Sunday performance but he sent someone from the Office instead who reported: 'Considerable alterations have been made to the script, as originally submitted for Licence, and in its present form appeared to be innocuous'. An invitation to send in a revised script was offered but not taken up, probably because the play had received a bad press. Then the over-lessee of the Garrick Theatre, where the play was being performed, told the Lord Chamberlain that tickets were being sold, thus making the performances public ones. Both the Home Office and the Director of Public Prosecutions were consulted. The case became so complicated as to who should be prosecuted – the lessee, the licensee, the Society which put on the play or the actors and actresses – that a decision was taken not to proceed. All except the over-lessee, a Mr Dott, were much relieved!

Fata Morgana (by the same author as *Harem*) was licensed in 1925 in the form in which it was submitted, even though that included a 'seduction scene' of a young man by an older, married woman. There were a number of complaints and the producer was asked to modify 'the business'. Apparently he was unable to persuade the actor and actress to restrain themselves, and so the manager of the Criterion Theatre, on his own initiative, decided to cut the scene. When the play went on tour, however, the controversial but licensed scene was reintroduced and more complaints followed. A final warning was given by the Lord Chamberlain that, if these increased in number, he would withdraw the licence, but in the event this did not prove necessary.

In 1926 there was to be a season of Gilbert and Sullivan

operas at the Princes Theatre, opening with *The Mikado*. The First Secretary at the Japanese Embassy came to the Lord Chamberlain's Office to express the hope that the Lord Chamberlain would be able to ensure that any feature which could possibly hurt the susceptibilities of the Japanese Imperial Family might be toned down. Lord Cromer decided to take a stronger line than Lord Althorp had taken in 1907 (see Chapter 2) and wrote to the Chief Clerk of the Office:

> Surely the Japanese are becoming over sensitive about plays! We have no justification for thinking that the new production of this play will transgress in any offensive manner upon Japanese susceptibilities. It would be ridiculous of me to interfere beforehand with a classic like *The Mikado*. Anything said to the producers at this stage would straightway find its way into the Press which would scoff at the idea of interference. If later on when the play has been actually produced the Japanese have any tangible ground for complaint over this time-honoured 'fairy tale', let them come along and say so.

The opera was produced and the Japanese did not return. The Comptroller himself went to see it and found it 'difficult to criticise adversely this charming and classic Comic Opera'. The Lord Chamberlain minuted, 'I see no just cause for interference.'

In 1927 the Public Morality Council complained of a production of Wycherley's play *The Country Wife* at the Everyman Theatre, Hampstead. As this play was written before 1843 it did not have to be submitted for licence. The Lord Chamberlain therefore told the Council that he had no power to make alterations to classic plays, but only to prohibit their performance, and this he was not prepared to do with *The Country Wife*. It was up to the producer to make any alteration he saw fit to make it suitable for presentation.

The theme of a husband's impotence appeared once again in *Who Knows?*, a play by 'John Lord' submitted in 1928 for production at the Savoy Theatre. It is a story of a wife, Julia, who divorces her husband, Richard, on the grounds of his supposed adultery with Margery who has thrown herself at him. Richard marries Margery who then discovers he is impotent. Both the reader, Street, and the Lord Chamberlain were against giving the piece a licence, whereas the members of the Advisory Board were divided. Lord Cromer minuted, 'I do not feel prepared at present to admit impotence as a fitting theme for a play.' The author agreed to revise the play, which he did, modifying the impotence theme. This time the reader recommended a licence, but Lord Cromer disagreed. The script having again been revised, the play under the changed title of *For Better For Worse*, by May Edginton (the author's real name) was given four performances at the Arts Theatre. It was well reviewed, but when it was seen by the Assistant Comptroller he did not advise that the ban be removed.

In 1935 Lord Cromer had little hesitation in refusing a licence for *Shroud of Forgiveness* by John McKenna, a play fantasising on the identity of the Unknown Warrior, the unnamed soldier of the 1914 war whose grave is in Westminster Abbey. He appears in the play and says he was convicted of murder, escaped from Dartmoor Prison, enlisted in the Army and was killed whilst rescuing a comrade. The Lord Chamberlain recorded, 'A most unsuitable theme for a play and the impersonation of the Unknown Warrior at all will be resented by most people, especially if the murder element were to remain.' That same year Lord Cromer also banned *Why Keep A Diary?*, by Ladislas Fodor, translated by Edith Ellis. In this play a baby is left on the doorstep of a man who has had many love affairs and he starts speculating which woman he was with nine months previously.

Naturally it was the 'banned' plays which created the greatest interest, which is also why so many of them are mentioned in this book. During Lord Cromer's sixteen years as Lord Chamberlain nearly 13,000 plays were licensed, an average of 820 a year, but in his later years that average annual number rose as high as 1000. Under 200 plays were refused a licence, an average of twelve a year.

The present Earl of Cromer writes:

Historically the relationship between the theatrical managements and the LCO had, prior to my father's day, tended

> to be constantly fairly strained and so the presentation of a particularly pretty silver coffee set by the Society of West End Theatre Managers to my father on his retirement showed how much my father's enlightened interpretation of his duties had been appreciated by the theatrical world.

This presentation was made by a deputation of theatre managers at the end of June, 1938. Their spokesman was the Society's President, Walter Payne, who said:

> On your retirement from the High Office as Lord Chamberlain, we . . . ask your acceptance of a tribute, which, seeing that speech (even in the theatre) is silver, we have enshrined in that metal. Few public offices are more difficult than that which involves the licensing of plays and theatres . . . What better proof could be afforded of your success in this onerous task than that those who are primarily affected should thus wish to demonstrate abiding gratitude for courtesy and patience in which you have never failed, and for the sagacity which you have constantly displayed.

As for Cromer's sagacity, the distinguished actor and director Raymond Massey tells two stories in his autobiography *A Hundred Different Lives* about how the Lord Chamberlain 'came through for the theatre'.

In the American play *Spread Eagle* (1927), by George S. Brooks and Walter Lister, the final line spoken by Massey was to be, 'You son of a bitch! Stand up!' Cromer told Massey, 'I cannot allow the word "bitch" to be spoken on the English stage . . . except denoting the female of the canine kind.'

Massey thought he would have to abandon the play, which needed a strong last line, said so, and prepared to leave. Lord Cromer stopped him: 'I cannot be responsible for preventing the production of this play. It's a fine play. Would "goddammed bastard" satisfy you, Massey?'

On a later occasion Raymond Massey was staging *The Man in Possession*, a cynical and, for its time – 1930 – daring farce by H. M. Harwood in which Isabel Jeans played a lady of pliable virtue. Massey wrote:

There is, of course, at least one seduction scene in most farces. In my direction of *The Man in Possession* I staged the scene on the proven theory that the 'unhooking' of a lady was a deal more intriguing than a progressive strip-tease, especially when the seducee was Miss Jeans, encased in one of Norman Hartnell's tightest gowns. The curtain fell on the second act as I struggled with the last recalcitrant hook, and rose after the interval with the entrance of the lady's maid carrying a torn garment which she displayed to a moderate laugh from the audience. I kept wondering why that laugh wasn't bigger.

We had been running for a month or so when I got a call from Lord Cromer to come and see him at once. When I passed the sentries at St James's Palace I was in a bad state of jitters. Lord Cromer wasted no time.

'What is the garment which the maid displays at the opening of the third act?' He didn't even mention the name of the play.

'I don't know what they call it. I think it's a chemise, or slip, or something.'

'Exactly. I saw the play again the night before last – it's an *intimate* garment, and that is not what is mentioned in the script which I licensed.'

He read from a copy of the play he had in his desk. 'The maid is carrying *some garments* . . . there's nothing about "intimate" or "underclothing" . . . and that's not good enough, Massey. I am having a deuce of a time with Mrs Hornibrook and the Bishop of London . . . and there are a lot of other letters too.'

'I don't know what to do about it, Lord Cromer. I've got to convey the impression that these two people acted by Miss Jeans and myself were not just holding hands and looking at old photograph albums after the second-act curtain! . . . After all, I've played fair with you as to those garments the maid brings in. I don't see that a torn shoulder strap is so awful . . . and, remember, I couldn't undo the last hook.'

Then the man who could control the mode of fashion in the Royal Enclosure at Ascot gave me a lesson in the direction of risqué farce. Quite deadpan, and in a confidential tone, he offered this suggestion: 'What about a maid carrying on a replica of Miss Jeans's dress which you had tried to unhook? It could be . . . oh . . . eh . . . appropriately damaged.'

That night, and on every subsequent performance of a long run, the damaged dress got a shout of laughter.

Raymond Massey summed up Lord Cromer as:

> a nobleman whose urbanity and dignity concealed the fact that he was stage-struck. Lord Cromer had a genuine respect for the theatre. He was an avid playgoer, and in the countless decisions he had to make as censor (a word he detested) he was guided as much by his concern for the playwright as by his duty to protect public taste.

Chapter Seven

The Deity, the Royal Family, and Living Persons

Humbert Wolfe – the poet, satirist and man of letters who was also a distinguished Civil Servant – wrote:

> C is for Censor
> Who keeps the stage clean
> By ruling out God and the Crown as obscene.

If it had fitted the rhyme he could have added 'Living Persons'. Although not specifically mentioned in the 1843 Act, it had been traditional for the Lord Chamberlain to disallow, on the stage, any representation of the Deity, the Royal Family, living persons and those recently dead. It was therefore not illegal to do so but, on the other hand, successive Lord Chamberlains felt it was essentially a matter of good taste.

The Deity

An absolute ban on the impersonation of Christ or the Deity on the stage was maintained until 1966. This was discussed from time to time with the ecclesiastical authorities, who, until that year, advised retaining the ban. When it was found that the various Churches no longer supported the ban, it was lifted for the last two years of the administration of the 1843 Theatres Act, from which point plays depicting Christ on the stage were considered individually and on their merits. Regard was always paid, however, to the advice of the 1909 Committee that stage plays should not 'do violence to the sentiment of religious reverence'.

The ban, of course, had only been applied to post-1843

plays. The old Mystery, Miracle or Morality plays did not require the sanction of the Lord Chamberlain. Similarly, it was not his custom to have to give a licence to any truly religious play – whether or not Christ was impersonated – which was performed in a church, as this was not considered to be 'a stage entertainment'. (Nor did the Lord Chamberlain's authority extend to oratorio, to concert performances or public readings.) In the theatre, however, a bright light or a voice offstage was required to be substituted for the Deity.

Some authors were adept at introducing Christ-like figures into the story. One example was Jerome K. Jerome's only remembered play, *The Passing of the Third Floor Back*, written in 1908, in which Forbes-Robertson starred as the mysterious stranger who rents the back room on the third floor of a Bloomsbury lodging house. He interviews separately all the other boarders and so influences them that they make up their minds to lead better lives in the future.

Although *A Scent of Flowers*, by James Saunders, contains no representation of the Deity, its controversial religious theme caused it to be licensed (in 1964) with a warning that there must be no intoning of the mock burial service by the priest and that he was only to mime it. The play is about a young girl, Zoë, who is dead and her coffin is on stage. All the characters can, and do, talk to her and about her. She has committed suicide after having had a fixation on a priest and also falling in love with a married man who rejects her. Surprisingly perhaps, an amateur dramatic society decided to put on the play in Coventry Cathedral, and their drama director wrote to ask if the lines of the burial service could be spoken (and not mimed) because the play was being enacted in a church. The Provost of Coventry Cathedral was consulted and, as he was unhappy with the society's choice of play, he did not support this request. It was not granted.

Possibly the most controversial play of its time was *The Green Pastures*, by the American dramatist Marc Connelly. It was based on Roark Bradford's stories of the Negro's conception of Old Testament history, and it was first submitted for a licence in 1930, to be performed at the Haymarket Theatre. The managing director of the theatre was told it was an accepted rule of censorship that the Deity was not to be represented on stage, and especially as in this play he is depicted as an old gentleman, black, and dressed in a white shirt with a bow tie, a long black alpaca coat with black trousers and congress gaiters. The great moment of the play is when the old gentleman is seen to be God and a speaker says, 'Forgive me Lawd, I did not see de Glory.'

The Lord Chamberlain (Lord Cromer) refused it a licence on the advice of the Archbishop of Canterbury. He then sent the play for King George V to read, who told the Lord Chamberlain he thought he was quite correct to refuse a licence.

Shortly afterwards the play was broadcast on the radio. In 1934 an inquiry was made as to the possibility of a licence being given if the Deity was not represented and a reply was given that this would depend on how the revised text would read. The following year Sir Oswald Stoll applied for a licence on the grounds that the play had had a successful run in New York, where it had won a Pulitzer Prize. Lord Cromer repeated his earlier objection and Sir Oswald did not proceed further. In 1936 a film was made of the play, with Rex Ingram as 'De Lawd'.

After the War, in 1948, permission was sought to perform one scene from the play, but this was refused by Lord Clarendon. Two years later Thane Parker of the Mask Theatre tried to obtain a licence and the Archbishop of Canterbury (Fisher) was again consulted. He had seen the film but did not recommend a stage performance. In 1957 Bernard Miles asked to put it on as one of the first productions in the newly built Mermaid Theatre but the Lord Chamberlain (Scarbrough) did not give permission. Soon afterwards it was performed privately by students of a drama college and received good notices.

Further inquiries were made in 1961 and 1964 but Archbishop Ramsey felt that no exception should be made to a ban on the representation of the Deity. So over a period of thirty-four years *The Green Pastures* was not given a licence. One of the Examiners, Geoffrey Dearmer, says that it is a lovely play to read and he is surprised it has never been acted, nor has he seen the film repeated or the play broadcast on TV.

In 1950, after he had retired as a play reader, Henry Game

wrote to Geoffrey Dearmer who was still an Examiner. Apparently the then Bishop of Chichester wanted the ban lifted:

> He plumps for God on the stage much more definitely than I expected. Of course it has nothing to do with Parliament and is merely a question whether the LC of the day has enough common sense and courage to revert to medieval custom. I softened up the boys [i.e., LCO staff] on the question; but do not yet throw your cap in the air . . . Meanwhile the Lord [God] can hardly keep still on His throne with jealousy. There is His Son starring at Oberammergau, and the Lord is not even allowed to appear in some obscure production of *The Death of Adam* by amateurs! I am surprised the LC has not been struck dead in the street by a well-aimed thunderbolt.

In the 1960s other plays were refused a licence because they contained impersonations of Christ or the Deity, including *The Jesus Revolution*, *The Boy Who Carved Birds* and *Simple Golgotha*. Another was *A Man Dies*, written by Ewan Hooper, a Presbyterian Minister, and Ernest Marvin, which was submitted in September 1965. The Lord Chamberlain wrote to the Archbishop of Canterbury (Ramsey) who thought the play 'reverent and well-conceived' but said he would prefer to see it staged non-commercially or in churches. It was shown on television and as a result the Lord Chamberlain came in for much criticism for having refused it a licence. The following year, in the debate in the House of Lords on theatre censorship, the Bishop of St Albans spoke against the blanket prohibition, and the Lord Chamberlain then decided to license the play. Lord Cobbold in fact lifted the total ban not only by licensing *A Man Dies* but other plays too which portrayed Christ.

At about the same time *Will The Real Jesus Christ Please Stand Up?*, a one-act play by J. R. Baldock, was submitted. In this play a group of actors, all dressed like the conventional pictures of Christ, are auditioning for the part of Jesus in a television show. The reader, with hesitation, recommended a licence, as did I but without reservation, and a licence was given.

Yet, even as late as June 1968 the blue pencil was used on a play with a religious theme, namely *Car Cemetery* by Fernando Arrabal, translated by Barbara Wright. The play begins as a satire on suburban community living and ends in a blasphemous crucifixion scene on a bicycle. It was described by the reader as 'a kind of surrealist Passion Play, larded with petty indecencies'. It was staged in London in 1969 after the end of censorship.

One is left wondering what good the ban ever did, particularly with regard to so sincere a play as *The Green Pastures*.

The Royal Family

Sovereigns and members of the Royal Family have always been popular material for playwrights, and plays portraying them came under especially careful scrutiny. A licence for such plays was usually refused, or at least until well after the death of the person or persons portrayed.

An early example was *Pains and Penalties*, which dealt with the trial of Queen Caroline, consort of George IV. Written by Laurence Housman, it was first submitted in 1910 and a licence was refused by Lord Spencer. In 1922, after considerable pressure, one was granted by the Duke of Atholl. Initially there was much correspondence between the Lord Chamberlain's Office, the Home Office and the Attorney-General. Although Lord Chamberlains were not obliged to give a reason for refusing a licence, Lord Spencer in 1910 did so in the case of this play, saying:

> The play was disallowed because it dealt with a sad episode of comparatively recent date in the life of a lady of Royal rank.

In 1922 the King's Private Secretary (Lord Stamfordham) wrote to the Comptroller, Lord Chamberlain's Office (Sir Douglas Dawson):

> I spoke to the King about licensing *Pains and Penalties*. He remembered the question coming up before. Although naturally not anxious to put the story of Q. Caroline before

> the public, HM realises the objections to refusing a licence, but approves of the play being submitted to the Advisory Board on the understanding that he [i.e. the LC] may, should he think fit and on further consideration, exercise his veto.

The Duke of Atholl recorded:

> I am not of the opinion that the play need be submitted to the Advisory Board, as it is a matter of politics affecting the Crown, and not a matter of public decency – and I cannot therefore see how the Board is more qualified to judge than HM's advisers. I consider that the play should receive a licence.

He did, however, check with the King who gave him leave to pass the play.

In 1924 Basil Dean submitted a play by Louis Parker, *Queen Victoria*, which the Lord Chamberlain (Lord Cromer) sent to the King to read. It was returned by Lord Stamfordham with a memorandum: 'The King has read Mr Louis Parker's play *Queen Victoria* and considers it is vulgar and in many instances historically incorrect: and permission for its performance ought never to be given in HM's lifetime.'

Laurence Housman, who was the younger brother of the poet A. E. Housman, was a great lover of the Victorian era because, he said, 'I am a Victorian.' He was born in 1865 and lived until 1959. In addition to *Pains and Penalties* he produced many religious and historical plays, including *Angels and Ministers* (1921) which, with other playlets he wrote later, were collected into *Victoria Regina* (1934). These were all refused a licence until 1937. *Victoria Regina* was put on privately at the Gate Theatre, London, in 1935 with Pamela Stanley in the title role and after 1937 enjoyed great popular success.

In April 1935 *Vickie*, a chronicle play illustrating the life and character of Queen Victoria from the age of seven to her accession, was submitted. It was read by Street:

> For my part I cannot imagine any possible harm in it – quite

> the contrary. But if it is a rigid rule that Queen Victoria, even as a girl, must not be put on the stage I suppose that ends the matter.

Lord Cromer refused a licence, recording:

> I agree it seems a pity to interfere with this sort of play, but still I am bound to prohibit the impersonation of Q. Victoria during the present reign.

Two months later it was performed under the auspices of a club at the Little Theatre, Bath. The Chief Constable was asked to investigate and he was of the opinion it was tantamount to being performed publicly. A successful prosecution took place (conducted personally by the Chief Constable) at which George Titman (Secretary, Lord Chamberlain's Office) gave evidence and the defendant was fined £10, with seven guineas costs.

In 1936, following King George V's death, Lord Cromer sounded out the Duke of Connaught about removing the ban then existing on the portrayal of Queen Victoria on the stage. The Duke in turn consulted Princess Louise and Princess Beatrice (Queen Victoria's surviving daughters) who were opposed to the ban being lifted. However as the centenary of Queen Victoria's accession would fall the following year, the Lord Chamberlain felt the public was entitled to hope for a relaxation of the existing restrictions. With King George VI's approval, therefore, a press notice was issued in December to the effect that, as from June the following year, the Lord Chamberlain would be prepared to consider plays dealing with the life of Queen Victoria. Thus *Victoria Regina*, *Vickie* and *Queen Victoria* were given licences in 1937.

However that same year Hugh Ross Williamson's play *Mr Gladstone* was refused a licence on the grounds that Queen Victoria was offensively portrayed. The play had been put on at the Gate Theatre and its director Norman Marshall, in his book *The Other Theatre*, said that it was so successful he decided to transfer it to another theatre, 'but the Lord Chamberlain refused a licence because of two scenes in which Queen Victoria appeared. Admittedly Williamson was more critical of the Queen than Housman had been in *Victoria Regina*, but he limited himself as far as possible to the actual words of the Queen, taken from her published letters. The Lord Chamberlain by his action thus granted official sanction to Housman's portrait, while protecting him from competition by any other playwright who was disposed to take up a more critical attitude.'

In 1951 an operetta *Victoria and Albert*, by Norman Ginsbury and Eric Maschwitz, was refused a licence because of 'many historical inaccuracies'. At about the same time a duet in a revue *We Are Amused* between Victoria and Disraeli was also disallowed. However in 1953 Anna Neagle playing Victoria in *The Glorious Days* was allowed – and to sing – on the grounds that she only *dreamed* she was Queen Victoria when under concussion.

Another play, *Portrait of a Queen* by William Francis, was licensed in 1965. Charles Heriot was the Examiner:

> An interesting play about Queen Victoria, made from extracts from her diaries, letters, speeches and other papers and speeches of the characters in the play . . . The main fault of such a play is that it lacks movement: the characters stare out in front of them and recite their lines . . . No scandal, no John Brown thank goodness, and no mention of the Royal Family except in passing. The play is in fact a dignified affair, adhering closely to the rules that nothing is invented. What a pity that it should be the least bit dull.

In October 1967 the English Stage Company submitted *Early Morning* by Edward Bond, in which Queen Victoria figures. Charles Marowitz has neatly summed up the story of the play: 'A fantasy based on the premise that Queen Victoria was a dyke and had a lesbian affair with Florence Nightingale while the British government, led by a sadistic Gladstone and a Machiavellian Disraeli, ran the country like a branch of Murder Incorporated'.*

Two readers did not recommend a licence, nor did I: 'I cannot conceive anyone wanting to see this play except

*Quoted in *Offensive Literature: Decensorship in Britain, 1960–1982* by John Sutherland.

possibly in anticipation of the zany treatment of Q. Victoria and her lesbian relationship with Florence Nightingale.'

When a licence was refused William Gaskill, the Artistic Director of the Royal Court Theatre, asked why. I replied on 18 January 1968:

> The play *Early Morning* comprises mainly historical characters, who are subjected throughout to highly offensive and untrue accusations of gross indecency. They are selected for insult apparently as being nationally respected figures with long records of devoted service to their country and fellow citizens . . . If allegory is required then the characters should be allegorical.

The following month Gaskill came to see me to find out if the Lord Chamberlain might change his mind. I repeated that the fundamental difficulty was the linking of historical personages with various unsavoury practices, including cannibalism. As the author did not wish to remove the recognisable historical passages, Gaskill eventually decided to put on two club performances at the Royal Court with Queen Victoria played by Moira Redmond and Florence Nightingale by Marianne Faithfull.

Having informed the Director of Public Prosecution's office of this, we went along there with the papers. We told them that the Lord Chamberlain felt strongly about the play and suggested that the Director might wish to consult the Attorney-General, which he did. They decided to await public reaction to the first performance. A vice squad Inspector became a club member without any difficulty and attended that performance. This was surprising as Mary Fisher from the Lord Chamberlain's Office was not so successful. As a result of the police going along to interview the management of the Royal Court, Gaskill cancelled the second performance and the Attorney-General decided not to take proceedings over the first one.

In his book *Sense of Direction* William Gaskill wrote: 'The play was not well received – neither Tynan nor Harewood, two of my staunchest allies, was behind it. While this was going on George Strauss had been piloting his [Theatres] Bill through the Commons . . . The general feeling was that I had been rocking the boat.'

The play was performed publicly in 1969 but has not been revived since.

In 1963, King Edward VII having died over fifty years previously and with no sons or daughters of his still alive, the Lord Chamberlain (Lord Cobbold) decided there would be no further objection in principle to plays in which that Sovereign figured. Henceforward such plays were to be judged entirely on their merits and were passed if correctly factual, but refused a licence if fantastical let alone merely scandalous. Into the latter category fell some sketches dealing with King Edward VII's love life.

The Scandal at Tranby Croft in 1966 was the first play representing King Edward to be allowed by the Lord Chamberlain. It told a true story about one Gordon Cumming being accused of cheating at cards. A number of cuts were called for before a licence was sent, particularly concerning details of Cumming's private life as his daughter, Mrs Mure, was still alive. Both Lord Cobbold and the producer, John Roberts, communicated with her to obtain her consent to the script.

The Snowdropper by Alan Richards, submitted in 1968, was a fictional story about an attempted assassination of Prince Charles at his Investiture as Prince of Wales, and the involvement of the Free Welsh Army. The reader did not recommend a licence. When I read the play my inclination was to allow it because there was no actual representation of Prince Charles. The Lord Chamberlain agreed with this view and sought the advice of the Queen and the Prince himself. However, as there was no set date or place of production a licence could not be given.

Although it was not submitted for a licence, Sir Alec Douglas-Home (as he then was) sent to the Queen's Private Secretary in the mid-1960s a play *Heir Apparent*, written by his brother, William Douglas-Home. I was invited to read and comment on the play, which I thought was not a good one. I also felt that the Queen, the Duke of Edinburgh and the Prince of Wales were all portrayed out of character. These and similar comments from other people were passed to Sir

Alec and the upshot was that his brother wrote to say he had decided not to put on the play.

The 1968 Theatres Act, which abolished the Lord Chamberlain's censorship powers, made no provision to prevent the portrayal on the stage of living members of the Royal Family. Four years later the Haymarket Theatre put on *Crown Matrimonial*, a play by Royce Ryton, dealing with the events leading up to the abdication of King Edward VIII. The dramatis personae consisted in the main of members of the Royal Family. These included Queen Mary, the abdicating King and the future King George VI, and two who are still living, namely, the then Duchess of York (now Queen Elizabeth the Queen Mother) and Princess Alice, Duchess of Gloucester.

In April 1972 the presenter, Michael Codron, had sent to the Queen's Private Secretary a copy of the script and asked for his comments, but none were forthcoming. The manager of the Haymarket telephoned me in August, telling me the play was under consideration, and asked privately for my views. I replied saying that, however good it might be as a play, it would surely be criticised for being performed so soon after the Duke of Windsor's death and portraying on stage members of the Royal Family living and recently dead. Having been sent a copy of the script, I read it and sent it with a synopsis and my comments to the Private Secretary on duty at Balmoral. Although it could only be guesswork on my part, much of the dialogue appeared to be out of character. I was also asked to send a copy of my synopsis to Queen Elizabeth the Queen Mother and to inform Princess Alice's Private Secretary. I was told that the Queen had read the play with interest, but had found a number of errors mostly in the way many of the characters were portrayed.

The play, which was set in Queen Mary's private sitting room at Marlborough House, opened at the Haymarket Theatre on 19 October 1972, directed by Peter Dewar, with Wendy Hiller as Queen Mary, Peter Barkworth as King Edward VIII and Amanda Reiss as the Duchess of York. I attended one of the earlier performances. It received some good notices and continued at the Haymarket until 9 February 1974 before going on tour.

The ban on portrayal of the Royal Family in plays was, in my opinion, unnecessarily strict. For example, good and inoffensive plays such as *Victoria Regina* and *Vickie* should have been licensed when first submitted. The banning of *Early Morning*, on the other hand, was more understandable. Perhaps Lord Chamberlains over the years could quite reasonably have been more flexible in their judgements.

In the preface to his *Happy and Glorious: A Dramatic Biography* (1943) Laurence Housman complains of the treatment given to his plays by the censorship. He goes on:

> The law still permits a single official to deprive an author of the reward of his work on no better grounds than his own private judgement. Though these plays are neither indecent, nor libellous, nor blasphemous, nor liable to cause a breach of the public peace (which are the grounds on which the censorship is supposed to operate) I have no right of appeal against a decision which has cost me . . . many hundreds of pounds.

He surely had a point.

Living persons and those recently dead

Two of the grounds suggested in the 1909 Joint Select Committee Report on which the Lord Chamberlain should be entitled to withhold a play licence were:

(c) To represent on the stage in an invidious manner a living person, or any person recently dead.
(f) To be calculated to impair friendly relations with any Foreign Power.

Lord Chamberlains since then complied with these proposals, but they used their common sense when interpreting 'in an invidious manner'. In later years they looked upon public figures, such as politicians, as being fair game in sketches and revues. An example was *Beyond the Fringe* in 1961 in which Peter Cook wittily 'sent up' Harold Macmillan, then Prime Minister.

In 1935 a play about the life of Dante Gabriel Rossetti was submitted but the Lord Chamberlain (Lord Cromer) said he would only license it if the surviving relatives had no objection. A member of the Rossetti family wrote to Lord Cromer, 'I would wish to protest against the licensing of this play which is gross in itself . . . cannot fail to be offensive to relatives and all who have any sympathetic knowledge of the persons concerned.' On the strength of this a licence was refused.

A further play about Rossetti, *We Dig for the Stars*, was submitted in 1945. This too was not licensed, again because one of his descendants raised an objection.

In October 1945, Terence Rattigan's *The Winslow Boy* was submitted. The reader's view was that although the plot was based on the Archer-Shee (1911) case it was first-rate theatre and so recommended a licence. Although it was known that a number of Archer-Shee relatives were still alive the Lord Chamberlain, Lord Clarendon, instead of consulting them, decided to advise the management to print a note in the programme to say that, 'This play was inspired by the facts of a well-known case but the characters attributed to the individuals represented are based on the author's imagination and are not necessarily factual.'

In 1950 Michael Walsh submitted for licence his play *The Baker's Daughter*. It was the story, thinly disguised, of Seretse Khama's marriage to an English girl, Ruth Williams, in 1948. Seretse Khama was to become Prime Minister of Bechuanaland in 1965 and in the following year he became the first President of the country, now Botswana. He died in 1980. Although he need not have done so Lord Clarendon consulted the Commonwealth Relations Office, which agreed that the play was clearly based upon the actual circumstances of the marriage and that a number of the characters were identifiable with real persons. Consequently the author was told the play could not be given a licence because it was the Lord Chamberlain's rule not to permit the portrayal of living persons on the stage.

Lord Cobbold (Lord Chamberlain 1963–71) kept an open mind on the question of 'living persons'. In 1965 the Royal Shakespeare Company submitted *In the Matter of J. Robert Oppenheimer*, by R. Spiers, for the Aldwych Theatre. This was a documentary type of play based on a transcript of the American Atomic Energy Commission's Loyalty Hearings in 1954 to establish whether Professor Oppenheimer, the doyen of atomic researchers in the United States, was a security risk because of his past communist affiliations. As all or most of the people involved were still alive, the play reader did not feel able to recommend a licence. Another of his concerns was that the play represented an actual trial of recent date.

The Lord Chamberlain decided to seek the views of David Bruce, US Ambassador in London. As to the representation of a living person, Cobbold said he had it in mind to ask Oppenheimer if he had any objection; and as to the re-enactment on stage of a recent American trial, that he would welcome American opinion and would like to know if the play was going to be put on in the States. The ambassador, having taken soundings, told Lord Cobbold that since the hearing was not before a Court of Justice there was no parallel with the re-enactment of a trial in the British Courts of Justice; and he felt that the American government could not validly object to the licensing of the play.

On the Lord Chamberlain's instructions I wrote to the Aldwych Theatre asking them to give an assurance that neither Professor Oppenheimer, nor anyone else principally involved, objected, and that the proceedings at the hearing would be adhered to on stage. Meanwhile the play was already being performed in London at the Hampstead Theatre Club as well as in many countries worldwide. When the RSC lost interest a new submission with a revised script was made by Perdita Productions. Lord Cobbold read this script and said in a note to me: 'I certainly do not regard the play as offensive to Oppenheimer. Some of the witnesses sound a bit silly, but so long as they are correctly quoted that does not worry me much . . . On balance, and in light of its history in other countries and at Hampstead, I think it would be foolish to refuse a licence.' *In the Matter of J. Robert Oppenheimer*, notwithstanding the representation of living persons, was given a licence.

In November 1966 *MacBird*, by Barbara Garson, was submitted by the Michael White management and, as a satire using *Macbeth* as a vehicle for commentary on the alleged activities of the former President of the United States and the Kennedy family, it caused quite a stir. President Johnson was 'cast' as Macbeth, his wife as Lady Macbeth and President Kennedy as Duncan. It accused the Kennedys of attempting to set up a presidential dynasty; and it accused the Johnsons of luring Kennedy to their home state of Texas and engineering his assassination.

Lord Cobbold wrote to Sir Paul Gore-Booth, the Permanent Under-Secretary at the Foreign Office, to ask for his informal view of the play. His view was that it should not be shown in Britain until it had been put on in the United States. Cobbold also wrote to David Bruce, who admired the style and ingenuity of the author but he, too, hoped the play would not be put on. I told Michael White that there could be no licence for the time being, but that the Lord Chamberlain would re-consider it if the play ran in the States for a considerable time and without undue unfavourable comment.

In March the following year the Theatre Royal, Stratford, in East London, submitted the play after it had opened in New York. The Lord Chamberlain was still reluctant and therefore the theatre, which had been closed for some time, turned itself into a Theatre Club and put on the play. Lord Cobbold wrote to the Director of Public Prosecutions to tell him about this, but not requesting him to take any action provided the performances were genuine Club performances. The police were asked to check and it seemed that they were. The Director of Public Prosecutions, having consulted the Attorney-General and in view of the pending Joint Committee on the Censorship of the Theatre, decided to take no action. In the event the play had a short run.

That same year (1967) another play on the assassination of President Kennedy was submitted. This was Gordon Kennedy's *The Day That Will Not End*. The play reader's interpretation of it was that it was a documentary investigation, but when I read the play it seemed more fictional in style.

As the wife and mother of Lee Harvey Oswald (the presumed assassin) were represented and were still alive, the author was told:

With regret the Lord Chamberlain does not feel able to

allow those parts of the play that involve the impersonation of living persons, and the attribution to them of dialogue and actions of your choosing.

The author was given the opportunity to seek the permission of those concerned, but this he declined to do and so no licence was given.

A particularly interesting and controversial play was *Soldiers*, by the German playwright Rolf Hochhuth. A provisional translation was submitted in December 1966 by Kenneth Tynan as its literary advisor for production at the National Theatre at some future date. The fictional story covered various events in 1943, accusing Winston Churchill of the death of his Polish ally, General Sikorski, in an air crash (thought by the author not to have been an accident); and of criminal inhumanity in the bombing of Dresden. The characters included Marshal of the RAF Sir Arthur Harris, then alive, and Churchill, Field Marshal Lord Alanbrooke, Bishop Bell of Chichester and Lord Cherwell, all recently dead. The play also cast doubt on the moral basis of much of the Allies' war effort, such as saturation bombing.

The Lord Chamberlain (Lord Cobbold) decided to consult privately Viscount Chandos, Chairman of the National Theatre, who said he was opposed to the National putting on this play. We played for time by telling Kenneth Tynan the Lord Chamberlain was not prepared to make any comment until there was a formal submission of a final script. This was received in March 1967 with notification that the Theatre Board members were going to discuss the play the following month. Lord Cobbold continued his private line of inquiry with Lord Chandos, who told him the script had taken him three and a half hours to read and he was sure it would be turned down unanimously by the Board. In view of this I wrote to Tynan on 6 April and told him the Lord Chamberlain was not prepared to make a decision until plans for production were formally submitted on behalf of the Board of the National Theatre. Tynan's response came in his letter to me of 10 April 1967, which is quoted in full:

I am at a loss to understand your communication of April

6th. Nothing in the Theatres Act (1843) stipulates that a theatre manager must guarantee production of a play before the Lord Chamberlain expresses an opinion on it. I am therefore compelled to repeat my request, which is made to you on behalf of Sir Laurence Olivier and the Board of the National Theatre: *will you kindly fulfil the function laid down for your office in law – namely that of informing us whether or not you will grant a licence for the public performance of the play in question?*

To drive the point home still more clearly: whether or not the National Theatre subsequently decides to present the play is – quite obviously – none of the Lord Chamberlain's business.

The reasons for your procrastination are, of course, perfectly obvious. The implication is that you propose to judge the play by one standard if it is presented at the National Theatre, and by another standard if the National Theatre decides against it and some other management undertakes the production. This is quite clearly an indefensible attitude for your office to take. I need hardly tell you that there would be a considerable outcry in the press and in the theatre as a whole if it became known that the Lord Chamberlain's Office was granting favours to the subsidised theatres which it withheld from the commercial theatre.

My reply was short and to the point:

Section 12 of the 1843 Theatres Act makes it obligatory upon the Lord Chamberlain to give a decision on a play only when it is submitted by the manager of the theatre and giving the date of the production.

There was silence until July, when a further version of the script was sent in. Tynan was then told that the Lord Chamberlain required evidence that Sir Arthur Harris and the families of other people portrayed in the play raised no objection. He inquired about the possibility of a Theatre Club production and he was advised to consult his solicitor. He asked if he and Sir Laurence Olivier, Director of the Theatre, might come and see the Lord Chamberlain. In the event

Tynan came alone as Olivier had had to go abroad. He asked Lord Cobbold to reconsider his attitude about the play, but this was declined. Tynan said he had a firm offer from the Mermaid Theatre for a Club production and asked for an indication as to whether or not there would be a risk of proceedings being initiated, but Lord Cobbold gave no such indication. The Lord Chamberlain wrote to Lord Chandos along these lines, copying his letter to the Director of Public Prosecutions. The National Theatre decided not to take any such risks and the play was postponed until after the Theatres Act 1968 became law. In the event it was performed, not at the National but at the New Theatre under Michael White' management from December 1968 until April 1969.

There is a postscript to this story. In 1969; Edward Prchal, the pilot of the plane in which Sikorski was killed, brought a series of libel actions as the play purported to show that Prchal had deliberately piloted the plane into the sea. He was awarded substantial damages.

A quite different type of play, *A Life in Bedrooms* by David Wood and David Wright, had been produced privately at the Traverse Theatre Club, Edinburgh, in 1967. It was a musical based on the life of the Reverend H. F. Davidson, the Rector of Stiffkey, who was defrocked in 1932 by an Ecclesiastical Consistory Court for being found guilty of misbehaving himself with numerous young ladies.

Although Davidson's widow had since died, before any licence could be given for this musical to be performed publicly we required written evidence from his descendants that they had no objections. No trace of any children could be found and the co-authors wrote to me:

> We think it logical to assume that if any of the Davidson children are alive and living in England, they can have no objection to any work being produced about their father. During the last four years a nationally screened BBC film, a best-selling paperback book, and now a play, have all been produced about the Rev. Davidson and his trial without any response whatsoever from any of the children who may be living.

This was a convincing argument and a licence was offered but it could not be taken up because the production plan for a public performance fell through.

After Lord Cobbold gave evidence before the Joint Committee in 1967, supporting the view that censorship of plays should be removed from the Lord Chamberlain, Atticus in the *Sunday Times* drew attention to his continued activity:

> Despite his evidence before the Joint Committee on Censorship of the Theatre that his own office was anachronistic the Lord Chamberlain, Lord Cobbold, is not withering away. His abhorred shears still snip and snap. Principal current victim is *Mrs Wilson's Diary*.

Mrs Wilson's Diary had been submitted by Gerald Raffles earlier that year, for production by Joan Littlewood at the Theatre Royal, Stratford. The shears indeed had been busy. There were three pages of disallowances and five of substitutions, following considerable correspondence with Gerald Raffles and following too the Lord Chamberlain's directive that he was inclined to license the piece (with cuts) because he felt sure it would be a mistake to advertise it by refusing a licence. (*Private Eye* had published the 'original' and the musical play was described as 'an affectionate lampoon' by Richard Ingrams and John Wells, its authors.) Lord Cobbold talked to Harold Wilson, then Prime Minister, about the play and sent him the script to read. I understand he was not too bothered by it but that Mrs Wilson had some reservations and so too did George Brown, then Secretary of State for Foreign Affairs.

At the invitation of Gerald Raffles I attended the first night on 21 September 1967 and was spotted by a journalist who saw me sitting in the stalls and taking notes. I minuted the next day to the Lord Chamberlain: 'It was a jolly romp with humour, good-natured and harmless and no way malicious.'

I also wrote to my host thanking him for his invitation and saying I had noticed a few deviations from the licensed script, due presumably to requirements becoming apparent during last-minute rehearsals. I added, 'No doubt your running order and routines will have settled down in the next few days and, if necessary, you will be sending me any additional material; after which I am sure you will take care to see that the licensed version is adhered to.' After that there were no further problems, and no formal complaints were raised. *Mrs Wilson's Diary* played at Stratford for a month and then it transferred to the Criterion Theatre.

I believe there can be little adverse criticism over the decisions taken by successive Lord Chamberlains on plays that featured living persons and those recently dead. Shaw, however, would not agree. On 26 June 1909, soon after his sketch *Press Cuttings* was refused a licence, he wrote a letter to *The Times* in which he drew attention to the 'living persons rule':

> This wholesale prohibition of holding the mirror up to nature does not, of course, mean what it says. On what it is understood by the Lord Chamberlain to mean I have to observe, first, that I have myself been 'represented on the stage', with the Lord Chamberlain's full approval, in a little fantasy by no less well-known an author than my friend Mr J. M. Barrie, and that on another occasion my appearance was so exactly imitated that a near relative of my own was deceived by the resemblance.
>
> After this it is hardly worth stating that unless a grotesquely imaginary Prime Minister under the well-worn *Punch* name of Balsquith, and a wildly impossible Teutophobe general whom I christened Mitchener in order to clear him of all possible suspicion of being a caricature of Lord Roberts, are to be considered as representations of living persons in any more serious sense than the topical people in our Christmas pantomimes, I feel so little guilty that I cannot bring myself to believe that the reason given for destroying the value of several weeks of my work is the real reason.

CHAPTER EIGHT

'The Right Type of Advice'

When the Earl of Clarendon was appointed Lord Chamberlain in 1938, one of the first decisions he took was to ask his predecessor, Lord Cromer, to become a member of the Advisory Board, an invitation which was accepted. After the war two more members were appointed – the Rev. Dr A. C. Don, a chaplain to the King and later Dean of Westminster; and Peter Fleming, the author and journalist for *The Times*, who also had theatrical associations as he was married to the actress Celia Johnson.

The latter appointment was on the advice of Sir Terence Nugent, the Comptroller. Peter Fleming wrote a characteristically witty letter of acceptance on 26 January 1946:

> I am very much honoured by the Chamberlain's invitation and will be delighted to serve on the Advisory Board, where I feel confident I shall soon become indispensable. Even if I do not my position there will, I flatter myself, improve the prospects of two not unimportant dramas which I have recently completed. Of these *Passion's Harvest* (written under the pseudonym of Lettuce Merridew), dealing as it does with lesbianism, incest and flagellation, is the kind of piece which might easily fall foul of the old-fashioned type of censor; while *Gomorrah and Gomorrah and Gomorrah*, a more scholarly but no less salacious effort, purporting to be written by a boy at Eton with the object of proving that Macbeth was a pansy might also, in the bad old days, have been something of a border-line case. It is a great relief to me, and also no doubt to the Lord Chamberlain, to know that the right type of advice will now be available to the Censor in respect of these two pieces, and of any others from the same source.

By this time, changes had also taken place among the Examiners of Plays. In 1930 Henry Game had been appointed joint Examiner with G. S. Street. Game, who had served throughout the First World War, had studied at the Slade School of Art and in his younger days had been an amateur actor.

A curious financial arrangement was made. Street had no salary whereas Game was given one of £250 p.a. However Street kept all the reading fees until he had earned £250, after which each retained the fees of the plays they read. In the 1930s the annual number of plays licensed was about one thousand, which meant that Street was probably receiving in reading fees more than £1,500 p.a.

In 1935 Street, who was then aged sixty-eight, asked if he could stay on until he was seventy as the post was not pensionable; but before a decision was taken, he became ill and died the following year. In 1936 therefore Game was promoted to Senior Examiner and retained his salary of £250. When, that year, he was joined by Geoffrey Dearmer, Dearmer was given no salary but, like Street, he kept the fees for

Geoffrey Dearmer, Examiner of Plays 1930–58; Chief Examiner, 1953

the plays he read. This seems to have been a more equitable arrangement. These two play readers worked in ideal harmony and remained good friends after both had retired, Game in 1953 and Dearmer in 1958. Oddly Street had never read pantomimes although Game and Dearmer did. Dearmer cannot recall, however, any pantomime needing the blue pencil.

Geoffrey Dearmer regarded Game as a very good and shrewd Examiner and a man of great charm. He remembers asking him what his policy was on double entendres and was told always to give the playwright the benefit of any doubt. About Shakespeare's frequent bawdy there could never be any doubt as Game, as an actor, well knew. He was never pornographic, and not one of his accepted editors ever tampered with his bawdy.

After Game retired Dearmer used to receive letters from him, in one of which, written in 1957, he wrote:

> Plays seem to me, judging from the notices in the papers, to have become most turgid and I don't think I should understand a good proportion of them if I still had to read them for the Lord Chamberlain.

The following year Game added:

> Censoring seems very remote to me now. I fully expect if I now read some of my judgements, I should think them damned silly. All I can plead, when up before the judgement seat, is that I did my poor best.

When Game died it was Geoffrey Dearmer who wrote his obituary for *The Times*:

> This is not the place to chew the rag about the censorship, but the severest critics of that office admit that since and including the era of George Street, whose assistant Henry was when he first went to the Lord Chamberlain's Office under Lord Cromer, nobody ever justly questioned his tolerance, good sense and great sense of humour . . . He showed in his careful and considered reports a knowledge

> and love of the theatre, and his acute mind and ready turn of speech enabled him to recommend for licence many a 'difficult' play which on paper might appear, in whole or in part, unacceptable . . .

Geoffrey Dearmer had been recommended to Lord Cromer by St John Ervine, the dramatist, and was first taken on temporarily during Street's illness in 1935–6. He had been a free-lance writer, a play reader, and, on Shaw's recommendation, a member of the Council of the Stage Society. In the First World War he fought at Gallipoli. During the Second he had joined the BBC *Children's Hour* programme as editor of the department, becoming known as 'Uncle Geoffrey'. Subsequently he returned to reading plays for the Lord Chamberlain until he retired in 1958. Now, in his late nineties, he lives in Kent.

In a letter in 1988 Dearmer defined how he saw the job of an Examiner: 'To protect and promote, to be positive not negative, to be a help not a hindrance and to say quite simply "Here is something good, and good enough for Royal Approval".'

Although Dearmer retired some five years before Lord Cobbold became Lord Chamberlain in 1963, there was a link between them. Lord Cobbold had in 1930 married Lady Hermione Lytton, eldest daughter of the second Earl of Lytton. In 1922 Geoffrey Dearmer spent a happy year in India where Lord Lytton was Governor of Bengal, as tutor to Hermione (then aged fifteen), her brother and her sister. He was not a very good tutor, he told me, but he enjoyed the job and he and his charges got on well together.

Dearmer rarely went to St James's Palace as the plays were sent to his home to read. He recalls very few plays he did not recommend for licensing, and always enjoyed his work and all aspects of the theatre, including music-hall:

> They are very funny low comedians. Some are pure as distilled water on paper. George Robey was always rather worried that we would cut any of his lines and we never did.
>
> There were two glorious old low comedians (male, I think) who toured the country as a couple of two very old

dames gossiping outside pubs. Their act always ended with someone shouting (off) 'They're Open' which gave them the best of motives for a hurried exit. Their names were 'Biddy' and 'Fanny'. Biddy – or was it Fanny? – had been in service in a stately home where French was the language on the menus for meals. Fanny – or was it Biddy? – had been in less exalted service and was shocked to hear the men used French . . . Oh Biddy! I wish I had seen them but I never did.

Charles Heriot joined the team of Examiners in 1937, one year after Dearmer, who claims the credit for his recruitment. He was a former actor and producer, and was educated at Glasgow University. Hearing that the Lord Chamberlain was looking for another Examiner, Dearmer spoke to his friend Clifford Bax, author amongst other things of *The Rose Without a Thorn*, who immediately responded with Heriot's name. During the later years of the censorship Charles Heriot was a lecturer at Morley College, University of London.

I found that I usually agreed with Heriot's recommendations as to whether or not a play should be licensed. One exception was *Duel at Durango*, a sketch by Alan Steel submitted by Glasgow University Union in 1967. The story was about the planning of a revolution in a South American country where the idea was to assassinate the President and his wife by an explosive contraceptive. Charles Heriot did not recommend a licence because of the nature of the plot and I minuted to the Lord Chamberlain, 'I have read the play and I think it is harmless enough to be licensed as it stands.' The Lord Chamberlain replied, 'I would not fuss about this light bit of nonsense and agree with the Assistant Comptroller.'

Heriot had a wry sense of humour, and was skilled in the writing of a synopsis of a play. He described a short play by Paul Foster submitted in 1968, entitled *Balls*, saying: 'Of course it is . . . a dialogue for the most part between the corpse of a sea captain hanged for treason and a cripple . . . They are visited by lovers who lie on their tomb and by school children who relieve themselves on the grave.'

Meanwhile, shortly before Henry Game's retirement, Lieutenant-Colonel Sir St Vincent Troubridge was appointed as Assistant Examiner in 1952. An ancestor of his was Nelson's commander-in-chief and the victor in the Battle of Cape St Vincent in 1797. Troubridge himself had a successful military career in both world wars and was interested in theatrical research. He too was a superb writer of play reports, for example, of *The Lily White Boys* by Harry Cookson, with songs by Christopher Logue and music by Tony Kinsey and Bill Le Sage, which played at the Royal Court Theatre in 1960:

> It is a curious reflection upon the intentions of the legislations of 1843 that, under present circumstances, I am about to recommend for licence, with a few verbal alterations, a play that is not only revolutionary, but indeed anarchistic in what it conveys to a Sloane Square audience, since it attacks and propounds by jeers the tearing down of *everything*, right, left and centre.

Troubridge died in office in 1963. Overlapping him was Maurice Coles, an Examiner from 1958 to 1965. In 1964 I. Kyrle Fletcher, a theatre historian and antiquarian bookseller, was appointed; and, in the following year, Timothy Harward, who recalls:

> I was actually quite surprised to be asked to be a Reader . . . I had been working as a freelance journalist for the *Irish Times* and doing book, theatre and some films for them, and my university background was literature and theatre. I was lecturing at the London Polytechnic at the time. I was fascinated by the prospect and immediately accepted.

He showed me a note from Charles Heriot saying that his report on the first play he read was 'just the thing we want' and sending him Charles Wood's play *Dingo* to read next on the grounds that, having served six years in the Army, he might be more au fait with army slang! Edward Bond's play *Early Morning* (see Chapter 7) also came his way which, he says, was a memorable difficulty. He once described to me how he set about the business of reading plays:

> I used to read a play straight through to visualise it as a piece of theatre, first; then again to pick up bits of 'business' that might conflict with the guidelines; and finally to detail suspect words and stage directions. I then wrote up a general summary with my view on it as a play, and gave my recommendation: for or against a licence. In the vast majority of cases, I was for a licence subject to small changes. I think Charles Wood and Edward Bond gave me some exercise . . . But the excitement lay in reading new plays often by very interesting writers before they were staged. That was a unique opportunity for somebody like me who was fascinated by the theatre . . .
>
> Looking back at it now I see it as a curious but rewarding episode; a sort of minor time warp in history.

Heriot, Kyrle Fletcher and Harward were still in office at the time of the Theatres Act, 1968.

There was one other notable Examiner, 'Jones the Censor'. In 1931, when an increasing number of Welsh plays were being submitted, Lord Cromer decided to appoint a Welsh Examiner. Previously Welsh playwrights had had to submit English translations. The man selected was the Rev. Albert Evans Jones (Cynan), a poet and dramatist, who had just won the Bardic crown at the Eisteddfod. A Presbyterian minister, he was quoted as saying in 1966, 'Very rarely does censorship arise in Wales.' He too was still in office in 1968. He was knighted in 1969, at the time of the Investiture of the Prince of Wales, for services to Welsh Literature, and died the following year.

The importance of the role played by these Examiners in the final thirty years of the censorship can scarcely be overestimated.

CHAPTER NINE

Indecency on the Stage

On 16 April 1940 Lord Clarendon convened a Stage Conference at St James's Palace. This was attended by representatives of the Home Office and the police; the London County Council, the County Councils' Association and Association of Municipal Corporations; and all branches of the entertainment industry – theatre, music-hall, cinema, and hotels. A shorthand writer was present to make a transcript of the proceedings.

When Lord Clarendon welcomed the dozen or so delegates, he outlined the theme of the conference and his own hopes for it:

> I am quite satisfied that we shall all be agreed that in these times, when the efforts of everyone should be devoted to securing the complete Victory in war of the Allies and ourselves, it is very desirable that the whole standard and tone of public entertainments, whether in theatres, music-halls or any other places, should be maintained on a decent level of propriety.

The debate which followed centred around nudity, 'objectionable' gags and 'business', and the undesirable growth of striptease and bottle parties. A gratifying measure of unanimity was evident and a communiqué was issued summarising the conclusions:

> 1. That immediate steps should be taken to check the greater tendency which has become evident since the war of greater displays of nudity and more impropriety of gesture and speech;

> 2. That the powers of control over places where music, dancing and other entertainments (i.e., bottle parties and cabarets) are given, which are not subject to any form of licence, should be greatly increased and that the Government should promote legislation for this purpose at an early date.

This second resolution was, of course, not the concern of the Lord Chamberlain but with regard to nudity in revues the Lord Chamberlain maintained his criterion of allowing only static nude posing (see below and Chapter 10).

When the Stage Play Licence had been revised, in 1912, it included five regulations for the particular attention of managements. One of these read: 'No indecency of dress, dance or gesture to be permitted on the stage.'

Most earlier Lord Chamberlains had held the view that this regulation did not cause as much difficulty as might have been expected, for in the case of nudity it was possible to formulate a clear set of rules:

> The Lord Chamberlain has for many years applied some arbitrary rules for the regulation of dress (or rather undress) on the stage:
> (a) Actresses in movement must not wear less than briefs and an opaque controlling brassière.
> (b) Actresses may pose completely nude provided the pose is motionless and expressionless; the pose is artistic and something rather more than a mere display of nakedness; and the lighting must be subdued.
> (c) Striptease as such is not allowed in a stage play.
> To date requests for males to pose in the nude have not been received.*

Many complaints over the years were received from members of the public about indecency on the stage and different Lord Chamberlains found it necessary from time to time to warn theatre managers about impropriety of costume. In 1869

*Quoted from the written evidence supplied by the Lord Chamberlain's Office to the 1966 Joint Committee.

Lord Sidney had sent out a circular calling attention to the costumes of ballet dancers and asked the managers for their co-operation in checking these. He had to send out another in 1871. In 1872 the Rev. Newman Hall complained of the performance of Lady Godiva at Astley's Theatre. The manager was consulted and he reported that there was nothing objectionable and this was corroborated by a member of the Lord Chamberlain's Office. At about that time the can-can had arrived in London and was occasionally featured on the stage. In 1874 there were numerous complaints about this dance at the St James's Theatre and so the Lord Chamberlain decided to see it for himself. Apparently he highly disapproved of the dance but he did not take any steps to stop it as the show only ran for a few performances.

In 1913 two plays were licensed with warnings. *Sumerum*, 'a wordless play' by Frederick Freska with music by Victor Hollander, had been put on at the Coliseum in 1911. Now the manager of the Coliseum was given a warning that proper decency must be observed with regard to the clothing of the woman who danced in the harem scene. Another play, *A La Carte*, was licensed with a warning to avoid indecency of dress and gesture. Considerable notoriety and advertisement was given to it by the local clergy who, after lodging a complaint with the Lord Chamberlain, then published the exchange of letters in the press.

In 1914, in the play *Alice Up To Date*, the Lord Chamberlain took exception to the suggestive costumes of the chorus girls, who were dressed on one side only! In the following year's LCO Annual Report, concern was expressed over the growing number of reports received by the Lord Chamberlain of a tendency towards suggestiveness, impropriety in language and scantiness of dress in revues. Some producers and managers were summoned and they promised to co-operate by a closer and more personal supervision of their theatres.

That same year the manager of the Ambassadors Theatre gave an undertaking over the play *Odds and Ends* that certain undress was to be kept within the bounds of decorum. When performances were witnessed on several occasions it was found that the manager's idea of decorum did not coincide with the wishes of the Lord Chamberlain. He was repeatedly warned. Later *The Whirl of Town* was licensed subject to the restriction that the bare-back costumes must not be lower than a lady's conventional evening dress.

In 1915 *Look Out* was licensed with a caution as to the 'business' by which the clothes of any girl standing on a magic mat became transparent; while *Sheba* was licensed subject to the omission of a reference to King Solomon's sleeping arrangements.

That same year complaints were made about *My Lady's Undress* at the Ambassadors Theatre, as a result of which the following memorandum was sent to the theatre manager:

> The following business must be omitted from the performance of *My Lady's Undress*:
> 1. The lifting of the drawers so as to show the leg above the top of the stocking.
> 2. Her advancing to the footlights to tell the audience that she has to retire to take her remaining garments off.
> 3. The loosening of the drawers and lowering them in front of the audience.
> 4. The placing of white garments over the top of the screen behind which the actress is supposed to be undressing.

In 1917 an Examiner of Plays went to see a performance of *Chu Chin Chow*, which had been first staged on 31 August 1916 and ran for 2,238 performances. The play was by Oscar Asche and the music by Frederick Norton. The Examiner reported on the scarcity of dress and some over-emphasis in action. So the Lord Chamberlain went to see the show himself and to reprimand the manager. Two years later Lord Sandhurst, considering *As You Were* by A. Wimperis, forbade the use of certain dresses worn by Madame Delysia and by some of the chorus for being too indecent.

In *Judith* by Arnold Bennett, Lord Sandhurst called for an alteration to the dress worn by Lillah McCarthy so that less of her body should be displayed. After seeing the first production of *Judith*, at the Devonshire Park Theatre, Eastbourne, Arnold Bennett wrote in his *Journal*:

> Her tent costume frightened one of the lessees of the theatre. Above a line drawn about ½ inch or 1 inch above the '*mont de Venus*' she wore nothing except a 4-inch band of black velvet round the body, hiding the breasts, and a similar perpendicular band of velvet starting from between the breasts and going down to the skirt and so hiding the navel. Two thin shoulder-straps held this contrivance in position. Bracelets and rings, of course. The skirt was slit everywhere and showed the legs up to the top of the thigh when she lay down at Holofernes's feet. She looked a magnificent picture thus, but a police prosecution would not have surprised me at all.

The Public Morality Council was active in the 1920s and 1930s, and repeatedly complained to the Lord Chamberlain (Lord Cromer) about nudity or near-nudity in revues. In 1925 the Council endeavoured to secure from the leaders of religious and social work a pronouncement in regard to 'Sex Plays'. In a pamphlet the Council stated that some American actors and actresses protested against indecent and indelicate plays and disliked acting in them. They thought that sex in a crude form as the subject of a play was becoming what some had always thought it, rather boring. In London some leading actresses felt compelled to decline parts which they considered went beyond the limits of decency and good taste.

Owen Nares, a well-known actor and a matinée idol, held strong views about dresses worn by chorus girls: 'They are obviously designed to make a sexual appeal to the man in the audience. Don't think I blame the girls! They can't help it, poor dears. They have to earn a living. What one protests against is that in order to earn a living they should be compelled to dress – or undress – in so extraordinarily vulgar a way.'

The *Daily News*, on 20 February 1925, reported that one of the best-known of West End actresses entirely agreed with Owen Nares. She was quoted as saying: 'Sometimes when playing an indelicate part, I have felt inclined to apologise to the audience, especially when I have noticed nice-looking families of father and mother with young sons and daughters obviously feeling uncomfortable.'

In 1932 and 1935 the Public Morality Council sent a deputation to the Lord Chamberlain's Office to discuss the exploitation on the stage of the semi-nude. In 1937 Lord Cromer chaired a conference attended by representatives of the London County Council, the Society of West End Theatre Managers, and the Theatrical Managers' Association amongst other groups. The LCO Annual Report for that year recorded that no conclusions were reached: 'and the Lord Chamberlain stated he preferred to leave these matters to the discretion of managers but he was concerned that in some cases intensive competition might lead to their endeavouring to outstrip [*sic*] each other in undesirable directions'.

There was another deputation to the Lord Chamberlain from the Public Morality Council in 1938 which argued that the new standard of nudity in ordinary life did not justify scantiness of clothing on the stage. The Lord Chamberlain replied that this was not objectionable so long as there was nothing obscene or suggestive about it.

The majority of actual prosecutions brought under the 1843 Theatres Act were minor ones, mostly in the provinces. The cases, which averaged four or five per year, were usually instigated by the police, but not necessarily with the knowledge of the Lord Chamberlain, who was normally reluctant to start proceedings and only did so when there appeared to be a clear-cut breach of the law. On these occasions he would consult the Office of the Director of Public Prosecutions (now the Crown Prosecution Service) and the Director would often consult the Attorney-General before bringing a charge.

The most common charge was for presenting an unlicensed play, or unlicensed material in a play, 'for hire', and would be brought against producers, managers and actors. Until 1925 a conviction under Section 15 of the Theatres Act automatically resulted in the theatre concerned losing its licence; but since the passing of the Criminal Justice Act that year magistrates were able to impose fines instead.

In 1939, Lord Clarendon instituted a summons against the manager of the Chelsea Palace Theatre where, in a revue called *Cosmopolitan Merry-Go-Round*, a male actor dressed as a woman did a partial striptease. The magistrate dismissed the charges as the Lord Chamberlain had licensed 'a female impersonation by Gerald du Vere assisted by two girls'. He expressed the view that this entitled the actor to give any sort of female impersonation he wished, as no detailed description of the actions had been submitted. This put Clarendon on the spot and he decided to remind managers and producers that all scripts submitted for licence must include full particulars of stage directions, actions or 'business' and complete description of dumb acts. An announcement was made to this effect in the press.

In the same year the manager and stage manager of the Grand Theatre, Clapham, and the producer of a revue *Going Gay*, were prosecuted for presenting unlicensed material in three scenes. In one of these a woman who performed the 'Dance of the Seven Veils' appeared nude from the waist upwards after discarding the last veil. The second complaint was about a scene in which two dictators in Europe, as they saluted in farewell, made vulgar noises at each other. In the third scene, entitled 'Tut Tut', portraying an Egyptian tomb, much vulgar use was made of a certain domestic utensil instead of a golden chalice mentioned in the script. The three defendants pleaded guilty and were fined with costs.

During the Second World War complaints about plays were occasionally received from members of the public or from the police and sometimes the local Chief Constable was requested to submit a report. This usually resulted in charges and the case being heard either by a stipendiary magistrate or by lay magistrates. In the Lord Chamberlain's opinion, the latter usually meted out fines and costs of an appropriate size whereas the former tended to be too lenient, and he so told the Lord Chancellor's Office.

Most of the prosecutions during the 1940s were against revues and almost all were successful; but it is worth noting that the famous Windmill Theatre revues (see the next chapter) were never prosecuted. Whenever a plea of 'Not Guilty' was entered, the Secretary of the Lord Chamberlain's Office would usually give evidence to the effect that the revue contained certain dialogue or 'business' which had either been disallowed, or, if submitted, would not have been allowed.

An example was the revue *Pin-up Parade* performed at the Hippodrome, Chesterfield, in 1945. When the script was submitted for licence, pictures of some poses, taken from a magazine, were also submitted; but these being regarded as unacceptable, actual photographs were requested. The photographs were disallowed on the ground that the artistic standard was too low and that they appeared to be merely an excuse for a display of nudity on the stage. The producer was informed and the licence endorsed accordingly. When the offending scene was included in the revue, summonses were issued against the theatre manager, the producer, the licensee and the artiste. The Chief Constable himself prosecuted. The theatre's defence was that the banned scene was not presented, and another had been substituted in which the artiste was not nude as she was covered by a flesh-coloured bra and pants. This evidence was contradicted by a police inspector *and* a police sergeant *and* a policewoman. Verdicts of guilty were brought in. The three defendants were fined £10 each with costs and the artiste was dismissed under the Probation of Offenders Act on payment of 4s. 0d. costs. One hopes that her salary 'covered' that!

Another Chief Constable in 1946 himself prosecuted eight defendants over a revue *Soldiers in Skirts*, but he failed to impress a bench of lay magistrates. They dismissed the case and this cast doubt on the validity of the Lord Chamberlain's control over much that went on in revues. An appeal was considered but, to the relief of the magistrates, not pursued. Instead the case was reviewed in the Public Prosecutor's Office. There followed a recommendation that, in the future, the prosecution should always be conducted by a legally qualified person and that the police should arrange for at least two inspections of every show to prove that the variations were not just casual departures from the scripts.

In 1948 the Christmas pantomime at Salford was *Aladdin*. Many versions of this favourite show had been licensed over the years, but apparently not this one. How was the case proved? A shorthand writer visited a performance and made a transcript of the dialogue. When this was checked in the Lord Chamberlain's Office against the version licensed in 1939, about one-third was revealed to be new material. The proprietor, company manager, producer and licensee were found guilty and fined varying sums for putting on an unlicensed version of *Aladdin*. The case made managers realise that they could not take liberties even with pantomimes.

In the 1950s nude posing acts were still a cause of concern to the Lord Chamberlain's Office. Some producers were increasing the lighting, altering poses and even introducing some which had been banned. Numerous warnings and cautionary letters were sent, but certain licensees told the Lord Chamberlain that, with the advent of television, the 'posing' act was the only attraction capable of bringing an audience to their theatres.

The Lord Chamberlain's policy continued unchanged, but by 1955 there was increasing evidence that the limits he set – considered by some to be quite lenient – were failing to satisfy audiences. The Public Morality Council continued to be critical and that year sent another deputation, this time headed by the Bishop of London, to discuss the issue of nudity and to suggest the banning of nude posing, a proposal which the Lord Chamberlain turned down.

In March 1958 a Cambridge University professor wrote to the Lord Chamberlain to ask for the precise terms in which a person is defined as 'nude' or 'not nude' for stage purposes. A tongue-in-cheek reply was sent:

> It is impossible practically to stipulate the minimum permissible dress and so his Lordship treats as nude any female whether otherwise clothed or not (i) who exposes the nipples, (ii) whose breasts are largely uncovered and not firmly supported, (iii) who exposes the region of the base of the trunk.

Was the learned professor any the wiser? Presumably too he was concerned about female nudity as the Lord Chamberlain's Office letter gave no definition of male nudity.

Despite the care taken by the Lord Chamberlain, the trend towards indecency on the stage continued to increase and his difficulties were not lightened by the passage of the Obscene Publications Act, and the test case under the Act in which

Penguin Books successfully resisted the Director of Public Prosecution's contention that the unexpurgated edition of D. H. Lawrence's *Lady Chatterley's Lover* (published by them in 1959), was obscene.

In 1960 the *Ballets Africains* was staged at the Piccadilly Theatre. The manager expressed concern about bare-breasted ladies performing a ritual dance, involving considerable movement of their bare breasts. The Comptroller hastened along to watch a rehearsal, as a result of which he established that this was a ballet and not a stage play and, therefore, not subject to the control of the Lord Chamberlain but to that of the London County Council. Incidentally, neither the Lord Chamberlain's Office nor the LCC considered the dance to be indecent.

In 1963 the Chief Constable of Edinburgh wrote and asked for the Lord Chamberlain's advice about some of the activities of an International Drama Conference which was taking place in that city. As to one of these activities, the reply was crystal clear: 'I can say categorically that the Lord Chamberlain would not allow a nude woman to be wheeled across the stage in a wheel-barrow.' In a later letter the Chief Constable (who had continued to seek the help of the Lord Chamberlain) was told: 'I am afraid that as the Edinburgh Festival Nude Case was one with which the Lord Chamberlain was not concerned, the incident having taken place in the course of a Conference, I have no official knowledge of it.' However, the following advice was proffered: 'Where the Lord Chamberlain's requirements are not observed you will realise that it is not necessary for him to prove indecency. He merely has to prove that the action complained of is not included or described in the manuscript of the piece which he has licensed.'

Even as late as 1967 and 1968 the Lord Chamberlain was still keeping a wary eye on questions of decency. In *The Italian Girl*, a play by James Saunders and Iris Murdoch, based on her novel, there was a stage direction, 'Isobel changes her clothes on stage'. The licence was marked, 'At no time must the actress be on stage dressed in less than briefs and a brassière.' In *Investigation*, by Leslie Sands, the direction, 'She undoes her blouse and pulls it down to reveal a swelling bruise' is marked 'She must not reveal her breast'. In

The Making of Theodore Thomas: Citizen by Michael Weller, the direction 'She pulls up her skirt' is marked 'The actress must not be naked under her skirt.' This play was submitted in July 1968, only a few weeks before the Theatres Act was passed. Even so, I doubt that the actress was naked beneath her skirt.

Persons in bed together were thought to be indecent for the stage, and this was not allowed. Various means were tried to get round the difficulty and one of the most ingenious occurred in *Don't Let Summer Come* (originally entitled *A Mid-Winter Night's Dream*), a play by Terence Feely and submitted by Bernard Miles for the Mermaid Theatre in 1964. In the play there are two scenes with actors in bed together but the producer put forward an argument that they were ON the bed and not IN the bed. Bernard Miles drew for us on the title page two sketches showing George ON the bed with a complicated system of coverlets (see opposite). When the Comptroller, Eric Penn, and I went to see the play in rehearsal, we found it harmless enough and so were able to recommend to the Lord Chamberlain that this clever device be allowed, which it was. However, a warning was issued with the licence saying that the stage directions must be carefully adhered to and at no time must George get INTO bed with the girls.

A similar warning was issued by the licence for *The Bed Sitting Room* by Spike Milligan and John Antrobus in 1966: 'Martin and the girl race for the bed and jump in. One person only is to get into the bed'. Again in *The Italian Girl*: 'Elsa gets into bed with Otto. The actor and actress must not be in bed together'. In *Jack Sheppard* by Ken Campbell (1965) the Lord Chamberlain tried to be helpful with the stage direction: 'make love on a couch'. He said he would be prepared to consider some other stage direction, such as 'caressing on the couch'.

Just before the curtain was pulled down on the 1843 Theatres Act, an unusual piece was submitted by H. M. Tennent in June 1968. *You Know I Can't Hear You When The Water's Running* was the title of a group of four one-act plays by Robert Anderson, the American author of *Tea and Sympathy*. In his report on the first play the reader wrote:

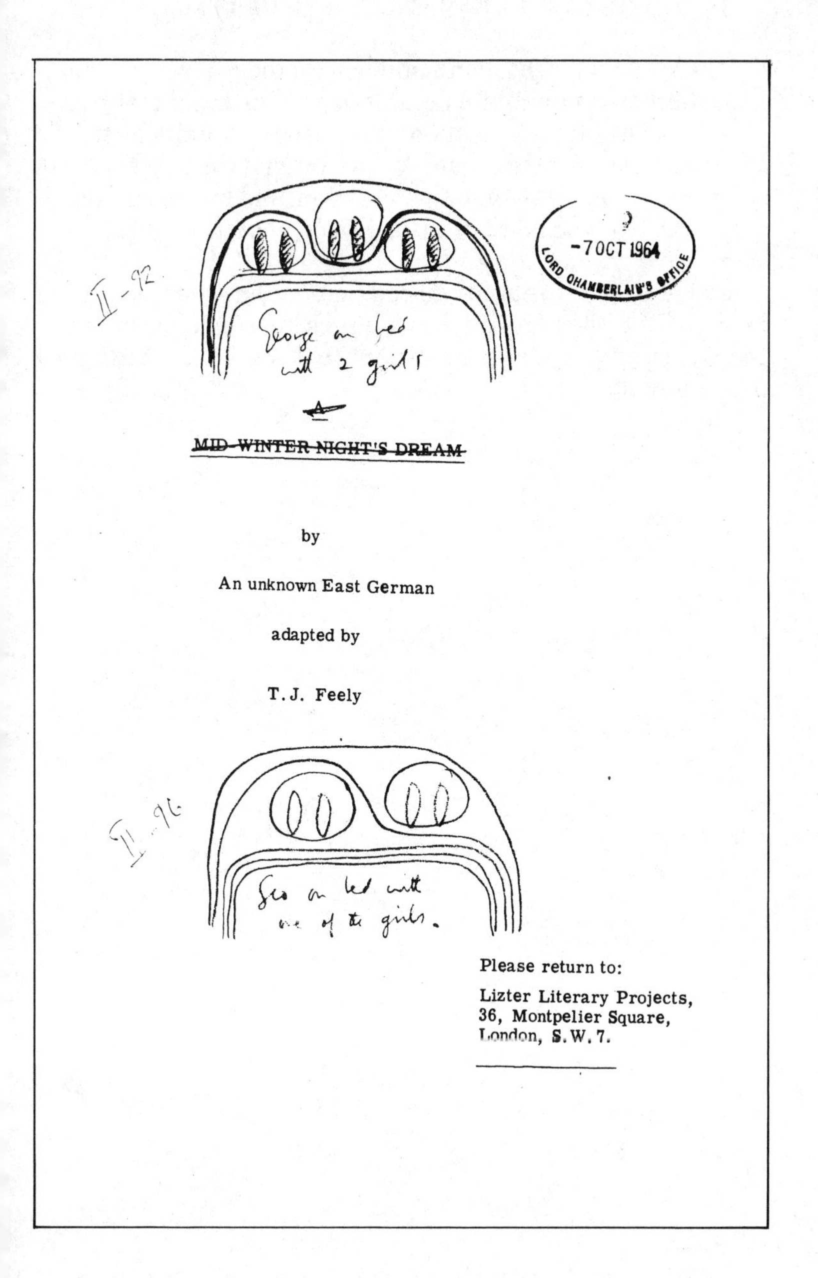

A sketch by Bernard Miles, for a play by Terence Feely, showing how three actors could be on a bed but none of them *in* it

> One scene has a husband and wife in their bedroom. He is in the bathroom and when his wife calls him he appears, nude. The author explains he wishes to emphasise the ridiculousness of the male sex organ; that the audience will recognise themselves in this situation; and laugh; and that it will destroy the myth of the big male phallus.

The blue pencil was not required here as the scene was not to be acted out, the play consisting largely of a dialogue between the writer and producer of a script that was being *considered* as a production!

Chapter Ten

The Windmill

The Windmill Theatre in Great Windmill Street, near Piccadilly Circus, was converted from a cinema in 1931. The following year Laura Henderson and her manager Vivian Van Damm introduced a policy of continuous variety entitled 'Revudeville' and no less than 341 revues were staged there over the next thirty-two years. After the death of Vivian Van Damm in 1960 Revudeville continued under the management of his daughter, Sheila. A cordial relationship existed between the Lord Chamberlain's Office and the Van Damm family, especially during the Second World War when, at times, the Windmill was the only theatre to remain open in London.

Many well-known comedians, such as Jimmy Edwards, Harry Secombe and Tony Hancock started their careers there. But it was the Windmill Girls, appearing in nude tableaux, who mainly drew the audiences and became a part of London life. The Lord Chamberlain, of course, permitted nudity on the stage provided that the girls were static, took up and left their positions unseen by the audience, and provided that the pose was artistic and in a subdued light (see page 127, above).

There being no written script for a nude, photographs were submitted instead. Not all were approved. These photographs, probably taken with a flash bulb, often gave a false impression as to what the subject looked like on the stage under a subdued light. Vivian Van Damm therefore used to send round some transparent coloured sheets to be placed over the black-and-white prints.

The revues consisted not only of nude tableaux but also of sketches and song-and-dance acts. There was seldom a shortage of volunteers from the Lord Chamberlain's Office to pay visits from time to time to check that the comics were sticking to the gags which had been licensed and that the nudes were complying with poses which had been approved.

As a result of one such visit, early in the war, a letter was sent saying, 'It has been brought to the notice of the Lord Chamberlain that certain additional dialogue would appear to have been added . . . in that the comedian, in reply to an inaudible remark by one of the girls, says "I can't without my gooseberries". The Lord Chamberlain desires to be informed whether the above remark had been interpolated and, if such is the case, it should be omitted in future.' Vivian Van Damm found this to be true and he warned the comedian. However, when the 'offence' was repeated he dismissed him – and that despite three years' service for the Windmill.

After another visit, this time to Revudeville No. 148 in 1941, a letter stated that fault could be found regarding dress in three scenes, in one of which 'The nude is too brightly lit and her position should be slightly changed, as a certain detail was visible from where I sat . . . Lord Clarendon will not permit breasts being visible when the girls are moving, either through a flimsy covering or on account of absence or looseness of costume.'

A bishop in 1941, having visited one of these revues, told the Lord Chamberlain he had heard that a Windmill show was shortly coming to his diocese to perform on a Sunday. He asked, 'Is it really the case that public performances are allowed now where all but completely naked women are so clearly displayed on the stage?' The Lord Chamberlain replied by saying that, two years previously, he had called a meeting of interested parties to discuss the possibility of doing away with nudity on the stage but the majority of licensing authorities and the theatrical people wanted to retain it. He expressed the hope that the forthcoming performance in the bishop's diocese would not include the excerpts which the bishop had seen.

Incidentally, as a result of the bishop's letter a visit was paid to the next Revudeville (No. 149) and there is a note in the file that it was lucky the bishop had not attended that particular performance because a hula-hula girl, wearing a string skirt and a brief garland of flowers, had a slight mishap – it had slipped down!

That same year Vivian Van Damm asked the Lord Chamberlain's Office why the Phoenix Theatre was apparently being allowed to do more than he was. He was told that the Phoenix show was a variety performance which did not come under the jurisdiction of the Lord Chamberlain. The ever-resourceful Van Damm then asked if his revues might be classified as variety performances. The 1843 Act was quoted for his information, which, not surprisingly, he found difficult to understand. He pleaded, 'Although I appreciate that the Lord Chamberlain's fiat still controls the running of the theatres, will you please help me out of the morass of unintelligible words?'

George (later Sir George) Titman, Secretary of the Lord Chamberlain's Office, endeavoured to do so, explaining that, in his view, the performances at the Windmill fell just outside a road show (which did not require a Stage Play licence) and just inside a revue (which did), and went on to say:

> Either you must continue to run your 'Revudeville' as a Stage Play as heretofore and conform to the Lord Chamberlain's requirement of which you are well aware; or you must change it to 'Varietyville' by entirely separating the various acts and eliminating any idea of a theme running through the show.

Surprisingly perhaps, Van Damm did not opt for the latter course. After thanking George Titman for the trouble he had taken in dealing with his query, he continued: 'In view of what you say there is little question that we are far safer to continue under the Lord Chamberlain's department in spite of the drawbacks at this end in the way of physical work it means we have to undertake, and I can only say that I hope we get on as happily in the future as we have done in the past, in spite of my being such "a naughty boy" on certain occasions.'

Van Damm continued to be anxious not to upset the Lord Chamberlain, even when he or one of his staff seemed to be rather demanding. For example, in Revudeville No. 145 Van

Damm was told, 'The two girls with the large balloons were also insufficiently covered about the breasts, considering the violent movements they perform. The covering would probably be sufficient if it was fixed, but as it is it will hardly do.'

In his reply Vivian Van Damm said: 'I have taken this up with the Wardrobe Master and it appears that during this exceptionally hot weather the elastic holding the tops, which is not of as good quality as normally, is inclined to become slack after a day or so. I have therefore given instructions for this to be renewed whenever necessary.'

In March 1942 George Titman went along to see Revudeville No. 152 and sent the Lord Chamberlain a note saying that, with one minor exception, he found nothing wrong either with the dialogue or with the 'undress' of the girls. The minor exception was in Scene 6, in which a girl wearing a bolero over an otherwise naked top half showed her breasts when doing the rumba. This apparently was caused by too loose a drawstring. After the performance Titman saw Mr Van Damm and Miss Mitelle, in charge of costumes, and asked them to attend to this small matter. He minuted, 'They told me they also had noticed it (I wonder if they had?) and the girl would be worried if she knew what she was showing (I wonder if she would?). Anyhow, they promised to rectify the matter forthwith.' Lord Clarendon added in his own hand, 'This is very satisfactory and perhaps Van Damm's views are undergoing a change!!'

Two years later, in 1944, George Titman found the 170th edition of Revudeville rather better than usual. It featured several nudes and he commented that their positional posing under subdued lighting brought them well within the limits allowed and that he found no adjustments necessary on this occasion.

No. 176 caused a member of the public to complain (the first for a long time), saying that unless the Lord Chamberlain took some action he would be alerting the Director of Public Prosecutions. A visit was paid and although not all the allegations were confirmed, a letter was sent calling attention to certain points. To quote from a long and detailed letter from Van Damm:

> No one tries harder to keep in line with the desires of Lord Clarendon and your department than myself . . . a fault has occurred in one or two instances due to the tremendous heat during which the girls have been working, causing the very poor war material to sag slightly in the crutch . . . to be quite frank, I was unable to trace the slightest sign of the genital organs being displayed by any single girl, as apart from the outer skirt there is a strap running from the waist right between the legs and fixed to the waist behind which utterly prevents anything being seen.

Vivian Van Damm was so anxious to meet the Lord Chamberlain's wishes that he had new straps made! In another scene he had an extra covering of net put on a girl: 'but I am certain that if you did see the nipples it must have been entirely due to the side lights being put on to full instead of three-quarters'. This was due, he said, to having to employ a low standard of electrician who, in his and other theatres, never lasted more than about two weeks. There was a complaint about the frock of one of the girls in a later scene. 'To be very candid, I do not agree with you as to this item, but to meet your desires, I am putting a second thickness of net inside the costume.' Apparently Lord Clarendon had paid a recent visit to the Windmill and found nothing to which he could take objection. Vivian Van Damm suggested the letter of complaint might have been written by some jealous competitor: 'as we know to our cost on occasions that many in the Profession are extremely jealous of the work and business we are doing here and would stop at nothing to interfere with our success'. He concluded by saying: 'However, please believe that I wish to meet you in every respect and would thank you and Lord Clarendon for the consideration that is shown us on all occasions when these difficult questions arise.'

In later years very few complaints were received in the Lord Chamberlain's Office, nor very often did the Office have cause to complain. The Assistant Comptroller in 1955 went to see Revudeville No. 273 and reported that the fan dancer made such dexterous use of her fans that it was impossible to tell whether she was wearing anything or was completely

The Windmill Theatre: in the case of revues the Lord Chamberlain had to approve poses from photographs: a) 'Desert scene'; b) a pose that was probably allowed; c) Approved; d) 'Anyone for tennis' – No

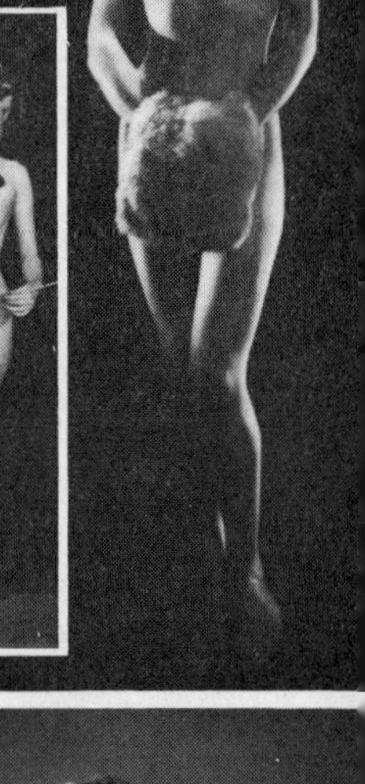

nude. Similarly the geisha girl was so skilful with her transparent sunshade, which she twirled all the time in subdued lighting, that it was difficult to prove she was nude if the management said otherwise.

No complaint was made on that occasion but one was sent the next year about No. 282: 'There is also a growing number of "inadvertent" breast exposures . . . and the conclusion cannot be avoided that such inadvertence is not by accident.' Vivian Van Damm replied that he continued to take endless trouble to comply with the Lord Chamberlain's wishes, even to the extent of employing a man and a woman, at an annual cost of over £2,000, whose primary duty it was to watch every performance and to rectify, on the spot, even minor discrepancies. A nice touch of Van Damm's was to invite to the dress rehearsal of each new revue the parents of the girls in the show.

In 1963, the Public Morality Council did file a complaint about Revudeville No. 331. When the next Assistant Comptroller visited the theatre he found the performance perfectly in order and entirely inoffensive except for two minor dress matters.

Sadly the Windmill, whose motto had been 'We Never Closed', did finally close in 1964 for the simple reason that, by then, their shows were almost too respectable and the strip clubs had taken over. It was typical of the courtesy and consideration of Sheila Van Damm that I was invited to attend the final performance in August that year. I was unable to accept then, but did attend one of the last performances as her guest, being given a box to myself!

Chapter Eleven

The Clarendon Years, 1938–52

Like his predecessor, Lord Cromer, Lord Clarendon was much liked and respected by the London theatre managers. His contribution to the censorship was not large, but in the Second World War few theatres were open for business. During those years his blue pencil was mainly confined to keeping Revudeville at the Windmill, and other revues, in some sort of discipline.

To alleviate the shortage of drama in the early part of the war, the Home Secretary, in 1941, considered allowing the opening of theatres on Sundays. When the Lord Chamberlain was consulted, Lord Clarendon foresaw difficulties and possible opposition from religious bodies. The Government nevertheless decided to go ahead by means of a Defence Regulation so that, in some areas, theatres could be open on Sunday for the benefit of servicemen and industrial workers. However, when the subject was debated in the House of Commons and allowed a free vote, there was a majority of eight against the proposal (144–136). The matter was dropped.

Almost the first play with which Lord Clarendon had had to deal when he took office in July 1938 was *The Flashing Stream* by Charles Morgan, the novelist and drama critic of *The Times*. This play is a story of love and intrigue set on an island in the Atlantic where a group of naval men (and one girl scientist) are carrying out experiments on a new type of pilotless plane. The reader (Dearmer) drew the Lord Chamberlain's attention to the inclusion of that well-known phrase 'where the monkey puts the nuts' but recommended its retention. Lord Clarendon, preferring to be consistent, asked for its deletion or substitution. The manager of the Lyric Theatre (H. G. Stoker) was told and he replied, saying that the author was away in Bwlch in Wales and that he had asked him to suggest a substitution. Stoker received the following telegram in reply:

> SUBMIT SUBSTITUTE SQUIRREL FOR MONKEY STOP IN MATTER NUTS SQUIRREL REPUTATION UNTARNISHED STOP REFERENCE IS TO KEATS LA BELLE DAME SANS MERCI THE GRANARY IS FULL AND NO BIRDS SING –
> CHARLES MORGAN

Mr Stoker's letter continued:

> I regret that Mr Morgan has slightly misquoted, displacing 'the harvest's done' for 'no birds sing' from another verse, but this may reasonably be explained by the probable lack of adequate reference facilities in Bwlch, Wales. I now express my humble duty to the Lord Chamberlain in requesting if he can see his way to reconsider the matter and permit the substitution of squirrel for monkey.

The Assistant Comptroller, Norman Gwatkin, relished this sort of exchange and minuted, 'I would still prefer nothing puts nuts anywhere though squirrels and nuts do go together.' With the consent of Lord Clarendon, he wrote back to Mr Stoker:

> I quite agree that the squirrel has an unblemished reputation in comparison with the monkey who has said and done some extraordinary things; but the fact remains that the general public would concentrate on the nuts and where they are popularly supposed to be put and not upon the actual vehicle of putting.

Good light-hearted stuff. Charles Morgan accepted this decision by keeping the monkey and not mentioning the nuts.

During 1944 a unique event took place, namely the revoking of a licence. *Felicity Jasmine*, by Gordon Sherry, was licensed with two small endorsements. The play tells the story of Mrs Mainwaring and her two daughters entertaining two American soldiers and centres around the use of 'Felicity

The 6th Earl of Clarendon, Lord Chamberlain 1938–1952. Portrait by Roy de Maistre

Jasmine', a supposed aphrodisiac but in fact only water. It opened in Brighton and then played in Bournemouth before coming to the St James's Theatre in London, where it received bad notices and few people saw it. George Titman went to see the fourth performance and managed to persuade those concerned to take it off. In his view, the play should never have received a licence. (It had been read by Geoffrey Dearmer who recommended the licence.) Lord Clarendon took the unusual step of asking the author to surrender the licence which he did under protest. The following notice was then inserted in *The Stage* and *The Performer*: 'I, the Lord Chamberlain of the King's Household for the time being, do by virtue of my Office . . . forbid the acting or presenting of the stage play . . . *Felicity Jasmine*, absolutely.'

This incident can only be accounted for as being an extreme and exceptional instance of the difficulty of judging from the written word alone how a scene was to be played on the stage. It showed up an inevitable shortcoming of pre-censorship.

Geoffrey Dearmer recalls: 'The play was a record flop . . . There was never any need to withdraw the licence. There was nothing indecent or offensive in dialogue or action. That one of the daughters of the house went to bed with an American officer billeted in it was not a reason for banning it. Public opinion was much better than censorship.'

The incident resulted in concern being shown by the League of Dramatists that perhaps the Lord Chamberlain's licence would not in future afford producers and managers the same protection as hitherto. Lord Clarendon wrote to their Chairman, Gertrude Jennings:

> A Lord Chamberlain's licence is certainly a guarantee to authors or producers against legal prosecution whilst it is in force; but under the law, the Lord Chamberlain has the power to withdraw his licence, if circumstances arise which make such action advisable.

He went on to explain that although the play had been taken off at the St James's Theatre there remained the possibility that it might later be produced elsewhere, which would have been unfair to the original management (which had withdrawn it); and thus he was left with no alternative but to cancel the licence. He concluded his letter: 'I exercised my powers to meet an exceptional situation, but my action in this case should not be taken to inaugurate a new policy or to establish a precedent.'

The League appeared satisfied with this explanation.

In 1946 *Tobacco Road* by Jack Kirkland, from the novel by Erskine Caldwell, was submitted for licence. It had been produced on Broadway in 1933 and had had a run of 3,182 performances. In London it was performed privately before the war at the Gate Theatre. The scene of the play is a derelict farm in the cotton-raising back country of Georgia and deals with the oppressed and degraded lives of the Lesser family.

Henry Game was the reader and he recommended a licence, subject to many alterations, but Lord Clarendon decided to withhold one. The play was resubmitted the following year for the New Lindsey Theatre Club, but again a licence was refused. Robert Henderson appealed on the grounds that he and only he was allowed by the author to produce the play and he gave an assurance that he would put it on in a manner acceptable to the Lord Chamberlain. It was seen in rehearsal by the Assistant Secretary, and the Assistant Comptroller attended a private performance. Neither were prepared to recommend a licence and the Lord Chamberlain minuted, 'I have read this play right through. It is quite horrible and no amount of blue pencilling will really improve it. I have therefore decided to stick to my original decision to refuse to license it.'

At the end of 1947 a licence was given to a revised version at the time when John Ford's 1941 film was showing in London. When, in 1949, the play was produced at the Playhouse Theatre, however, the Public Morality Council drew the Lord Chamberlain's attention to 'the caricature of religion throughout the play' and 'the grossly offensive sex incidents'. Norman Gwatkin wrote to the General Secretary of the Council describing how the play came to be licensed and ended his letter: 'The play is not erotic, it is a picture of the depths to which human beings can descend and, as such, is an object lesson. It was felt that to insist upon even further cuts would so alter the character of the play that the type it portrays would be put in an unnatural light and would appear purely as immoral rather than amoral and degenerate, thus removing the force of the lesson, such as it is, that the play was intended to give.'

In August 1950 *Tobacco Road* played in Oldham. The police reported that the performers were stressing the sexual side of the play and that some 'business' and dialogue were not in the licensed script. The Public Prosecutor was notified but he was against a prosecution on the grounds that it was difficult to produce accurate evidence of 'business' overstepping the mark, adding, 'and in my view nothing has been imported by the "business" which is not implicit in the situation'. Robert Henderson was given a warning and requested to return the licence so that it might be suitably endorsed and this was done. *Tobacco Road* played again in London and continued on tour for some months under Henderson's careful direction and no more complaints were received.

An unusually interesting American play, submitted to the Lord Chamberlain in 1946, was *Pick-up Girl* by Elsa Shelley. The action takes place in a juvenile court in New York and is a realistic representation of a case of juvenile delinquency. A fifteen-year-old girl has been caught in bed with a middle-aged man, and previously has had an abortion and contracted syphilis. Henry Game said in his report: 'A very unsavoury theme . . . Censoring becomes impossible unless one at least tries to act on rational lines . . . Apart from giving sensation seekers the thrill they seek the play cannot do any harm . . .' and so recommended a licence with certain cuts. Lord Clarendon agreed: 'The theme of this play is certainly unsavoury and will probably make the squeamish squirm! But as it is sincere and brings home the great importance of parental responsibility it can receive a licence subject to all the cuts recommended being agreed to.' Although these were not many, Elsa Shelley would not agree to any of them.

When Peter Cotes put on the play at New Lindsey Theatre Club it was well received. Norman Gwatkin saw it and so did the Home Secretary. Queen Mary caused quite a stir by visiting the play on the eve of her seventy-ninth birthday. She had recently become much concerned with juvenile delinquency and approved the piece's sensitive treatment of a difficult subject. Lord Clarendon promptly gave the play a licence without any alterations or cuts being made and it transferred successfully to the West End at the Prince of Wales Theatre.

In 1947 some lines were cut from a revue *Between Ourselves* as they were thought to be offensive to certain members of the

Labour government. This excited the press into claiming that the government had intervened directly to stifle criticism, and that political censorship had returned. The resultant storm in a tea-cup produced eddies as far away as Canada where it was reported, 'The Lord Chamberlain instructed London pantomimes that this Christmas there must be no jokes against the government.'

In 1948 Lord Clarendon decided to license *The Lion Tamer*, a translation of a French play by Alfred Savoir. It had been submitted in 1927, 1928 and 1930 and Lord Cromer had refused it a licence each time because, in his words, of 'the objectionable feature of procuring seduction and infidelity treated with levity'. It is a quasi-philosophical comedy about a man who follows a lion tamer about, hoping to see him devoured, and who hires someone to seduce the lion tamer's wife. A modified version was again submitted in 1932, but still Lord Cromer would not be moved. Curiously when it was next submitted in 1939 Lord Cromer, now a member of the Advisory Board, recommended a licence but the new Lord Chamberlain did not agree! It took another nine years and a further submission for him to change his mind.

There were a number of other plays which Lord Clarendon felt should not receive a licence. One such was *Marriage*, a Hungarian play on the theme that marriage is war, by Johenne Vaszany, of which, when it was first submitted in 1938 just before he retired, Lord Cromer had disapproved. Many alterations were called for and another version was submitted in 1940 under the title *Marriage in Mayfair*. The reader, Geoffrey Dearmer, recommended a licence, with certain reservations. The Comptroller (Major C. L. Gordon) was less sure and asked Lord Clarendon to read it. He responded: 'This is a most revolting play and even with all the suggested cuts I cannot license it. My predecessor was evidently very doubtful as to the wisdom of passing it even if revised, and I am satisfied that if I granted a licence with the cuts recommended by you and Dearmer, it would, if it ever appeared on the stage, cause a storm of protest and justifiably so, from all sorts of quarters.'

Another was *Follow My Leader* (1938), a farce which satirised the Nazi regime and burlesqued its leaders. Terence

Rattigan, who was already famous for *French Without Tears*, was part-author. The play was referred to the Foreign Office, which recommended that the Lord Chamberlain should not give it a licence.

Lord Clarendon also banned *To Stall The Grey Rat* in 1942 on the advice of the Director of Military Intelligence, as the play told a story (albeit a fictitious one) of an escape organisation in Occupied France. The following year he banned *Deryn Dierth*, a Welsh play, as it contained libellous matter on the Gorsedd of Bards, an elected body of poets and authors.

During Lord Clarendon's fourteen years as Lord Chamberlain the number of banned plays decreased in proportion to the licensed ones: over 13,000 were granted a licence and only 79 were refused one. During the war only about 500 manuscripts a year were submitted, whereas in 1952 this figure had increased to 1,300. Although Lord Clarendon banned fewer plays than did Lord Cromer – in proportion to the number that were licensed – this was probably because in his time fewer difficult plays were being submitted, as during the war most playwrights were otherwise occupied.

After the war was over, amidst the general feeling of liberation, the majority of informed opinion seemed to favour the abolition of censorship. At the British Theatre Conference in March 1948, chaired by J. B. Priestley, there were 450 delegates and only three voted for its retention. This prompted a question in the House of Commons to which the Home Secretary, James Chuter Ede, replied that there was no prospect of legislation to amend the Theatres Act.

This was followed a year later by the Censorship of Plays (Repeal Act) Bill 1949 known as the Benn Levy Bill. It was a Private Member's Bill – Benn Levy was a playwright who was also Labour member for Eton and Slough from 1945–50 – intended 'to amend the law relating to the censorship of plays and licensing of theatres, so as to exempt the theatre from restrictions upon freedom of expression in excess of those applicable to other forms of literature . . .' The Bill was introduced by a Conservative MP and playwright, E. P. Smith, who had written such plays as *Ladies in Retirement* and

The Shop at Sly Corner under the name of Edward Percy. He was supported by the Labour MP, Michael Foot.

The Government decided to adopt a neutral attitude but the Home Secretary (who voted against) spoke and drew attention to its technical shortcomings. However, in its written evidence to the 1966 Joint Committee, the League of Dramatists wrote, 'We believe the Benn Levy Bill marks the high-water mark of clear and practical thinking in legislative terms about stage censorship. Its Second Reading was carried by 76 votes to 37; but it suffered the fatc of many Private Members' Bills and never reached the Statute Book.'

In fact the Bill *was* considered by the House's Standing Committee and all its clauses approved, but pressure of business and an impending General Election resulted in the Government deciding that no more time could be made available for Private Members' business. This killed the Bill with practically no comment from the press and scarcely any reaction from the public.

Lord Clarendon decided to stand off from the proceedings and not intervene. Thus he was not seen to be either for or against the Bill. He did however prepare for the Home Secretary a short paper on how he administered his statutory function.

As was expected, the majority of playwrights (notable exceptions being Sir Alan (A. P.) Herbert and William Douglas-Home) supported the Bill for, as they said, the existence of the censor had a stultifying effect on free expression. Conversely the theatre managers contended that the censor's authority alone prevented local and unofficial censors from interfering and thus making it financially impossible to produce controversial plays. Seemingly, and unlike in 1909, none of the more prominent actors or actresses intervened in the agitation. Maybe the whole matter was being raised just too soon after the end of the war? However, it is probably true that, had the Benn Levy Bill been passed, not only would the censorship have been brought to an end much sooner than 1968, but the trouble and difficulties of the later 1950s and 1960s, particularly over theatre clubs, could have been avoided.

Lord Clarendon retired in 1952, by which time he was

seventy-five. He had been King George VI's Lord Chamberlain for all but the first eighteen months of his reign. He died three years later, when the title passed to his grandson, the present (7th) Earl of Clarendon whose father, Lord Hyde, had died in 1935 when his son was only two years old. Nicholas Villiers, the 6th Earl's younger son, remembers how his father would go to see a play, usually incognito, but was invariably recognised, especially when he lit up a cigar in the theatre despite all the warning 'no smoking' signs!

Chapter Twelve

The Earl of Scarbrough: an increasingly difficult task

Whereas Lord Cromer had questioned the advisability of the Lord Chamberlain continuing to be the censor since the appointment had been made non-political, Lord Scarbrough was the first Lord Chamberlain to make a positive move to be relieved of what was becoming an increasingly difficult task in administering the Theatres Act of 1843.

Roger, Earl of Scarbrough (who had succeeded his uncle as the eleventh Earl in 1945) was born in 1896 and appointed Lord Chamberlain in 1952. He served in the First World War and was destined for an army career. His elder brother's death in the war changed his future and he decided to take up politics. As Roger Lumley he was a Member of Parliament from 1922–37 when he was knighted and appointed Governor of Bombay (1937–43). The present Earl of Scarbrough has told me that his father almost never talked about his job as Lord Chamberlain; he remembers him occasionally coming home howling with laughter but when he enquired the cause of his mirth he was told he would not see it. He remembers too accompanying his father when he took the Queen to see *Beyond the Fringe* – 'that was considered quite daring'. He was also a fan of the Crazy Gang and said they were impossible to censor for they ad-libbed so much. Dickon Scarbrough concluded, 'As you will know, Father was most discreet and we were, quite rightly, Lord S's children and nothing to do with the Lord Chamberlain.'

On 24 May 1957 Lord Scarbrough wrote a note to be seen only by the Comptroller and Assistant Comptroller. He asked the Queen if he might have approval to examine the matter of the censorship, and he outlined the arguments for and against

The Earl of Scarbrough, who found the 'censorship' an increasingly difficult task in the 1950s

censorship and for and against the Lord Chamberlain continuing as censor. She gave her approval.

On 4 June 1957 he went, at his request, to see the Home Secretary (R. A. Butler) to discuss censorship generally and the particular problems of the theatre clubs (see Chapter 16) and plays with a homosexual theme (see Chapter 13). He told

Butler that if he was to continue as censor he would like to have his hand strengthened by an amendment of the law to give the Lord Chamberlain authority to attach conditions to licences for plays so that some could be licensed for adults only. He felt this might reduce the criticism to which the censorship was inevitably exposed. In the minute summarising this meeting, he wrote,

> My own view was that the censorship should be watchful to see that it kept on terms with central responsible criticism. I did not mean that we should go ahead of such critics or even keep pace with them, but that we should not be too far away from that kind of central opinion. I thought it was time to say that over many years the censorship had done that by gradual and cautious adjustments to changing attitudes.

The Comptroller, Sir Norman Gwatkin, followed this up on 31 July by going to see Mr Gwynne, a senior Civil Servant, at the Home Office, and giving him a copy of the Lord Chamberlain's note of his meeting with the Home Secretary. Gwynne said that the Home Office was, in principle, in favour of an amendment of the Theatres Act to bring it more in line with the times and, in particular, to enable the Lord Chamberlain to grant different degrees of licence to correspond with the Cinematograph Censorship. The difficulty was how to bring this about and Gwynne held out very little hope of achieving this by means of the Commons ten-minute rule as so many MPs would wish to speak that the matter would be talked out. The chances for a Private Member's Bill were slim because so few were successful in the ballot. He was pessimistic about a government-sponsored Bill, because there was a long waiting-list of these and, as the subject could hardly be called an urgent one, it might well be many years before the Bill could be presented. He did offer, however, to try and get the Cabinet to sanction the drafting of a Bill.

On 26 February 1958, there still being no sign of any move by the Home Office, Lord Scarbrough wrote to the Home Secretary underlining that the campaign against the censorship was continuing and explaining how, with the formation of new theatre clubs putting on unlicensed plays, it was becoming increasingly difficult for him to carry out his parliamentary duty. He went on:

> I fully understand the difficulty of finding time for legislation, but from my point of view there would I think be much advantage in making it clear that I would welcome an amendment of that kind (i.e., grades of licence). I wonder, therefore, what you would think of this suggestion? That I myself should put down a motion in the House of Lords which would in effect say that an amendment of that kind should be considered.

He went on to say that, naturally, he would only take this action if it had the sympathetic support of the Government. He felt it would not be improper for the person on whom the statutory duty falls to suggest an amendment to that statute.

The Lord Chamberlain and the Home Secretary met again on 26 March, when the latter said he had been advised against an amendment to the Theatres Act on the lines suggested. His advisors thought the Lord Chamberlain might incur greater criticism if he were given power to choose what plays should be seen by adults only; and that he should not be exposed to increased criticism of that kind. Lord Scarbrough minuted:

> I replied that in my opinion that situation had already arisen, and it was a fact that the Lord Chamberlain, as head of The Queen's Household, was already involved in undesirable criticism which had some reflection upon the throne; and that it was on that account that I had put forward my proposal for a slight amendment to the Theatres Act.

The Home Secretary expressed the view that the censorship was being very well carried out and that there were probably many people who would not like to see a change. Lord Scarbrough pointed out, however, that he had noticed a tendency for authors to refuse to make minor alterations and then claim that their plays had been refused licences. His suggested amendment, he felt, would provide him with a neat weapon for countering this.

Lord Scarbrough went on:

> The Home Secretary asked me if I thought the censorship should be taken away from the Lord Chamberlain's Office. I replied that I thought it would probably be a good thing in view of the criticism to which the Lord Chamberlain and, at times, the Queen, was through ignorance exposed, but that I would not welcome any move towards that end unless it were done decently and did not appear to have come about through any failure of the present system of censorship.

He realised that, by proposing an amendment to the Theatres Act, there would be discussion on the whole question of the censorship and that the Government would have to decide whether *any* form of censorship should be continued. They touched on the fears of theatre managers at no longer having the protection of a Lord Chamberlain's licence and being exposed to the vagaries of Watch Committees, and the probability of the Churches and others opposing no form of censorship. The Home Secretary did not favour the Home Office being saddled with it and, if a change were to be made, he would prefer some kind of Board under, perhaps, a distinguished retired Civil Servant. The meeting ended with the Home Secretary agreeing to take the Lord Chamberlain's request for an amendment to the Theatres Act to the Home Affairs Committee of the Cabinet. Lord Scarbrough ended: 'He (Butler) made it clear that this should be regarded as very confidential, and it was desirable that I should not let my own views leak out.'

So the Lord Chamberlain, having made his own views quite plain, had also made the first move to amend or do away with the Theatres Act of 1843, but it took another ten years for the latter option to become a reality. Useful though these talks had been to clear the air, little was to come of them for, on 11 August, Butler wrote to Lord Scarbrough:

> Following our discussions about the censorship of plays, I have now discussed with my colleagues your suggestion that legislation should be introduced to give power to make

> it a condition of your allowance of a play that it should not be shown to children.
>
> Our feeling is that it would be unwise to subject the censorship of plays to Parliamentary discussion. Modest though your proposal is, Parliamentary discussion of it – whether on a Bill introduced by the Government or by a Private Member – would inevitably lead to a debate on censorship generally and might result in a demand for the substitution of some method of control less acceptable than the present arrangement. I am sorry to have to tell you, therefore, that the Government cannot support your proposal for a Private Member's Bill.

As this letter had no doubt been drafted for him, the Home Secretary had the courtesy to add a postscript in his own hand:

> This letter would be incomplete if I did not say that my colleagues marvel at your success and say in fact 'leave it to the Lord Chamberlain and he will tighten up where he thinks fit'.

So the Government of the day, presumably encouraged by the Home Office, wanted none of it.

At about this time an article appeared in *Theatre Industry*, a trade journal produced by the Theatre Managers' Association, which covered the whole ground of theatre censorship and concluded:

> It will be seen that those who propose that the Lord Chamberlain's powers under the Theatres Act should be abolished or placed in other hands have failed to appreciate some of the overwhelming considerations in favour of the present system.

On 15 May 1958 an article in *The Times* by its drama critic, A. V. Cookman, was headed 'Blue Pencil in the Wings'. It opened:

> A curious air of unreality hangs over every discussion of the censorship. It may be that the majority of those who are satisfied to retain the censorship in its present form have chiefly in mind its convenience to the theatrical industry, while the majority of those who call for the abolition of the censor are concerned to free the drama from restrictions they consider unnecessary.

Any censor, the critic went on, is vulnerable to criticism but the Lord Chamberlain had not been set an impossible task. Although his powers were breathtaking, in recent years they had been used with tolerance and good sense. Nevertheless, it was natural for playwrights to assert their unfair treatment compared with other branches of literature or indeed with any other art. Even so, he pointed out, a play forbidden the stage could be made into a film or projected into the home on television or radio.

After giving a résumé of the story of the censorship from Tudor times, the writer continued:

> The Lord Chamberlain has won respect as a civilised judge of the treatment of stage subjects. It is the responsibility he bears for deciding what subjects are fit to be treated on the public stage that today exposes him to criticism . . . The question now being asked is whether his powers require modernising in some form which will enable him to broaden the range of subjects open to playwrights while keeping the public stage free from plays seeking to make pornographic capital out of the permitted new subjects.

He argued (as Lord Scarbrough had already done) for licences being issued with certificates indicating the nature of the play, and concluded:

> Such a modest extension of the system would have several clear advantages over more root and branch methods of clarifying the present situation. It would modify the grievance now felt by authors; it would leave the theatre managers still under the protection of the Lord Chamberlain;

and it would leave the public free to pick and choose from the subjects they wished to see treated.

On 23 July 1958 the President of the West End Theatrical Managers' Association, Frederick Carter, accompanied by Tom Arnold, Emile Littler and Sir Bronson Albery, went at their own request to discuss the censorship with the Lord Chamberlain. Their discussion ranged over a possible amendment to the Theatres Act, homosexual plays, theatre clubs and television. They said they were unanimously in favour of the present regime and hoped there would be no change.

In March 1961 John Temple MP suggested to the Home Secretary that a Parliamentary Committee be set up to give the Lord Chamberlain stronger and more rigid directions about censorship. The Lord Chamberlain's Office's views were sought and the Home Office was told that whereas the Lord Chamberlain would welcome being given a stronger hand, he was not keen to back Mr Temple's request which, he was certain, would receive little support. As a result, the Home Secretary took the view 'that it is best to leave things as they are' (the Minister of State's reply to Temple) and for the Lord Chamberlain to continue to be guided by the advice of the 1909 Committee. The Home Secretary wrote:

> The acts of a censor are inevitably always a matter of controversy, but I think it is time to say that we here receive fewer complaints about stage plays than about works in other media. There is a body of opinion which argues that the theatre is an adult form of entertainment which should not be subject to any censorship at all, apart from the general law against obscenity.

This turned out to be an accurate prognosis of what was to happen in 1968. The letter concluded:

> The view of successive Home Secretaries has been that, while the system of censorship by the Lord Chamberlain is anomalous in theory, it works well in practice and achieves a good measure of satisfaction in a field in which difference of opinion cannot be avoided.

In 1954 the Scunthorpe police, having first consulted the Lord Chamberlain's Office, had prosecuted Phyllis Dixey for a striptease act and her husband, Jack Tracey, for certain 'filthy business' and jokes. They were both found guilty and fined.

In 1957 the Lord Chamberlain was troubled by *You Weren't Always On Top* at the Theatre Royal, Stratford. Although the piece had been given a licence, considerable parts of the script had been rewritten and some of the new material was felt to be offensive. An example was one of the actors who imitated the voice of Winston Churchill when opening a public lavatory. After some delay the Director of Public Prosecutions decided to take them to court. All five defendants, who included Joan Littlewood, pleaded guilty and small fines were imposed on the plea of poverty.

But from some quarters there was criticism of the Lord Chamberlain being too lenient a censor. Henry Sherek, a leading impresario, in 1961 spoke on the radio and elsewhere of his 'embarrassment at the filth the Lord Chamberlain allowed to go on in the theatre'. It was reported in the *Daily Sketch*:

> The Lord Chamberlain . . . censor to the stage . . . must be used to being scolded by the theatre people who think he is too strict. Yesterday he must have felt a little startled to receive a sharp reproof for being too lax. It came from that top class Purveyor of Fine Drama, Henry Sherek.

Sherek made a plea for an X certificate for plays dealing with sex. Lord Scarbrough minuted at the time: 'A year or two ago I asked the Home Secretary for authority to use some form of differential licence: but the answer was it would need legislation. There were other considerations also.'

Henry Sherek and Norman Gwatkin (Comptroller) knew each other well and their letters contain some amusing exchanges. In one Gwatkin wrote: 'I think playwrights and theatre managers should take the beam out of their own eyes before they start poking about for motes elsewhere. Risk bankruptcy, produce good clean plays and educate your public, my dear Henry.'

Sherek replied: 'Let me declare again that I have always

found your department to be most considerate, but I feel you are being a little too considerate . . . It would probably amuse the populace if a lady (or gentleman) were to undress in the middle of Piccadilly Circus, and if her (or his) protector were to pass round a hat he would conceivably receive quite a lot of money, but public decency steps in represented by a Bluebottle, and they are both hauled off to gaol. Surely your department's function, in which I heartily concur, should be of a similar nature.'

Sherek told Gwatkin he supposed he would keep all the splendid letters he had written and, after his death, sell them for a large sum of money. Not so, replied Gwatkin, 'they are intended for the Bodleian'. In a letter dated 28 July 1961 Gwatkin wrote:

> The Lord Chamberlain cannot, even if he wished to do so, for ever travel in a horse carriage: he is now in a motor car and many people are trying to force him into a spaceship . . . You would probably be surprised to know how much we cut out in words and how much we warn about business, but since the evidence at the trial of 'Lady Chatterley' I am beginning to wonder who one is trying to protect . . .

Some time later Sherek wrote to invite Norman Gwatkin to lunch at the Empress Restaurant, Berkeley Street, beginning his letter 'Mon cher Norman' and ending 'Votre devoué Henri'. Their friendship clearly had not been strained.

The next event of importance in this controversy did not take place until 1962, when Dingle Foot (Labour, Ipswich) was refused leave in the Commons to introduce his Censorship of Plays (Abolition) Bill which was to make it optional to submit a play to the Lord Chamberlain for a licence and to make it legal to perform an unlicensed play. This, of course, had been the recommendation of the 1909 Select Committee. Foot's arguments centred around the difficulties of improvisation and the representation of living people on the stage. There were 77 members who voted for the proposal but as many as 134 voted against. One of the opposing speakers was W. R. Rees-Davies who said of the Lord Chamberlain: 'Could this House find anybody who was more impartial politically, more independent financially, a man of greater integrity or whose endeavours in this matter could be more truly impartial than the Lord Chamberlain (Scarbrough) who does not cost the nation a penny piece?'

The general press comment was one of disappointment, and Lord Scarbrough, now close to retirement, apparently felt the same for he wrote a private and personal letter the next day to the Home Secretary, now Henry Brooke, asking if he might come and discuss the censorship question. He offered to send some notes which he had drawn up for his successor, and specifically asked, 'whether under the law as it stands it is possible for me to allow improvisation on the stage. I am doing my best to find a solution but it is doubtful whether one can be found without rendering the censorship of plays practically impossible.'

They duly met on 3 January 1963 and Brooke reaffirmed his keenness for the Lord Chamberlain to continue his censoring role. A few days later Lord Scarbrough handed over the blue pencil to his successor, Lord Cobbold.

During Lord Scarbrough's term of office a number of unusual and contentious plays came before him. In 1956 *My Fair Lady* was submitted, a musical version of Shaw's *Pygmalion* which had been licensed in 1912 and in which, contrary to popular belief, the Lord Chamberlain (Lord Sandhurst) had allowed Eliza to say 'not bloody likely' when asked if she was going to walk home. Sir St Vincent Troubridge read *My Fair Lady* and said in his report:

> For 1956 the adaptor has sought for some equivalent 'coup de foudre' that would shock without disgusting. They have found this in the Ascot scene where Eliza, having backed a horse, when watching the race with a lot of impassive socialites, adjures the horse at the top of her voice, 'Move your blooming arse'.

He suggested these words should be allowed, continuing:

> In fact 'bloody' in 1912 is if anything more startling in relation to its date than is 'arse' in 1956. Though generally

> cut, this is a homely word, well understood by everybody . . .

Lord Scarbrough agreed, but when the musical opened at Drury Lane the phrase was altered to 'move your ruddy arse' as this had had a better reception. Permission was given.

That same year John Osborne's *Look Back in Anger* was licensed after some alterations had been agreed. The reader wrote, 'This impressive and depressing play breaks new psychological ground, dealing with a type of young man . . . a kind of intellectual that walked about passionately looking for a cause . . .' The play brought Osborne into prominence and was an outstanding success at the Royal Court Theatre. It marked a radical departure from the traditional West End play and many people considered that the Lord Chamberlain had been unusually liberal in allowing it.

The year 1957 saw the closure of both the St James's Theatre and the Stoll Theatre. Commercial television, with its superior resources, increasingly attracted the attention of the more important impresarios and a number of writers of talent. The gradual decline of the revue (and the roadshow) which resulted was shown by fewer such scripts being submitted to the Lord Chamberlain.

A licence was given in 1958 for *For Adults Only* to which Ludovic Kennedy took exception because of some unkind references to his wife, Moira Shearer, and himself. The following year Liberace also objected to a sketch in *For Amusement Only*, also licensed, in which he was portrayed as effeminate. In both cases legal discussion took place but there was no court action as the respective theatre proprietors each offered an apology and an ex-gratia payment. The Lord Chamberlain might have been liable as an accessory on both occasions, for he had, after all, licensed the pieces; but no approach was made to him or against him, possibly because it was believed he was safeguarded by privilege.

In 1959 a licensed revue *We're No Ladies* was performed at the Twentieth-Century Theatre in Westbourne Grove. On investigation it was found to be an all-male show although the dramatis personae were women. Was this an early example of modern camp theatre? As the licensed script was in the main being followed, the Lord Chamberlain took no action other than to inform the London County Council which had licensed this church hall type building as a theatre.

In the LCO's Annual Report of 1960 reference is made to a continuing trend towards 'realistic plays', usually written by young authors at odds with 'the Establishment', sometimes formless and plotless, and relying for their appeal less on plot than on characterisation. The main character was sometimes an 'underprivileged' hero who reacted to social conventions by aggression, or lechery, or by offering violence to women. Despite the care the Lord Chamberlain took over such plays, his task was made more difficult by the passage of the Obscene Publications Act and the successful outcome of the Lady Chatterley case. The following year a play, based on D. H. Lawrence's novel and called *Lady Chatterley*, written by John Hart, was staged at the Arts Theatre. To increase its appeal the actress playing Lady Chatterley climbed naked into bed with an apparently naked actor playing Mellors. This secured the Arts Theatre some publicity but the public reacted with indifference.

During the early 1960s a situation arose concerning a pantomime in a Midlands city. It had been reported to the Lord Chamberlain's Office that striptease was taking place during the performance of the licensed stage play *Cinderella*. A telephone inquiry was made to the manager of the theatre who replied that there was, of course, no striptease as such but that an imaginative and much enjoyed new element had been introduced into the story whereby the means of identifying Cinderella had been changed from the size of her slipper to the shape and size of her bra. This variation on the age-old story was enormously appreciated by audiences and the manager was delighted to say that the pantomime was playing to full houses and was being regarded in the city and elsewhere as a great success. When questioned as to the authority for such an alteration to the licensed script, and reminded of his responsibility for maintaining the law in accordance with the Theatres Act, the manager said that he would never dream of breaking the law; as a matter of fact, the city police station was almost next door and the police themselves were continually coming in and out of the theatre and 'they liked the performance very much'. Presumably the good-mannered manager was conveniently unfamiliar with the dividing-line between a licence for a stage play, issued only by the Lord Chamberlain, and a music and dancing licence, issued by the local licensing authority; neither of which, in fact, allowed for the manipulation of bras in public performances in theatres.

Some plays which included improvisation caused problems because no allowance was made for it in the Theatres Act. Improvisation was therefore illegal, and this meant that one brand of the actors' art could not be practised in Britain, however innocuous the composition. Lord Scarbrough, aware of this deprivation, turned a blind eye whenever he could; he did, however, keep an open one on *The Premise*, an American revue playing at the Comedy Theatre, which relied heavily on improvisation. Although it was acceptable in this case and public sympathy was on the side of the producer, some sections of the press tried to stir up trouble at the expense of the Lord Chamberlain, who believed that improvisation should be allowed if means within the law could be found to control it. The Home Office was unable to advise a way to achieve this and so *The Premise* was allowed to continue on the tacit understanding that nothing of which the Lord Chamberlain could have reasonable complaint would be introduced. It closed soon afterwards. Lord Scarbrough consequently warned the Society of West End Theatre Managers that it was becoming impossible for him to accept improvisation.

Lord Scarbrough's increasingly difficult task of carrying on the censorship was made no easier by the Arts Council increasing grants to subsidise the English Stage Company at the Royal Court Theatre, the Royal Shakespeare Company in London at the Aldwych and the new National Theatre at the Old Vic. These grants enabled these managements to challenge more easily the authority which Parliament had vested in the Lord Chamberlain by submitting controversial plays.

By the time Lord Scarbrough laid down his blue pencil in January 1963 he had, in ten years, licensed over 10,000 plays and banned no more than 30, a ratio of 333:1. Three years later, in February 1966, he spoke early in the debate on theatre censorship in the House of Lords. He supported the proposition that a Joint Select Committee should be appointed to consider the problem afresh, but declared that he was nonetheless in favour of some form of censorship. He was not sure what that should be but believed it should be removed from the Lord Chamberlain who, as Head of the Sovereign's Household, must not be involved in controversy and yet, in his censorship task, he was not always able to avoid it.

CHAPTER THIRTEEN

Homosexuality on the Stage

Until 1958 the Lord Chamberlain maintained an absolute ban on homosexuality as a stage theme.

In 1946, as a result of representations being made to him to modify this ban, the Lord Chamberlain, Lord Clarendon, decided to gauge public opinion on the subject. He therefore addressed letters to as representative a cross-section as he could devise of the leaders of national life, including eminent members of the clerical, legal, scholastic and medical professions. The majority were not in favour of lifting the ban on the grounds that there was much more likelihood of introducing the subject of an illegal practice to the innocent rather than accomplishing the reformation of the pervert. When the matter was looked at again in 1951, with much the same result, Lord Clarendon concluded that the ban should continue.

In 1957 the 'Report of the Committee on Homosexuality and Prostitution', known as the Wolfenden Report, was published. This recommended that homosexual relations between consenting adults be legalised. At that time there had been debates on the subject in the Convocation of Canterbury, the television companies were devoting much time to discussions of it; there were editorials in newspapers; and books were being published explaining or justifying homosexuality.

It was therefore inevitable that, when Lord Scarbrough went to see the Home Secretary, R. A. Butler in June 1957, one of the subjects they discussed was plays with homosexual themes. In his memorandum of the meeting Lord Scarbrough wrote:

Up to now I had maintained a rigid attitude, as had my

predecessors, on this subject, and allowed no mention of it on the stage. I maintained that attitude for one reason only: that to permit references or plays dealing with that subject would inevitably introduce some young people to a subject that otherwise they might never come into contact with. I doubted whether it would be possible for this attitude to be maintained much longer. For one thing this subject had now become one which was one much talked about, and it was bound to appear rather ostrich-like that it should never be mentioned on the stage. In addition to that an increasing number of plays, some of them good, and dealing seriously with this subject, were being written, and it was bound to appear absurd to quite sensible people to disallow any attempt to deal seriously with a subject which had now become, unfortunately, one of the problems of life.

Since Lord Scarbrough felt the topic had been so widely voiced that there was no point in continuing to debar it from the stage, he informed the theatre industry that in future, the subject would be allowed on certain terms, including:

(a) Every play will continue to be judged on its merits and only those dealing seriously with the subject will be passed;
(b) Plays violently homosexual will not be passed;
(c) Homosexual characters will not be allowed if their inclusion in the piece is unnecessary to the action or theme of the play;
(d) Embraces between homosexuals will not be allowed.

When, in 1932, Lord Cromer had licensed *The Green Bay Tree* by Mordaunt Shairp, the story of an unhappy wife of a husband with a homosexual tendency, a number of critics had read into the plot a homosexual relationship between the husband and his adopted son, which was not the author's intention. Equally, the licensing of this play had given some people the impression that the subject of homosexuality was no longer taboo. The play was seen by one of the Comptrollers and by G. S. Street, the Examiner, who recorded:

There is no suggestion of physical homosexuality in it and

indeed the play is inconsistent with it. The few critics who took the opposite view were, I think, influenced by a desire to appear knowing or by the unfortunate fact that homosexuality is in the air very much at present or at least in the theatrical air.

Geoffrey Dearmer remembered seeing the play with Catherine Lacey in the part of the wife. 'The play was strong and sympathetic, showing the problem (homosexuality) to be a real one and quite the reverse of being offensive. To have banned it would have been a great mistake. It had been quite a success at, I think, the St Martin's, and caused no unfavourable comment.'

Children's Hour by Lillian Hellman, dealing as it does with lesbianism, was in the public eye for many years. It was first submitted in 1935 – 'a horribly unpleasant play' (Street) – and Lord Cromer refused it a licence. It was later seen by one of his staff at a private performance at the Gate Theatre. He appreciated the quality of the production and the acting, but still felt unable to recommend a licence. The play was submitted again with the same results in 1936, 1939, 1942 and 1945. In 1950 it was seen by Sir Norman Gwatkin, then Assistant Comptroller, at the New Boltons Theatre Club and he described it as a most moving and sincere play.

The following year, 1951, a deputation went to see Lord Clarendon to try and persuade him to allow this subject on the stage, or at least this play, on the grounds that:

(a) According to the Law the act of lesbianism was not an offence;
(b) The play brought out the tragedy of the condition, and in no way encouraged it.

The Lord Chamberlain once again decided to seek the views of a wider audience. The majority were not in favour of allowing the subject on principle because – unlike homosexuality between men – it was believed to be confined to a much smaller circle and harm might be done by arousing the curiosity of adolescent girls.

Further attempts at obtaining a licence were made during

that decade and, on one occasion, the author offered to make changes, but Lord Scarbrough continued the ban until 1960 when he relented, although the play was not performed publicly until, in 1964, it was produced at the Guildhall School of Music.

In 1940 the play *Queer People* was submitted by the manager of the Duchess Theatre. It opens and ends with a farewell homily on the penalties of sodomy, spoken by a headmaster to a boy whom he is in the act of expelling. The story centres on a neurotic young man, who is about to be married, and who meets again a young man who was his lover at school. The play was read by Henry Game, who wrote:

> In my ten years' experience as an Examiner of Plays I have never read anything which was so impossible for public or private production . . . Not only will it have to be banned but every effort should be made to prevent it being produced by one of the bogus theatre clubs.

Lord Clarendon added, 'I entirely agree that this revolting play cannot be allowed and I sincerely hope that if any bogus theatre club produces it a prosecution will follow.'

The Comptroller wrote to the manager of the Duchess Theatre informing him that the Lord Chamberlain was unable to license *Queer People*, adding, 'I am further to inform you that His Lordship considers it a piece of impertinence that such a play should have been submitted.' The manager sent his sincere apologies and said the wrong play had been sent for licensing! The Comptroller replied, 'I cannot see that your explanation as to how this particular play came to be submitted is very convincing in that the title of the play, and even the author's name, is mentioned in your letter.'

The matter was raised with the Home Office, which in turn consulted the Director of Public Prosecutions, but no action resulted and no more was heard of the play.

Leslie and Sewell Stokes' play *Oscar Wilde* never received a licence. It was first performed before the war at the Gate Theatre and was refused a licence when submitted in 1946 because the play was about homosexuals. It was next performed at the Boltons Theatre in 1948 and was seen by both

Charles Heriot and by Sir Terence Nugent (Comptroller) who wrote to the Lord Chamberlain, Lord Clarendon:

> It is undoubtedly a good play but I do not recommend you to pass it. It is entirely about perverts, and as Game says in his 1946 report this subject is taboo as a dramatic theme.

Because it *was* a good play Lord Clarendon was reasonably criticised for withholding a licence. In 1957 Arnold Taylor, the producer, asked the next Lord Chamberlain, Lord Scarbrough, to reconsider the decision but was told that, as the policy regarding plays on homosexuality had not been changed, he would not license it. However, when the policy was changed the following year Arnold Taylor was told that he could resubmit the play provided Oscar Wilde's son (Vyvyan Holland) raised no objection. Lord Scarbrough received a letter from him saying:

> I have read the play which I consider to be in very bad taste and to give an entirely wrong impression of the whole wretched business. If put on publicly it would certainly cause distress to my wife and son. *I have therefore the most sincere objection to a licence being granted*, and would be very grateful if you could withhold it.

Lord Scarbrough did just that.

Also in the 1950s, the portrayal of homosexual love in Arthur Miller's *A View From The Bridge* was not allowed, nor at first was Ronald Duncan's *The Catalyst* which included lesbian leanings between a man's wife and his mistress. Despite its theme, the reader (Troubridge) recommended that *The Catalyst* be licensed as it seemed to him very good drama – 'So I advise that this is the exceptional play for which to loosen up.' Lord Scarbrough minuted: 'I have read this play with great interest and I should think it could be a real success, but I am not prepared to pick and choose between the good and the bad plays which deal with the subject of homosexuality and lesbianism, and so long as that policy prevails I regret I cannot license the play.' These and other plays dealing with homosexuality were given club performances in 1956 and 1957 at theatres such as the Comedy and the New Watergate.

A minor landmark in theatrical licensing was to allow, in 1953, *Serious Charge* by Philip King. The play hinged on an accusation of indecency by a young man against a clergyman. The reader, Charles Heriot, concluded his report: 'The play is strong and sensible. We are in no doubt at any time that the vicar is innocent of the "serious charge". Therefore, though the forbidden topic of homosexuality shadows this play, it does so in an inoffensive manner.' Heriot recommended a licence. Lord Scarbrough minuted:

> I am not convinced by the retort that because the accusation was untrue no question of propriety can arise. But neither am I convinced that the relevant part of the play should be cut out or altered. It is a straight play and though it is conceivable that some embarrassment might be caused, I think on the whole no great harm will be done and that the play should be licensed.

An American schoolboy accused of being a homosexual is the subject of Robert Anderson's notable play *Tea and Sympathy*. The play was widely acclaimed when it was performed in Chicago with Deborah Kerr in the lead as the schoolmaster's wife, but Lord Scarbrough refused it a licence in 1954. Mrs Franks, who owned the rights of the play, maintained that homosexuality was at no point condoned and that the theme of the play is one of loving kindness; she even offered to fly out Sir Terence Nugent, the Comptroller, to see it. In 1956 *Tea and Sympathy* was made into a film with the homosexual theme removed; and a play licence was finally given in 1958 to a virtually unaltered version, after the ban on homosexual subjects had been lifted.

In May 1963 the English Stage Company submitted *Spring Awakening*, Frank Wedekind's first play, published in 1891. Maurice Coles' opinion was: 'This is one of the most loathsome and depraved plays I have ever read. It is concerned with the turgid sexual fantasies and experiments of the awakening adolescent instincts of provincial German schoolchildren in the 1890s.'

The Lord Chamberlain's Office called for two scenes to be cut and gave two warnings about kissing between boys. The Royal Court decided not to put on the play publicly, and Terence Nugent and Eric Penn attended a Sunday evening performance. The following year the National Theatre said they were considering putting on the play and asked the Lord Chamberlain to reconsider his original disallowances. Kenneth Tynan, the National's Literary Manager, came to see me, as a result of which we gave some ground but still refused to allow the boys kissing. The National Theatre decided to drop the project. Instead, the following year the Royal Court made another attempt to obtain a licence for public performance. They continued to plead for the retention of certain 'business' (including kissing and simulated masturbating) but the Lord Chamberlain refused again. However a further version, without these elements, was licensed in April 1965.

That same year *The Killing of Sister George* by Frank Marcus was submitted. The part of Sister George, a character in a radio series, was played by Beryl Reid. Because of its lesbian content a licence was given with some diffidence. However, it was received without any complaint on that score and personally I enjoyed the play and particularly Beryl Reid's performance.

The lifting in 1958 of the stage ban on homosexual subjects marked quite a milestone in the history of the theatre censorship, but it did not, contrary to expectations, result in a spate of plays with such themes. Indeed public reaction was slight, perhaps because in this matter the Lord Chamberlain had been running behind public taste. Inevitably, though, some people criticised the Lord Chamberlain for his decision. To one such correspondent Lord Scarbrough set out to justify his action and ended his letter with the following words:

> With the freedom with which it is now discussed . . . it can no longer be held that a complete ban should be maintained on the stage alone in order to keep the subject away from young people. The complete ban has in consequence ceased to achieve its object and has lost any power for good that it used to have. That is the reason why I have made the change, which, I must point out, is not to allow complete

liberty on the subject but serious plays about it. It is possible – though time will tell – that serious plays on the subject will do more good than the wide publicity which such plays received through being banned.

Chapter Fourteen

The Beginning of the End, 1963–66

Lord Cobbold succeeded Lord Scarbrough on 29 January 1963. During his last five years Lord Scarbrough had done much to gain Ministers' sympathy for the view that some sort of change was necessary. It was now up to Lord Cobbold to persuade them into action.

There had been a similarity in the careers of the past three Lord Chamberlains, but Lord Cobbold's background was different. He had been a banker all his working life, becoming Governor of the Bank of England at the age of forty-five, an appointment he held for fourteen years. Born in 1904, he was aged fifty-nine when he became head of the Queen's Household. He was created a life peer in 1960.

Lord Cobbold did not keep a diary. In 1988, however, his widow, Hermione, sent me a memorandum about the censorship which he had written for his family. In it Lord Cobbold said:

> When I took it on there was a good deal of regular criticism and occasional outbursts about particular decisions.
>
> It was, however, generally admitted that the censorship had become much more tolerant and sensible under my immediate predecessors, largely because Terence Nugent (Comptroller, Lord Chamberlain's Office, 1937–60, except during the war) was a very popular figure in the theatre world, and also because theatre managements found it useful to have themselves, to a considerable extent, protected from libel or indecency actions.
>
> It had, however, become an obvious nonsense, particularly with the cinema censorship arrangements and the

growth of radio and television which had quite different and rather vague 'censorship' regimes, and with the interchange with an entirely free New York theatre, not to mention increasing freedom of general public taste, I soon decided that the position was going to become untenable. I was also strongly influenced by feeling that, although we ran it from St James's and not from Buckingham Palace, and though we did our best to maintain that it was quite a different function, there was increasing danger that it would reflect on the Monarch and give ammunition to criticisms that the Palace was stuffy and out-of-date. I was pretty sure that it was a job which, five or ten years later, nobody in their senses would take on.

I, therefore, started nosing around with Ministers and officials to see what could be done.

Nonetheless, and as he feared, Lord Cobbold quickly became accustomed to criticism, both from the press and the public, mainly on the grounds of being too 'stuffy'. But he also received complaints for being too liberal. A typical letter written to a complainant by the Assistant Comptroller on 2 August 1963 included the following paragraphs:

> May I thank you on behalf of the Lord Chamberlain for having taken the trouble to write about your experiences in the theatre. The Lord Chamberlain is under constant attack in the Press and elsewhere for any restrictive action which he takes. Comments in the opposite sense, such as are expressed in your letter, are therefore of the greatest help to him in his task of forming a balanced view.
>
> The Lord Chamberlain asks me to explain that he does not consider it his duty to forbid the expression on the stage of opinions which it would be legal to publish in other ways; he does try to ensure that such views are represented with reasonable regard to contemporary standards of behaviour and that they do not needlessly give cause for offence.

Because of attacks on him as censor of plays, Lord Cobbold did consider during his first year of office publishing an informed article on the censorship or inviting a journalist or

Lord Cobbold, the last Lord Chamberlain to administer the Theatres Act, 1843

distinguished writer to put together such an article with help from the Lord Chamberlain's Office. Nothing happened at the time but, in April 1965, he agreed to an interview with J. W. Lambert which was published in the *Sunday Times* on 11 April.

Meanwhile, in April 1964, Philip Oakes had written an article on censorship in *The Queen* magazine. It began:

> The best kept secret about censorship in Britain is that there is so much of it. Its salient features are plain as, say, the nose on Lord Cobbold's face, but censorship does not end with the tools of the Lord Chamberlain's Office . . . It is the filter through which all forms of public expression pass.

The writer went on to say that the Romans founded the office of Censor which was given to a senior magistrate whose chief duty was the drawing up of a register or consensus of citizens. It was this same person who was required to supervise public morals.

Although the Lord Chamberlain and his staff were frequently asked to give interviews, the policy was not to do so and the long interview between Lord Cobbold and J. W. Lambert was, I believe, unique. This provided a very good summary of the censorship in 1965 and still makes interesting reading twenty-five years later (see Appendix E, page 272). But, except in his answer to Lambert's first question, Lord Cobbold was careful not to reveal his own views on the future of the censorship.

During this discussion Lord Cobbold gave the fullest expression of his views on the workings of the censorship:

> Q: What is your personal view of the censor's function? Is it to maintain a norm of generally acceptable freedom?
>
> A: Norm is the operative word. If I may go a bit ahead of your question, we always think of ourselves as a licensing authority rather than as a censoring authority. The bias is always to give a licence unless there is very strong ground for objection. My personal objective is to try to assess the norm of educated, adult opinion and if possible to keep just a touch ahead of it. I find I have to make a positive effort to keep my own personal tastes, likes and dislikes right out of the picture. They are obviously irrelevant for censorship purposes. Of course, one must make some allowance for selectivity; people don't have to go to the theatre; they choose what they want to see and if they want to they can quite easily find out something about the play before they go.

Lord Cobbold believed it important to be on the same wavelength with Lord Harlech, his counterpart as censor of films. In 1965 he wrote a confidential note for the record:

> I asked Lord Harlech to come in on Nov. 12th for a private talk about censorship. I told him where I stood with Ministers and the DPP, giving him pretty full background of our thinking and actions over the past year or so.

Lord Harlech was grateful and agreed
(a) that the present arrangements cannot hold for many years;
(b) that it is wise to try and get all this looked at on a favourable wicket, i.e. when the Stage and Film Censorship are not under particular fire from the Press, etc;
(c) that the inquiry, if any, should cover films (possibly TV) as well as stage.

I asked him to keep this to himself leaving him discretion to tell Trevelyan privately as much as he thought necessary.

We agreed to keep in touch.

John Trevelyan, the Secretary of the British Board of Film Censors, and I already used to keep each other informed about our respective activities, and we continued to do so.

In the mid-1960s it was becoming apparent that those theatres which had the financial backing of public money were the ones which were staging the more contentious or controversial plays. On 22 April 1965 Kenneth Tynan, writing to the Lord Chamberlain about the play *Mother Courage* by Bertolt Brecht – which the National Theatre was to put on – maintained that the National had a special status, being the first theatre to have been set up by a government edict. Tynan said:

> It is run by government nominees and it is supported by a Treasury grant. It thus has a political as well as an artistic significance. In this respect it is unique, and this uniqueness puts it on a different footing from other theatre companies . . . the Board was created with a specific briefing and specific task to fulfil; namely to make available to the public a repertoire drawn from the best in world drama, ancient and modern, native and foreign. In this respect its public function is analogous to that of an institution like the British Museum – a repository where *any* book can be obtained . . .

He went on to develop this theme and to suggest that the Lord Chamberlain should take it into account when the National Theatre submitted plays. I replied on 5 May 1965:

> With regard to the general points that you have raised concerning the National Theatre, the Lord Chamberlain has asked me to make the following comment. Whilst he personally has the highest regard for the work being done by the National Theatre, he carries out, as Lord Chamberlain, duties imposed by Parliament. He has no authority to give preferential treatment to one management, whether state-supported or not, over another. He endeavours to take all factors into account and to deal equitably and, he hopes, reasonably with all managements.
>
> As you yourself are aware, it is not possible for the Lord Chamberlain to license a play to be performed exclusively by the National Theatre; a play licence under the present regulations is valid for all performances anywhere in the country . . .

Lord Cobbold sent copies of the exchange to Lord Chandos, the National Theatre Board Chairman, adding:

> Let us have a gossip about all this some time . . . I do not want your people and my people to get up against each other. It only complicates an already difficult state of affairs!

Lord Willis, the playwright Ted Willis, helped to keep the censorship question in the parliamentary eye. He asked in the House of Lords on 7 May 1964 whether HMG had considered 'the amendment of existing laws and regulations to allow for the abolition of the present system of censorship of stage plays'. Replying for the Government (Conservative), Lord Derwent, the Minister of State at the Home Office, said that no amendment was contemplated, and he continued:

> Even though the present system of censorship of stage plays by the Lord Chamberlain may appear anomalous in theory, the Government consider that it has worked well in practice and that no alternative system is likely to be found which would command general support.

Lord Willis pointed out that Britain was the only country in the world with this father figure as the dictator of what was put on the stage, and suggested some other system be found more in keeping with the times. Lord Derwent replied that 'we always do everything better than other countries' and doubted another system would have majority support. Lord Gardiner, who was shortly to become Lord Chancellor, then posed the question:

> Does not the noble Lord think it very odd that grown-up people in this country should not be able to see a play unless an official of the Queen's Household thinks they ought to?

Lord Derwent replied that some other official had been contemplated but the Government had not found the suggestion any more satisfactory; in fact, rather less so.

In 1965, the script of a revue *Nite Life New York* was submitted by the manager of the Royal Pavilion, Blackpool. A licence was delayed as some alterations to the script had been asked for. Meanwhile a revue entitled *Folies Strip-Tease* was being performed in its place and the Blackpool police were asked to investigate. They reported that the script of this revue was substantially the same as that submitted for *Nite Life New York* with certain innocuous variety acts being replaced by a series of striptease performances. The Lord Chamberlain sent the papers to the Director of Public Prosecutions who decided to prosecute both the theatre manager and the producer. When the case came before the Blackpool Magistrates Court in January, the defendants pleaded not guilty on the grounds that *Nite Life New York* was not a stage play and that *Folies Strip-Tease* was a completely different entertainment! The magistrates found both of them guilty and they were fined £40 with £35 costs.

Lord Scarbrough had made little use of the Advisory Board during his term as Lord Chamberlain. Now Lord Cobbold had no recourse to it whatsoever. In August 1964, soon after he succeeded Sir Norman Gwatkin as Comptroller, Sir Eric Penn wrote a memorandum to Lord Cobbold, presumably in answer to his inquiry:

> The Advisory Board has always been something of a mystery to me . . . I have asked Tim Nugent his views . . .

> He remembers some members of the Board being written to . . . He is of the opinion that the Board serves no useful function. It is entirely unofficial. It is always possible for the Lord Chamberlain to consult the most eminent authorities in the land concerning any particular play, as you yourself have already done . . . The Board cannot take away any responsibility from the Lord Chamberlain himself . . . In these circumstances, I think it may well be that you will wish to let the existence of this Board fade out.

Lord Cobbold's reply was short and to the point:

> Let us leave this dog to continue its slumbers undisturbed.

Thus this dog continued to sleep its way through the final four years of theatre censorship. But even when it was awake I doubt that it was ever a satisfactory working dog. The main practical disadvantage of the Advisory Board was the time it took to pass a playscript from one member to another, for each one to read and make a recommendation. One can imagine the frustration of the playwright or manager awaiting a decision about his or her play before the days of photocopying.

Lord Cobbold recorded in his memorandum to his family that he was making little progress over changing the Lord Chamberlain's responsibilities:

> The big difficulty was that nothing effective could be done without an Act of Parliament which was likely to be controversial and to take up a good deal of parliamentary time. I made no progress with two Home Secretaries (Brooke, Conservative, and Soskice, Labour), both of whom took the line 'You're doing very well, old boy, keep at it – it would really be very difficult to get a bill through Parliament'. It was only when Roy Jenkins became Home Secretary, who was interested in the subject and agreed with my views, that things got moving. A private member's bill got under way, a Select Committee was appointed, and the Act eventually went through without much difficulty. The main trouble was to find parliamentary time and we were

helped by one of those curious quirks of fate – we brought the car back from Italy/France on a Le Touquet/Lydd plane; one of the other cars being Dick Crossman's, who was then Leader of the House, and I spent the twenty minutes (not wholly wasted I think) encouraging him to find time for the Bill.

Lord Cobbold had been to see Sir Frank Soskice on 11 February 1965 for a general talk, on a 'thinking aloud' basis, about the censorship and what its future might be. He expressed doubts about being able to continue for much longer. He explained that the situation was changing because of the organised opposition to the censorship by some theatre companies, including the Royal Shakespeare Company, and the challenge of television. The Home Secretary told him he would prefer to let things ride for a while longer: a further example of Government playing for time.

However by the end of the year things had begun to move for the Government had agreed to a debate in the House of Lords. Roy Jenkins had just been appointed Home Secretary, and during the month of January 1966 the Lord Chamberlain had talks with both him and the Prime Minister. One suggestion Lord Cobbold made was to have an alternative form of theatre censorship, perhaps a Board of Censors similar to the Film Board. On another visit to the Home Office, Lord Cobbold talked to Roy Jenkins about the setting up of a Joint Committee to follow the debate in the Lords; and, if the Committee came up with a unanimous recommendation, he urged that legislation should follow speedily.

However, when it became known that there was to be a debate on the censorship there was plenty of support expressed for the Lord Chamberlain to continue as censor. Jack Minster, a director of Minster Productions, wrote to Lord Cobbold on 2 February 1966:

> I would like to say that speaking for myself and certainly other reputable managements, we think it will be a far less safe state of affairs should anything happen in this country to abolish the Lord Chamberlain's office. In the several dealings I have had over plays with yourself and your

> predecessors, I have never had anything but courtesy and a fair deal . . . Somehow the would-be abolishers of censorship always seem a good deal suspect.

This support of the theatre managers continued to the very end. Lord Cobbold replied:

> Many thanks for your nice letter . . . Amid the welter of criticism it is always pleasing to think that this Office does a good job.

The debate was set for 17 February 1966. Throughout this period, however, the work of the Lord Chamberlain's Office had been proceeding normally; indeed a remarkable number of new plays had been considered and licensed, many of which were memorable.

CHAPTER FIFTEEN

New Plays in the Mid-1960s

During the six years (1963–8) when Lord Cobbold administered the Theatres Act of 1843 he licensed 4,343 new plays and banned outright only sixteen, a ratio of 277:1. There were a number in a third category, namely those in which changes had been called for (e.g., John Osborne's *A Patriot for Me*) but which were not accepted by the authors or managements. These we referred to in the Office as 'waiting box' plays. From early in 1966, after the debate in the House of Lords, they grew in number as playwrights became less inclined to make alterations in order to obtain a licence.

Nonetheless this was a time when some particularly interesting plays were being submitted, on a number of which it was not easy to reach a decision. One of these was Rolf Hochhuth's *The Representative* in 1963, which deals with the Papacy and its attitude to the persecution of the Jews in the Second World War; this was because a former head of state, namely Pope Pius XII, was not only represented but also shown in none too favourable a light. However Lord Cobbold decided to allow the play as an expression of opinion, but the licence was made conditional on the management of the Aldwych Theatre printing in the programme a commentary from the Catholic Church giving a favourable view of the Pope's actions. (This did not, of course, have the force of law.) It seemed that the right decision had been taken, since there was little press comment, there were no disturbances, and only one complaint was made to the Lord Chamberlain.

Alfie by Bill Naughton, submitted by the Mermaid Theatre in 1963, was a study of the sexual adventures of a cockney 'wide boy'. A number of cuts in both dialogue and 'business' were asked for but Lord Cobbold's main objection was to an abortion that was enacted on stage behind a screen. A revised script was submitted with the abortion scene taking place offstage and a licence was given. There were still a number of complaints despite that and the play was 'inspected' twice. One complaint came from the Public Morality Council to whom Lord Cobbold wrote:

> This play certainly deals with unpleasant subjects and may not be to everybody's taste. This is not of itself a sufficient reason for banning a play. My endeavour is to form a judgement, admittedly not easy, as to whether such subjects are treated seriously or otherwise, whether the production would normally be regarded as an incitement or a deterrent to immorality; and whether particular scenes or words would . . . cause general offence to the theatre-going public. The present production (after considerable cuts and alterations at my request) seemed to me to justify a licence.

Alfie was a successful play, partly because it was funny. It transferred to the West End in July 1963 and was later filmed.

When Robert Bolt's *Gentle Jack* was put on at the Queen's Theatre that year, the author (so the actor Timothy West told me) came to see one of the Comptrollers at the Lord Chamberlain's Office to inquire why the Lord Chamberlain had taken exception to a passage about a lion 'shitting himself with fear'. He pointed out that the use of this excretory term had been permitted elsewhere but it was explained to him that for other animals, or indeed humans, it might be all right, but not for the symbol of British supremacy!

Language was, naturally enough, often a bone of contention and certain four-letter words, particularly 'fuck', were invariably cut. One example of how to get around this problem came in David Rudkin's *Afore Night Come*, when the Lord Chamberlain was readily persuaded to allow the substitution of the invented word 'firk'. As Timothy West recalled, 'In a Worcestershire accent the sounds were indistinguishable, but honour was satisfied.'

A 'waiting box' play of 1963–4 was *The Screens* by Jean Genet, translated by Bernard Frechtman, which was submitted by John Roberts for the Royal Shakespeare Theatre, Stratford-upon-Avon. The reader (Heriot) began his report:

> This is an enormous, sprawling, vaguely symbolic play by a self-confessed criminal and pervert, once patronised by Sartre . . . There is a cast of one hundred and the author has designed the play to be performed out of doors before screens on which the scenery is sometimes painted by the actors. The players wear grotesque masks and their costumes are violently coloured as in a crudely-tinted cartoon. The time is, apparently, during the recent Algerian war.

A number of the scenes are in a brothel and the dialogue contains a good deal of bad language. In fact the Lord Chamberlain's disallowances ran to as many as four pages.

In May 1964 the company carried out some experimental work with *The Screens*, performing privately some of the scenes at the Donmar Rehearsal Theatre in London over a period of six days. At their request, Ronald Hill from the Lord Chamberlain's Office went to see one of the performances and wrote a report for the Lord Chamberlain in which, whilst commending the play's technical excellence, he nevertheless did not feel it merited any specially sympathetic treatment. He supported the proposed disallowances. John Roberts was told that an entirely new script would need to be submitted for the play to be given a licence, but the Royal Shakespeare Theatre presumably felt it could not accept so many changes for a writer of considerable literary reputation.

An author who had regular dealings over the years with the Lord Chamberlain's Office was John Arden. He recalled two oddities, both of which arose from his play *Armstrong's Last Goodnight* which was performed at the Glasgow Citizens' Theatre in 1964 and also at the Chichester Festival in 1965. As Arden wrote to me, 'they were requested by the Lord Chamberlain's Office to furnish full details about the hanging of the hero, at the end of the play, from a branch of a tree. The stage direction simply reads "They hang him."'

Arden explained that at that stage of the production there were in fact no details, nor could there be until the stage manager had concerted arrangements with a flying ballet specialist (who apparently had a technique for hanging an actor). He continued:

> The demand caused some concern at the theatre, and no one could quite work out what was in the mind of the gentleman who had made it, until it was suggested that there was a good deal of current national controversy about capital punishment, involving some gruesome descriptions in various newspapers of death by hanging; and that perhaps the Lord Chamberlain's Office was afraid that the scene in the play would be used for a piece of politically-motivated 'grand guignol'.

This, of course, was not true. The intention was simply to ensure that the 'business' was not too horrifying. The other stage direction in the play to which exception was taken was, 'They are in the garden enjoying the pleasures of love', referring to two Renaissance gentlemen and two ladies. John Arden wrote of this:

> In fact, I intended – and I don't think anyone else involved in the production had understood it in any other way, given the style of the writing – that the scene should be languid and sensuous with perhaps a lute and a bottle of wine: but simulated sexual congress was becoming quite a feature of avant-garde (and not so avant-garde) theatre in the mid-sixties and obviously some suspicions had been aroused.

In the event the licence was endorsed, with the business of the hanging to be largely masked; while 'enjoying the pleasures of love' was to be played with the couples reclining at ease, as in a scene of dalliance.

Although *Listen To The Mocking Bird*, written by John Wells and Claud Cockburn and licensed in 1964 for the Nottingham Playhouse, seemed to be a heavy-handed political satire, it was allowed with a number of alterations. A Methodist minister wrote to the Lord Chamberlain expressing his deep concern that this play should have been passed for public performance. He said there were many young people at the performance he had attended and he was convinced that much in this play must have had a harmful effect on impressionable minds. I replied on the Lord Chamberlain's behalf on 9 October 1964:

> The Lord Chamberlain shares your views in that he considers this play does contain a number of scenes which are lacking in merit. However the law requires him to be not an arbiter of merit but the Censor of Stage Plays, and as such he must take account of contemporary standards, which are now so frank as to be controversial. Therefore, it is not unusual for him to be thought too lax by some in his decisions, or on the other hand too strict by others.

Charles Wood was no stranger to conflict with the Lord Chamberlain over a number of his plays. Apparently he was a little surprised when the National Theatre wanted to put on *Dingo* which Kenneth Tynan submitted towards the end of 1964, for presentation the following year. The play, set in the Western Desert during the Second World War, was described by the reader (Harward) as 'a bitter, pungent attack on war and heroism'. He recommended a licence subject to three pages of alterations to language and to some 'business'. I confess I did not like the play when I read it and was uncertain about a recommendation. Lord Cobbold decided neither to ban it nor to send a list of alterations but to invite Laurence Olivier and Kenneth Tynan to come and see him, which they did on 26 January 1965. He said he did not wish to have an open row with the National Theatre over a controversial play that might receive much publicity. Olivier and Tynan agreed to try and persuade the author to resubmit the script without the obviously unacceptable words and phrases.

Nothing further was heard from the National. A few months later Charles Wood was quoted in the *Daily Mail* as saying, 'He [the Lord Chamberlain] keeps talking about bad taste and I don't know what that is'. Presumably the author was not prepared to revise the script and the National Theatre dropped the idea of staging the play. Two years later the English Stage Society took over the Royal Court Theatre for three weeks to present *Dingo* to its members. The general manager wrote, 'I know that his Lordship will not grant a public licence for this play and we do not want to flout his wishes in any way.' We left them guessing as to what action the Lord Chamberlain might take, but he took none.

Another of Charles Wood's plays *Meals on Wheels* also

caused us a problem. This too was submitted in 1964, by the Bristol Old Vic, but the production was abandoned after no agreement was reached over cuts and substitutions. A further script was submitted six months later and with some reluctance a licence was issued. When the play was performed publicly at the Royal Court Theatre it was 'inspected' by a representative of the Lord Chamberlain who noticed a number of deviations from the licensed script. A reviewer, B. A. Young, wrote in the *Financial Times*, 'There isn't much to say about *Meals on Wheels* except that it's about the most empty, witless, pointless load of rubbish that I've seen for a very long time.' Other critics gave it somewhat better notices, however.

Lord Cobbold decided to take no action other than to send the Royal Court a reminder that they must keep to the licensed script, minuting, 'Generally I agree with the F.T. critic that all this is such drivel as to be inoffensive and incapable of corrupting a rabbit. It makes the Royal Court look ridiculous . . .'

William Gaskill, as Artistic Director of the Royal Court Theatre, at this time often visited the Lord Chamberlain's Office to discuss plays to be presented at that theatre. In March 1989, when we met again for the first time in over twenty years, we enjoyed a reminiscence during which Gaskill said, 'Any kind of restriction as to what can be done on stage is a limitation, particularly for authors who felt very strongly, not just for the subject-matter but for the way in which it limited their language. What they were not being allowed to do as writers seemed so out of step compared with what people in the street were saying that it was not a true representation of people as they were . . . It was a terrible irritation for authors.' Gaskill recalled how a member of the Lord Chamberlain's Office had, at the request of the Royal Court, attended a reading of *Endgame* by Samuel Beckett – an unusual occurrence. He had often wondered who the play readers were and what they said in their reports. He recalled some interesting battles with the Lord Chamberlain's Office, conducted with a great deal of energy, and admitted that, after 1968, he missed the challenge of taking on the Lord Chamberlain.

Harold Pinter's play *The Caretaker* had been licensed for

the Duchess Theatre in 1960. One of the disallowances then was the phrase 'Piss off'. In 1965 *The Caretaker* was put on at the Playhouse Theatre, Nottingham, and the management asked for the phrase to be reinstated on the grounds that it had been used in the recent film of the play. I checked with John Trevelyan, Secretary of the British Board of Film Censors, who confirmed that, whereas customarily they did not allow such language, they had done so in this case. In view of our policy of keeping in step with the Film Board, we agreed.

In December 1964 Michael Codron submitted Joe Orton's play *Loot*. It is a black comedy centred on the treatment of a corpse and is played for laughs. We required certain scenes to be rewritten and, after a talk with Michael Codron and the director, I wrote to Codron on 11 January 1965 to say that the Lord Chamberlain was prepared to consider a licence if some careful stage directions were written into the script, such as that the corpse is obviously a dummy and is not seen by the audience. The revisions arrived at the time of Winston Churchill's death, just when the Lord Chamberlain's Office was deeply involved in the arrangements for his State Funeral, so *Loot* and other plays inevitably took second place. Michael Codron jogged my elbow with a courteous telegram: 'Appreciate your duties unusually heavy at this time but may we have the Lord Chamberlain's decisions on *Loot*?' A licence was given on the understanding that a few more alterations were made.

I went to see a performance at the enormous Wimbledon Theatre which was played to an almost empty house. I did not much care for the play but it confirmed my view that it would have been wrong to withhold a licence. I said as much to Lord Cobbold but suggested he should not rush to see it. When *Loot* came to the West End in 1966 it enjoyed some success and won the *Evening Standard* award for best play of the year. None of the disallowances we had made crept back in and the stage directions required by us were carried out. The Lord Chamberlain, however, did receive a few letters of complaint. One said, 'I am exceedingly surprised that the play ever passed your censure. It breaks every canon of decent behaviour and is a shocking example to young people.'

Another complainant wrote, 'I do not think I have ever witnessed such an unpleasant and wickedly filthy-worded play in my life'; and after one performance a lady brandishing an umbrella came up to Michael Codron and hissed 'Felicity's 21st'. Apparently her selection of this play, starring Geraldine McEwan and Kenneth Williams, had turned out to be not the right one for a twenty-first birthday party!

The Lord Chamberlain was held up to a little ridicule in April 1965 when, just before the revue *Guarding the Change* opened at the New Lyric Theatre, Hammersmith, he banned two of the sketches. One was called 'Great Scott' and was a parody of Scott's last expedition in the Antarctic, mocking his heroism. The other was a send-up of relations between Britain and Australia which included a speech by Britannia. This speech was to have been delivered by the actress Virginia Osborn, who planned instead to read the Lord Chamberlain's letter banning the speech. But he refused to allow this. Instead, the next day, it was published in the *Daily Mail*. The speech read:

> Our dearest and most well-beloved subjects, people, compatriots and allies. It pleases us to be here in your country, especially in this dear and well-beloved season of the year, spring/summer/autumn/winter in order to carry out our duties at this investiture/opening/funeral/wedding/signing of death warrant. We declare this bridge/dam/arsenal/baby farm/open/closed/independent/abolished/knighted. Let Empire/Commonwealth/Loose Association of Nations with common interests/partners in trade/bitter enemies/rest assured. Our thoughts/good wishes/carpet salesmen/aircraft carriers/ are on their way towards you. And so on this beautiful morning/afternoon/evening/what else is there for us to say, but hallo/how-do-you-do/goodbye/well done/arise Sir Robert Menzies.

As Michael Frayn commented in *The Guardian* three days later:

> As a result of the Lord Small Chamberlain's astute intervention, the text of the banned Britannia number was

printed in the *Daily Mail*. The capacity of the New Lyric is 600. The readership of the *Daily Mail* is well over six million. To reach an audience of this size without Lord Cobbold's assistance the sketch would have had to play at the New Lyric for more than 30 years.

Passion Flower Hotel, a musical based on the novel by Rosalind Erskine, submitted in June 1965, depicts five girls at a boarding school who decide to teach the boys of a neighbouring school to lose their inhibitions about sex – and possibly their virginity too. The reader (Harward) did not recommend a licence. However, I had been amused by the book and considered the story to be light-hearted enough to recommend the Lord Chamberlain to give it a licence with a few alterations. For example, in one scene the boys are invited to indicate their requirements for particular services on a form of application. Part of this was disallowed, the service 'Nothing Barred Short of La Pénétration'.

When Schönberg's opera *Moses and Aaron* was put on at the Royal Opera House, Covent Garden, in the same month, directed by Peter Hall, the script showed that an orgy scene was to be included, with a request for some virgins to be half-naked and for some men to wear phalluses. Warnings were given by us and I attended the opening night by invitation. I left the Opera House to catch the night train to Edinburgh wondering what sort of report I should make the next day! I decided to sleep on it – in the sleeper – and take a look at the reviews in the morning's papers. As these were generally favourable I reported to the Lord Chamberlain that I thought the orgy scene was just all right – brilliantly staged and very spectacular. The *Daily Mail*'s headline was 'An orgy, but NOT erotic'. I reported that there was some nudity, but discreetly done; no phalluses were worn, but phallic-like objects were carried above the heads of the men. It seemed to me that the audience was in no way shocked, and anyway the scene did not seem out of place in an operatic setting. Lord Cobbold minuted, 'In the light of your report and of the reviews I have so far seen, I propose to let this alone.'

Another play presented by Michael Codron was *Travelling Light* by Leonard Kingston at the Hippodrome, Golders

Green. This comedy tells a story of two men and a girl sharing a room together, the parts being played by Harry H. Corbett, Michael Crawford and Julia Foster. Following considerable correspondence between the Lord Chamberlain's Office and the management we made clear by letter that,

> the stage directions had to be so precise as to prohibit any semblance of (a) sexual intercourse, particularly with a third person present; (b) two persons of the same or opposite sexes in bed together.

In the event Corbett and Foster were seen lying *on* a bed with the blankets drawn back, one below a sheet and the other above it. As one review read, 'It is the classic Tristram and Iseult situation. Only a sheet instead of a sword keeps the lovers apart.'

Michael Codron also presented David Mercer's *Ride A Cock Horse* which opened in Nottingham and came to London in 1965, with Peter O'Toole in the lead, and Barbara Jefford, Sian Phillips (Peter O'Toole's wife), Wendy Craig and Judy Wilson in the cast. The reader, Kyrle Fletcher, was doubtful about a licence, but a decision was taken to give one after a considerable number of language cuts were agreed to. I quite enjoyed the play although I felt it was too long; but one person walked out after the first act and wrote to the Lord Chamberlain,

> We had endured quite enough of the four characters – one a self-confessed lesbian; two, a drunken boor whose vocabulary was only fit for the dustbin; the third a middle-aged woman attempting suicide on stage with alcohol and drugs; and lastly a reefer-addict practising her folly on the bed . . . Certainly the play could be summed up in one word – ABYSSMAL [*sic*].

I showed this letter to Michael Codron recently. He told me he still receives letters like that now, and added that the play did well as long as O'Toole was in it: 'He was a big draw and people were clamouring to get in. I think our undoing was when the Snowdons came to see the play and announced they were going backstage afterwards. They obviously didn't like it and did not turn up backstage . . . O'Toole was waiting for them in his dressing-gown with drinks and took great offence when they didn't turn up. He went ill and did not appear again, leaving me and his wife without the star. So we had to play a few performances with the understudy and then had to close it.'

Codron said, much as William Gaskill had, that after 1968 he missed the cut and thrust of taking on the Lord Chamberlain. He particularly remembered one meeting at the Lord Chamberlain's Office about a play in which there was a scene of a man and a woman in a boat and objection was taken to the man saying something like he wanted to 'enter within her'. When Codron queried why 'enter within' was being disallowed he was told 'it was a straightforward case of rogering in a boat – in as much as rogering in a boat can be straightforward!' We agreed we had both enjoyed those meetings, and, looking back, he recalled that most of the plays which needed these discussions had had rather chequered careers and few ran for any length of time. He wondered if there was a moral there.

In February 1967 the London Traverse Company submitted for licence *Fanghorn* by David Pinner. It was described as a purple comedy, that is, a mixture of blue and black elements with a strong sexual theme, including lesbianism. It was read by two readers (Heriot and Harward), the Comptroller and a former Comptroller – as well as by me and, finally, by Lord Cobbold who did not consider it suitable for general audiences and therefore refused it a licence. At the time of its submission *Fanghorn* was being performed privately at the Traverse Theatre Club in Edinburgh.

Charles Marowitz, the director, accompanied by the author, came to see me and persuaded me to attend a performance in Edinburgh, making the case that the play was a spoof on a series of vices and played for laughs. In my report to the Lord Chamberlain I wrote, 'The play is definitely more light-hearted to see than to read . . . but the lesbian aspect is predominant . . . My companion aptly described the play afterwards as rather startling, but not shocking, and in her opinion unlikely to give offence.'

The Traverse Theatre only seats about fifty people, and on the evening I saw *Fanghorn* the front two rows were occupied by boys and girls of school age. I talked to them during the interval and all seemed to think it was funny and were enjoying it. I concluded my report, 'I have no idea how much of this play they (i.e. the children) understood, but I didn't get the impression that they were being corrupted.'

Lord Cobbold minuted, 'I appreciate that it might be possible to produce the play with such a light touch that it would minimise the offence of many passages. But, as we have so often said, I have to consider plays and *not* productions: once licensed the play can be produced anywhere by anybody. So long as this play is produced, as it has been in Edinburgh, in legitimate Theatre Clubs, when it is offered to specialised audiences, I should not for my part seek to intervene.'

However Lord Cobbold relented after a number of cuts and alterations were made and a warning given that there must be no kissing or fond embracing between the women. This was all reported in *The Times* on 31 March under the headline: 'Lord Chamberlain's change of mind'. The play was performed publicly in London later in the year at the Fortune Theatre, but did not have a long run.

An unusual and controversial play in 1967 was *A Day in the Death of Joe Egg*. This was submitted by Michael Blakemore, Artistic Director of the Citizens' Theatre, Glasgow, and when it came to the Comedy Theatre in London it was co-presented by Albert Finney's Memorial Enterprises Ltd. The author, Peter Nichols, was the father of a spastic child, and Blakemore wrote in his letter,

> It is to some extent an autobiographical work, the author having a child similar to the one described in the play. To most people the situation it presents is a shocking and disturbing one, but the intention of the play is certainly not to shock.
>
> A perfectly normal child actress will be asked to play the part, being permanently asleep . . . I believe the presentation of the child on stage will be far less terrible to see than it is to read about on the page.

The reader (Heriot) described the play as about an over-sexed schoolmaster and his wife with a ten-year-old spastic child (Joe). He considered that both the medical profession and the Church were libelled in a particularly juvenile way and that some doctors and clergymen might take offence. My own report to the Lord Chamberlain was less damning:

> I find this play a difficult one on which to give a clear recommendation. The theme is unusual if not unique. At times it is moving and the author undoubtedly has a message . . . I do not like the sex talk in front of the child . . . and I believe the play could upset a number of people. I cannot see how the part of Joe can be played except by a child actress. I should like to restrict the length of time she is on the stage.
>
> The Director's letter is honest and sincere. I think it might help if there was a note in the programme saying the author has a spastic child . . . On balance I feel it should be given a licence.

Lord Cobbold commented, 'I do not find any general difficulty in licensing this play, subject to the cuts and alterations recommended. The difficulty, I agree, is about the child actress – the producers clearly find the same difficulty. Would it be worth talking to them and seeing whether Joe could be offstage or in the wings most of the time?'

The author and director came to discuss the play with us and it was agreed that part of the script should be rewritten to meet our objections. A revised version was submitted, following which Michael Blakemore wrote:

> As we explained, the Citizens' Theatre in its press and publicity announcements has made a point of advertising the fact that the subject of this play is a chronically retarded child. The author has further volunteered that in all future productions he will include a paragraph in the contract requiring the management concerned to similarly publicise the nature and subject of the play. Thank you for the consideration you have extended to us over this controversial but, I believe, admirable play.

America Hurrah became one of our 'waiting box' plays. It is a group of three one-act plays, written by Jean-Claude van Ittalie, and was submitted by Michael White for production at the Jeannetta Cochrane Theatre in June 1967. The theme of the play is the deadening effect of the American way of life on its people. Some alterations to representation (President Johnson), stage directions and language (including the usual four-letter word) were requested. Michael White came to plead his case and then went to New York, where the show was playing, to consult the author. He, however, refused to make any alterations.

The English Stage Company put on the play for a four-week run in August for its members. I was invited to attend a performance, but I was advised to decline in case a prosecution was to follow – there being similarities to the *Saved* case (see Chapter 16). The Office of the Director of Public Prosecutions was informed but no action was taken. The play was then due to transfer to the Vaudeville Theatre (again for members only) but this did not happen.

Reports in the press accused the Lord Chamberlain of not allowing the Vaudeville production and we received a number of letters of complaint. Michael White had a further talk with us, as a result of which we relaxed some of the original disallowances, but again he could not persuade the author to make any changes. Finally I wrote to White, 'I am sorry to learn that the author is disinclined to agree to submitting alterations. I will inform the Lord Chamberlain who, I am sure, will be disappointed that it has not been possible to reach some compromise on this play so that it may be allowed for public performance.'

Lord Goodman, the Chairman of the Arts Council, was critical of the outcome and Lord Cobbold wrote to explain that, although we had been willing to make concessions, the author was not. In his reply Goodman said he had no doubt we had been co-operative but he was sad that the play could not be seen by the general public.

In August 1967 Simon Gray's *Wise Child* was submitted by Michael Codron. It is about two men on the run from the police, one (to be played by Alec Guinness) dressed as a woman. The reader, Charles Heriot, misjudged the plot and, thinking it had a homosexual theme, recommended a licence but with the utmost reluctance. I was on leave at the time and, at our request, Codron came to see the Comptroller and persuaded him that the audience would know from the start that 'Mrs Artminster' *is* a man, and that there really is no element of homosexuality. The Lord Chamberlain accepted the point, gave the play a licence, and it had a run at Wyndham's Theatre from 10 October 1967, directed by John Dexter. It was perhaps an example of one of the basic difficulties of pre-censorship – the need to form a judgement on reading a play and coming to a different conclusion when seeing it acted.

The year 1968 was, of course, the last year of the censorship. Two plays of particular note were submitted, the first, by the manager of the Richmond Theatre, being *A Fig For Eloquence* by Alec Coppel. The reader (Heriot) described it as 'one long snigger at the male genitalia'. It told the story of a colossal nude male statue, sculpted by a White Russian lady who gave it the features of her husband but a member with which he could not compete. The husband tries to find out whom his wife has used as a model. The statue is to be unveiled by a royal person, but shortly before the ceremony the statue is mutilated. The male member is missing . . .

Heriot did not recommend a licence. I read the play and found it amusing. Taking into account the ending of censorship I wrote, 'It is a harmless comedy and could be licensed if some undertakings are given.' One of these was that the statue should at all times be facing away from the audience. The Lord Chamberlain marked my note 'Oh, very well'. However, Terence Nugent, the former Comptroller, had also been asked to read the play, and he wrote, 'Since you ask me I feel bound to say it goes too far and personally I feel the Lord Chamberlain would be fully justified in refusing it a licence.' Lord Cobbold sent me a note, 'With apologies for wavering, I would honestly prefer to revert, having in mind also Tim's note, to my original view that this had better not be licensed. I think it *is* obscene and a bit prurient, though I agree it is light and funny.'

Looking back I believe we should have given *A Fig for*

Eloquence the benefit of the doubt, but at the time three wise people were against a licence. Not surprisingly, though, the decision was questioned by the management and I replied to their letter, saying:

> His decision is based upon the view that the theme of this play is largely concerned with the private parts of one of the 'characters'. Although he accepts it is treated in a light-hearted way, the Lord Chamberlain feels that such a theme might well give offence to a large section of the theatre-going public.

The other play of note in 1968 was the 'tribal love-rock musical' *Hair*, by Gerome Ragni and James Rado with music by Galt MacDermott. It was submitted in May by Harold Fielding Ltd for the old Saville Theatre (now the ABC Cinema, Shaftesbury Avenue). *Hair* had opened on Broadway the previous month when a rave review appeared in the *Sunday Times*, but the critic added that it was 'a show which could not conceivably be presented on any British stage'. The problem for the Lord Chamberlain was that there was a good deal of nudity, male and female and full frontal. There was also improvisation. The producer was invited to resubmit a version without nudity and improvisation, but this he declined to do and Harold Fielding Ltd decided to withdraw their application for a licence.

Another version was submitted the following month by James Verner Ltd. It was read by a different reader (Heriot), who also did not recommend a licence, with which the Lord Chamberlain agreed. This management was more open-minded about changes, and put forward the case that the piece was moving, beautiful and quite uncorrupting. Lord Cobbold continued to feel convinced, however, that such a play would be too controversial for British audiences.

A third, much-toned down script was submitted in July. This I discussed with James Verner and I told him a licence probably would be given subject to certain alterations. By then, of course, the new Bill had nearly completed its journey through Parliament and because of casting and other problems the production anyway was postponed. I was then told that *Hair* would open on 26 September, and by good fortune, I was able to reply on 30 July: 'In accordance with the Theatres Act 1968, which has now received the Royal Assent, new plays for a production on or after 26 September do not require a Lord Chamberlain's licence.' *Hair* opened, in fact (to be on the safe side?), on 27 September at the Shaftesbury Theatre, and there was a general sense of relief that we did not have a battle on our hands at the very end of the Lord Chamberlain's authority.

For the last three or four years of that authority, the Lord Chamberlain's Office had been discussing *A Patriot for Me* with the English Stage Company, who had submitted it in 1964, and with the author John Osborne.

The play, put briefly, is about an officer, Redl, in the Austro-Hungarian army in the early years of the twentieth century. Redl finds he has homosexual tendencies, which he practises, and, having been blackmailed, he shoots himself.

Lord Cobbold decided he could not give the play a licence and, in September 1964, I wrote to the Royal Court Theatre which hoped to stage it:

> There are various scenes in the play as it now stands which the Lord Chamberlain feels unable to license on the grounds that they exploit homosexuality in a manner that may tend to have corrupting influences. He cannot allow such scenes as a homosexual ball at which some of the men are dressed as women (including one who portrays Lady Godiva dressed in a gold lamé jockstrap); and others in which men embrace each other and are seen in bed together.

A protracted exchange of correspondence followed, during which the Lord Chamberlain continued to keep an open mind pending possible alterations to the script.

In July 1965 the Royal Court decided to put on the play as a 'club' production for the members of the English Stage Society. I wrote to inform the Director of Public Prosecutions and, at the end of the letter, said,

> The Lord Chamberlain would also wish to emphasise that he has no desire to interfere with the operations of genuine Theatre Clubs. He is solely concerned to avoid a position where the Law can be brought into disrepute by what is no more than a subterfuge . . . he feels if this production goes unchallenged it may be difficult later to establish any line between what is and what is not a genuine Theatre Club.

Lord Cobbold followed this up by going to see the Director of Public Prosecutions and he kept the Home Secretary (Soskice) informed. The Director, having consulted the Attorney-General, wrote that although the play was being presented more or less publicly the Law Officers did not wish to institute proceedings as it had been running for some time, attracted a great deal of public interest and a good deal of support. The Lord Chamberlain naturally had to accept this decision but he had hoped some sort of warning might have been possible.

A Patriot for Me opened at the Royal Court on 30 June 1965 and played to packed houses; it was also awarded the *Evening Standard* prize for the best play of 1965. Even so, with a large cast and a small theatre, and with no chance of a transfer without a licence, it lost £16,000 and John Osborne stood half the loss. As far as is known the theatre received no letters of complaint. Lord Goodman, as Chairman of the Arts Council, took up their cause and asked Lord Cobbold to think again. He was told he would only do so if a further script was sent or alternatives submitted to the disallowed parts.

On 5 August 1965 Anthony Page, the director, came to discuss the play with me and he too asked the Lord Chamberlain to reconsider our decision as the play had been well received. After I gave him the same answer as Lord Cobbold had given Lord Goodman he did come forward with some alterations and added that he hoped others could be provided. I sent a holding reply and the letter concluded, 'There are aspects of this play other than those raised in your letter and these, as well as the evident merits of the piece, will have to weigh with the Lord Chamberlain when making his decision.' Page said he would discuss further changes with

Osborne, but we heard nothing more and so presumably Osborne was not prepared to make any.

Meanwhile the Royal Court had asked one of us to come and see the play. As I had already been on the quiet as a guest of a friend who had joined the English Stage Society, the Comptroller, Sir Eric Penn, went. He recorded, 'I do not think that the tolerance of homosexuality in this country has yet reached the point where this play, *in its present form*, is suitable for public performances.'

However Lord Cobbold asked the actress, Irene Worth, for her feelings about the play and on 8 August she wrote to him, 'I saw it last Friday evening and I really didn't think it needed to be limited to a subscription audience. It seemed to me to be written with seriousness, dignity, humanity, and to be impartial.' She added that she thought the play too long and technically poor and went on: 'I wish I had great wisdom for I see that passing this play could set a precedent for an avalanche of inferior and tasteless copies, yet I don't honestly feel that Osborne's play should suffer because of that.'

The valued opinion of the actress did not, it seemed, sway Lord Cobbold. The Earl of Harewood also sprang to the play's defence and asked if he might come and discuss it. I replied, 'I do not think we can be of any help to you until we have had submitted either a fresh manuscript or amendments to those parts of the play which the Lord Chamberlain has not allowed.'

The next event of note was not until May the following year (1966), when Laurence Olivier came to see the Lord Chamberlain as the National Theatre wished to perform the play publicly. He was given the same response as that given to Anthony Page. Nothing further was heard from the Royal Court or the National Theatre.

Three months earlier, in the debate in the House of Lords (see Chapter 17) Lord Annan in his speech opening the debate had referred to *A Patriot for Me*:

> I cannot conceive of any play less sentimental towards homosexuality, more cold-eyed and ruthless in its exposure of the horrors of life with a particular kind of homosexuality, and less likely to induce anyone to go into this practice.

> The transvestite scene, to which particular exception was taken, was both pathetic and comical, but it was entirely integral to the play . . . Is this the way to reward one of our better playwrights?

The Marquess of Hertford said:

> Anyone who really wanted to see *A Patriot For Me* could quite easily have done so when it was at the Royal Court Theatre. But it was a bit of a bother: one had to fill in a form to join a club, and wait a few days before becoming a member before applying for tickets. Therefore, because it could not be shown to the general public, a lot of people missed a tremendous theatrical experience, an experience which left one sadder and wiser and certainly not inclined to any form of vice . . .

When The Joint Committee of Parliament examined John Osborne on 29 November 1966, he was asked by Lord Lloyd of Hampstead what had happened to *A Patriot for Me* in America, to which he replied that a production there was still being negotiated but the delay was not for any reasons of censorship. It appeared that the Americans were more concerned about anti-Semitic aspects of the play than about its homosexual content. Lord Lloyd asked what were the practical consequences of this play being banned by the Lord Chamberlain, to which Osborne replied that both he and the Royal Court Theatre lost a lot of money, despite it being seen by 25,000 or 30,000 people in its eight-week run of club performances. He went on to say that the Lord Chamberlain was adamant about cutting three scenes of the play, and agreed that, but for the Lord Chamberlain's demands, he would have been a more successful dramatist in practical commercial terms.

When Lord Cobbold was examined by the Committee on 6 December, Michael Foot asked him if the removal of three scenes would have knocked the guts out of the play, to which Lord Cobbold agreed it made quite a considerable difference. To a further question he also agreed that a single individual should not have the right to make such a decision without there being a right of appeal.

Lord Goodman, while recognising that the censorship had a liberal outlook under Lord Cobbold's administration, nevertheless said that he had made some grievous mistakes, and that one of them was over *A Patriot for Me*.

CHAPTER SIXTEEN

Theatre Clubs

Private theatre clubs were in existence before 1900. They originally operated on Sunday evenings when the Sunday Observance Act disallowed the opening of public theatres. Such clubs gave actors an opportunity to experiment in new parts or in plays of a non-commercial kind. They also enabled producers to put on plays without the necessity of a play licence.

These theatre clubs were well organised and run on a proper legal basis. It was the Lord Chamberlain's custom to take no action against a club that was a genuine club, established for the purpose of privately presenting plays to its *bona fide* members who had been proposed and seconded. He did not interfere in the performance of any play, even one which had been refused a licence, provided that the society running the club applied strictly the following rules:

(a) Tickets to be sold only to its members, on production of a membership card, who may bring up to four guests. (Note: There must be a specified interval between the application and granting of membership.)

(b) No tickets to be sold at the door or money taken there.

(c) Any advertising must clearly state that performances are for members only.

(d) No alcoholic drinks (to comply with the Theatres Act 1843).

By 1913 the earlier clubs/societies had secured lists of non-theatrical patrons and were operating as experimental theatre clubs in a modest way. Some, such as the Arts and Watergate clubs in London, developed into proprietary theatre clubs, with their own premises, catering for those interested in the theatre. It was the policy then to accept these theatre clubs as legal, although, as a strict matter of law, they were probably not so.

In the late 1920s both the Gate Theatre in Floral Street, Covent Garden and the Cambridge Festival Theatre were clubs with a reputation for staging banned plays, but no action was taken against them as their affairs seemed to be properly conducted. This was found not to be the case with the Torch Theatre Club, which was successfully prosecuted in 1940, and again in 1950, for giving what amounted to public performances of unlicensed plays. On the first occasion the proprietors were found guilty on the evidence of one person from the Lord Chamberlain's Office and a plain-clothes policeman going together to a performance, both having been made members on the spot by one shilling being added to the cost of the tickets.

At one level there were genuine clubs; at another level there were less authentic ones, which were running a secondary membership scheme by which it was fairly simple to purchase tickets for a private performance. Some clubs were formed solely for the purpose of putting on banned plays. These clubs were usually short-lived, since they depended on the existence of a controversy with the censor to induce members of the public to go to the trouble of filling in an application form.

In 1956 a written question was put to the Home Secretary in the House of Commons: 'Whether, in view of the recent performances of unlicensed plays in certain theatres, he will abolish or modify the present system of censorship of plays.' To which his reply was, 'No'.

The first sign of a real problem appeared that year when the Watergate Theatre Club, which had been compulsorily dispossessed of its premises, took a lease of a regular London theatre (the Comedy, which had relinquished its theatre licence), enrolled a membership of 68,000 on a basis of little more than mailing list requirements, and produced a series of plays which had not received the Lord Chamberlain's licence, including Arthur Miller's *A View from the Bridge*. At the same time the Arts Theatre Club was seeking to create a temporary annex in another London theatre, enrolling new members on unrestricted terms. The Lord Chamberlain,

Lord Scarbrough, kept a watchful eye on these activities and was considering testing the law when the Watergate/Comedy scheme foundered through lack of funds and because not enough unlicensed plays came their way.

The following year, on 4 June 1957, when Lord Scarbrough went to see the Home Secretary, R. A. Butler, to discuss various theatre matters, one of the subjects was private theatre clubs. In his record of the meeting, Lord Scarbrough wrote:

> I expressed my view that these were very useful adjuncts to the British Theatre in general. They could be regarded as experimental laboratories for the theatre, and I would be very sorry to see them interfered with. The New Watergate Theatre Club, however, had created a position in which the law and the censorship was becoming rather farcical.

Neither the Lord Chamberlain nor the Home Secretary were keen to ask for a prosecution of the Watergate Club. The Home Office apparently took the view that the 1843 Theatres Act was obscure in itself; still more obscure was an opinion given by the Law Officers in 1903, which seemed to imply that the Lord Chamberlain had power under the Act to prevent theatre clubs putting on unlicensed plays.

The situation of private theatre clubs was causing concern also to Actors' Equity, their trade union. Their solicitor visited the Lord Chamberlain's Office in August 1960 to discuss these clubs with the Assistant Comptroller and the Assistant Secretary. He said he was unhappy about the facilities afforded his members at some clubs' premises, which were unsafe, insanitary and sometimes verging on the improper. There were problems too over contracts. His opinion was that a successful prosecution was possible under Section 11 or Section 12 of the Theatres Act which did not differentiate between public and private performances. He expressed surprise that the law had not been tested. He was told that, for the past fifty or sixty years, Lord Chamberlains had given latitude to bona fide theatre clubs formed especially for the performance of experimental plays. He said his Council took a serious view of the situation and might institute a private prosecution. Equity may have decided not to do so for, if such a prosecution had been successful, it might have led to the closure of theatre clubs resulting in less employment for its members.

The Theatres National Committee was concerned enough to raise the matter with the Home Office. A copy of their memorandum, sent to the Lord Chamberlain's Office, opened: 'The Society of West End Theatre Managers and the Theatrical Managers' Association have become increasingly concerned over the growth of entertainment in establishments conducting business as "Clubs" . . .' Their main concern was with strip clubs rather than theatre clubs and, therefore, outside the jurisdiction of the Lord Chamberlain. By the early 1960s it was clear that the private theatre clubs were becoming less private and that some performances being put on by them were tantamount to public performances. The Lord Chamberlain now began to feel he was entitled to forbid any play anywhere provided it was one 'for hire', i.e. actors were paid and patrons were charged, but the situation became aggravated in 1965 when the Royal Shakespeare Company was staging disallowed plays at the Aldwych Theatre which, for part of the week, was being turned into a private theatre. The English Stage Society went further and for periods took over the Royal Court Theatre for its exclusive use. To make this commercially viable the Society had to expand its membership enormously. The Lord Chamberlain, deciding he could no longer turn a blind eye to all this, now felt obliged to test the Theatres Act regarding theatre clubs.

Some warning shots were fired. These were heeded by the Royal Shakespeare Company but not by the Royal Court Theatre which put on *A Patriot For Me* before it was licensed. The Director of Public Prosecutions was consulted; he approached the Attorney-General, who was inclined to view the performances as illegal but did not advocate action. So much for government support for the Lord Chamberlain! However, when the Royal Court Theatre put on Edward Bond's play *Saved*, Lord Cobbold tried again and this time the Director of Public Prosecutions did proceed.

The time-table of the events surrounding *Saved* was as follows:

1. The play was submitted by the management of the Royal Court Theatre in June 1965 for production later in the year.
2. The reader (Heriot) reluctantly recommended a licence but drew attention to large amounts of 'foul' language and to a scene in which a gang of youths torments a baby in its pram, rolls it in its excrement, and finally stones it to death.
3. I read the play and so did Eric Penn (Comptroller) and Tim Nugent (former Comptroller). Lord Cobbold, having read it too, was prepared to grant a licence if a large number of cuts and alterations was made. He did consider refusing it a licence but felt that this would give the Royal Court undue publicity.
4. I wrote to the director, William Gaskill, listing the alterations required. He came to see me and we discussed the main problem of the offensive scene which I said would have to be rewritten before any decision could be made. I told Gaskill, in answer to his question, that the Lord Chamberlain *had* considered refusing a licence but that, having sought various opinions, decided against doing so, and to ask instead for specific alterations. Gaskill told me he was doubtful of the author's willingness to make any changes and, if this was so, they would probably put on the play for the members of the English Stage Society. This is what happened, and *Saved* had an eight-week run under 'club' auspices, the Society acquiring 3,000 new members in the process.
5. On 8 September the LCO told the office of the Director of Public Prosecutions that this was going to happen, and on 6 October the Lord Chamberlain wrote to the Director asking what action, if any, he proposed. We were asked to send someone from the Lord Chamberlain's Office to see the play, and the Assistant Secretary (Ronald Hill) went, after becoming an associate member of the Society. He reported that the play contained all the elements objected to at the time the script was submitted.
6. The Director informed us he would be consulting the Attorney-General. The Lord Chamberlain went to see the Solicitor-General, Sir Dingle Foot, who said that the Law Officers were in something of a dilemma and had yet to reach a decision. Lord Cobbold expressed the hope that some action would be taken.

7. During November we received a number of letters complaining about the play, which had not generally been well received by the press critics.
8. On 22 November the Home Secretary held a meeting attended by the Lord Chamberlain and myself, at which were present some of his own officers. Lord Cobbold made it plain to the Home Secretary that there *were* grounds for a prosecution and, if a case did not follow because it was not in the public interest, then he would be obliged to tell Parliament that it was impossible for him to carry on his duties under the Theatres Act of 1843.
9. A police officer went to see the play, having had no difficulty in obtaining a ticket; and on 6 December the Director wrote to the Lord Chamberlain saying the Attorney-General had agreed to proceedings being instituted, subject to the results of interviews with William Gaskill and others. At the request of the police I made a written statement covering the facts of the case.
10. On 13 January 1966 we were told that a summons had been issued on the licensee of the theatre, Alfred Esdaile, the director of the play, William Gaskill, and the English Stage Society for presenting 'for hire' a new stage play before it had been allowed by the Lord Chamberlain, contrary to Section 15 of the Theatres Act 1843.

Thus, at last, the Lord Chamberlain had been allowed to test the law as to whether or not it was legal for 'club' performances to be staged of a play that was not yet licensed. The case was to be heard by the Bow Street stipendiary magistrate on 14 February. In the event there were three sittings and the case closed on 1 April. I attended the hearing; the Assistant Secretary, Lord Chamberlain's Office, was one of the prosecution witnesses and amongst those called by the defence were the Earl of Harewood and Sir Laurence Olivier. The defendants were found guilty and given a twelve-month conditional discharge and the English Stage Society had to pay fifty guineas (£52.50) costs. Notice of appeal was lodged but the defendants decided not to proceed.

The magistrate based his decision, it seemed, on his interpretation that any performance 'for hire' under the Theatres Act of 1843 *had* to be licensed. His ruling indicated that a 'club' performance of an unlicensed play did not give it immunity from prosecution. On 3 May the Director of Public Prosecutions wrote to the Lord Chamberlain saying that, unfortunately, the magistrate

> did not give any decision as to whether they were in fact public performances . . . and that in the result we have not got the advantage of any ruling upon this point, but the prosecution will probably have achieved the desired result of causing those responsible to cease presenting unlicensed plays at the Royal Court Theatre in the way in which they were doing.

Lord Cobbold was not unduly worried by this because a Joint Committee of both Houses of Parliament had just been set up to look into the whole question of the censorship of the theatre. In the event *Saved* was revived, after the ending of the censorship, in 1969.

When, some twenty years later, William Gaskill and I talked about *Saved*, he told me that Edward Bond felt his play had been badly treated by the censor. I showed Gaskill the play reader's report which, in his opinion, did not give a fair synopsis. He mentioned that *Saved* was the last play at the Royal Court produced by George Devine. During the many years Devine had run the Royal Court he had had a number of brushes with the Lord Chamberlain's Office, but the prosecution of *Saved* had brought about a heart attack from which he did not recover.

In his book *Sense of Direction* William Gaskill said: 'The *Saved* affair had brought to a head the case against the Lord Chamberlain's power of pre-censorship. The following three years were dominated by the fight to break his power, a fight we eventually won.'

Oddly enough, though, the Lord Chamberlain's hand had become strengthened by the outcome of the *Saved* prosecution. In 1967 the Theatre Royal, Stratford, in East London, staged Barbara Garson's *MacBird* which the Lord Chamberlain had refused to license (see Chapter 7), but the Lord Chamberlain took no action in this case as the promotors were reasonably circumspect in their club arrangements, and the play made little impact in Britain. There were other such 'club' performances but, in view of the existence of the Joint Committee, the Lord Chamberlain decided not to prosecute unless provoked. He nearly was provoked by Kenneth Tynan over Rolf Hochhuth's *Soldiers* but he held his fire.

The legal situation of private theatre clubs was further aggravated by the appearance of 'The Clubman's Club' which, on payment of a fee and on receipt of a signed application form, granted the applicant a membership of 225 clubs throughout the country. Included in the list was the Hampstead Theatre Club. A further complication was that the holder of a Camden Borough Council library ticket was automatically entitled to be a member of the Hampstead Theatre Club.

Followed the *Saved* case, Lord Goodman, Chairman of the Arts Council, sought the advice of Lord Cobbold about what should be the proper attitude of the Arts Council towards theatre clubs. Lord Cobbold minuted: 'I said that I had always been inclined, within reason, to turn a blind eye to theatre club productions which I regarded as a safety valve for specialised audiences. I had, however, always made it clear that if theatre clubs were silly I might have to test the law and this in fact had been done in the *Saved* case.'

He continued, saying that he did not wish to prosecute those productions which he regarded as acceptable for specialised club audiences, and only encouraged prosecution of productions which seemed to go beyond the limits. He emphasised that the decision rested with the Public Prosecutor and the Attorney-General. As a result of this discussion, the Arts Council decided to discontinue financial support for club performances on the grounds that, unless a play had been licensed by the Lord Chamberlain, *any* performance might be illegal.

As a postscript, mention should be made of the Theatre of Cruelty. This experimental type of theatre consisted of exercises, improvisations and sketches and, as described by Peter Brook, 'a collage, a form of surrealist revue composed of shots in the dark; shots at distant targets. It is not a programme of out-of-the-way plays . . . We are exploring theatre language.' Its name was taken from an idea originated by Antonin Artaud (1869–1948), an avant-garde French dramatist. Artaud was referring to life's cruelties and two of his aims were to make the audience uncomfortable and to undermine bourgeois culture. The Royal Shakespeare Company took up the Theatre of Cruelty in the 1960s. Pieces in this genre were written by Genet, Orton and Weiss, e.g. *Marat/Sade* by the latter. In no way could these be given a play licence by the Lord Chamberlain and so they were privately performed in theatre clubs in the spirit of Lord Cobbold's 'safety valve for specialised audiences'.

Chapter Seventeen

Debate on Theatre Censorship

The debate took place in the House of Lords on Thursday, 17 February 1966 and lasted nearly five hours. There was a good attendance. I was fortunate to be present, Black Rod having given me a seat in his box.

Their Lordships had previously put their heads together to plan the order of speaking. Lord Annan, who was interested in the subject, was invited to speak first with Lord Scarbrough – the previous Lord Chamberlain – to follow. Lord Cobbold had asked to speak towards the end of the debate and it was decided that Lord Stonham would wind up for the Government.

Lord Annan moved that it be desirable to appoint a Joint Committee of both Houses to review the law and practice relating to the censorship of stage plays. He had clearly taken much trouble over the composition of his speech, which lasted thirty minutes. He began with a résumé of the history of censorship; paid tribute to Lords Scarbrough and Cobbold and their officers; pointed out the anomalies of the system: how it infringed the freedom of the subject and how it violated freedom of expression; expressed sympathy for John Osborne and his clashes with the censor; and asked if there was a better alternative, quoting Hilaire Belloc's warning in his *Cautionary Tales*:

> Always keep a hold of Nurse
> For fear of finding something worse.

Lord Scarbrough, with the authority of having been Lord Chamberlain for eleven years, then recounted some of his own experiences and set out the pros and cons of the Lord Chamberlain being the censor. He praised in particular the Examiners of Plays: 'All of these have received little thanks and many kicks; but the credit for any success which is due must go to them.'

His objective had been to try and keep the censorship not too far away from the centre of public opinion, in the hope that the rude remarks made about him for what he had banned would be matched by the indignant protests against what he had passed. He supported the idea of a Joint Committee, for nearly sixty years had passed since there had been one, although on three separate occasions the House of Commons had considered the matter. Each time the Government had been scared of having to shoulder the responsibility, being content to leave it in the lap of the Lord Chamberlain. He came down in favour of censorship of plays but not by the Lord Chamberlain.

Lord Carrington (Leader of the Opposition) should have been the next speaker but he was indisposed and Lord Dilhorne took his place, speaking from Carrington's notes. As a former Attorney-General, Dilhorne set out the legal aspects of the censorship and touched on the Obscene Publications Act of 1959, expressing some reservations about its effectiveness. As a result he preferred censorship to reliance on the criminal law, but doubted whether a committee of parliamentarians was the right one to make recommendations. He preferred a Royal Commission.

He was followed by the Lord Chancellor (Lord Gardiner) who supported the idea of an inquiry. He maintained that the debate was not so much about censorship but about pre-censorship, and he was against that.

Lord Harlech, in a maiden speech, gave a brief account of the functions and powers of the British Board of Film Censors of which he had been President for only six months: 'Therefore I cannot claim any long experience with the blue pencil or, perhaps, more appropriately in my case, with the scissors', but he believed there could and should be a similar board for the theatre with a court of appeal from its judgements.

Lord Norwich (John Julius Norwich) was a writer and the son of Lady Diana Cooper who played the leading role in Max Reinhardt's play *The Miracle*. He argued for complete freedom of the theatre, the freedom to 'publish and be damned' with the ultimate deterrent of police prosecution. He had a good word to say for the present Lord Chamberlain, for his predecessor and their staffs saying, according to Hansard, that 'censorship has been wielded certainly more sensitively, more understandingly, more sympathetically and more perceptibly, than at any time in the past'.

The Bishop of St Albans added that, if the censor of the future was not the Lord Chamberlain, he should be someone who had the qualities of a Lord Chamberlain. He did not agree with the ban on the portrayal of Christ on the stage and, in his opinion, modern Mystery plays such as *A Man Dies* (see Chapter 7) should be allowed.

Lord Goodman, Chairman of the Arts Council, spoke of how he disapproved of and disliked censorship, and that he considered playwrights should only have the criminal law to contend with. Yet, paradoxically, he thought the Lord Chamberlain had in some ways been responsible for a more liberal theatre in recent years and that he had licensed a number of plays for the London theatre which, without the Lord Chamberlain, might not have seen the light of day. He was less complimentary about Lord Cobbold's decision to 'ban' John Osborne's *A Patriot For Me*. He thought that a case could be made for voluntary censorship, and he supported Lord Dilhorne's feeling of unease about a Joint Committee.

Lord Birkett, who later produced Peter Brook's film of *King Lear* (1970) and became a director of the National Theatre, spoke fluently, and at times amusingly, about certain plays including *The Passing of the Essenes* and *Entertaining Mr Sloane*. He concluded by quoting Lord Chesterfield's speech against the Licensing Act in 1737 (see Chapter 1). The next speaker, Lord Willis, the playwright Ted Willis, described himself as a dramatist who had had one or two brushes with the Lord Chamberlain:

> I would like to pay tribute to the Lord Chamberlain for the courtesy, delicacy and generosity with which he treats writers . . . but he is a gentle and kindly jailer . . . I do not want the theatre to be privileged. I want it to be subject to the same checks and controls in law as any other form of art or literature.

Lord Willis's view was that, if there *had* to be censorship, the method in use was by far the best; but he was opposed to censorship on principle and so was an abolitionist who wanted dramatists to have complete freedom: 'It is time we released the poor Lord Chamberlain from the whole tedious, sordid and revolting business.'

Lord Hertford also declared for abolishing it, but Lord Kennet (the writer Wayland Young) argued for voluntary censorship, as suggested by the 1909 Joint Select Committee, and, as if to comfort Lord Cobbold, observed that their Lordships were being rude about the office but not the holder of it. He referred to the Theatre Censorship Reform Committee which he had instituted in 1958 to draft a bill similar to Benn Levy's failed bill in 1949. He was critical of the development of theatre clubs; and he urged that the Joint Committee should look at the censorship arrangements in other countries – Spain, he believed, was the only other country with a system of pre-censorship.

Lord Strabolgi made the point that as earlier drama, such as Restoration plays, did not require a licence the Lord Chamberlain had become a censor of modern literature. He agreed the time had come for a review, while Lord Auckland suggested that the theatre should provide its own censor, much as the Press Council acts as a 'censor' of the press. He was against the idea of Parliament, still less the legal profession, taking on the job.

Four hours after the start of the debate Lord Cobbold rose to thank Lord Annan and others for the plaudits heaped on him, his predecessor, and the staff of the Lord Chamberlain's Office. He referred to the interview he had given ten months earlier to the *Sunday Times* as a good summary of his views, and took up a number of points made by various speakers where he disagreed with them. He said he would continue to do his best to administer the Act in the immediate future, however more difficult the task might become and whatever the outcome of the debate, but he doubted the wisdom of the censor being head of the Royal Household, even though there was an historical reason for this:

Originally when the censorship was exercised under the

> Royal Prerogative, it was, presumably, to protect the Court from offence. Later, when Walpole brought the question to another place, it was to protect the political figures of the time. Today the basic philosophy, at any rate as I see it, still centres on the conception of preventing offence to individuals, to sections of the community or the community at large.

It had always been his objective, Lord Cobbold explained, to license where possible and only to censor where he had to. Like Lord Scarbrough, he kept as near as possible to the centre of public opinion; and he tried also to follow the recommendations of the 1909 Committee, which he spelt out. Some form of censorship, he believed, should be maintained as a check against violence, over religious questions and offensive treatment of personalities. He saw no advantage in optional censorship. This was not the time or place, he said, to discuss whether or not there should be censorship and, if so, who should exercise it. That was to be the task of a Joint Committee, and he was strongly in favour of setting it up.

Lord Stonham, winding up for the Government, joined in the general chorus of thanks to Lord Annan for proposing the motion and he paid a special tribute to Lords Scarbrough and Cobbold for their contributions to the debate and for what they had done in administering the Theatres Act for the past fourteen years. It was clearly time for the whole system to be examined, he added, but he favoured a Joint Committee of both Houses rather than another body, adding, 'It also commends itself to Her Majesty's Government and I therefore invite the House to accept the motion.'

The motion was agreed to without a division.

A delay was to follow, however, for Parliament was dissolved the following month and the Joint Committee could not be set up until the new Parliament met. A few months later the Arts Council set up a committee which recommended the abolition of the censorship for a trial period of five years, but as events turned out, there was no need for this.

In his book *Banned*, published in 1967, Richard Findlater foreshadowed the advice that he, as a journalist and drama critic, would have given the Joint Committee:

Lord Cobbold may seem to us far better than his predecessors. But who knows what damage he has already done? Who knows what the *next* censor will be like? It is the office, not the man, that is to blame. The job is impossible – and unnecessary.

CHAPTER EIGHTEEN

Joint Committee on the Censorship of the Theatre, 1966–67

Following the debate in February 1966, on 19 May Lord Stonham moved in the House of Lords 'that it is desirable that a Joint Committee of both Houses be appointed to review the law and practice relating to the censorship of stage plays'. The Commons agreed to this resolution on 25 May.

On 19 July the House of Lords appointed eight peers to serve on the Committee. They were:

Earl of Scarbrough (Con.)	Baroness Gaitskell (Lab.)
Earl of Kilmuir (Con.)	Lord Lloyd of Hampstead (Lab.)
Viscount Norwich (Lib.)	Lord Annan (Ind.)
Lord Tweedsmuir (Con.)	Lord Goodman (Ind.)

Lord Kilmuir died while the committee was in session and was replaced by Lord Brooke of Cumnor, the former Conservative Home Secretary, Henry Brooke.

The Commons announced their team on 21 July:

Andrew Faulds (Lab.)	Sir David Renton (Con.)
Michael Foot (Lab.)	Norman St John-Stevas (Con.)
Emlyn Hooson (Lib.)	George Strauss (Lab.)
Hugh Jenkins (Lab.)	William Wilson (Lab.)

Thus altogether there were seven Labour members, five Conservatives, two Liberals and two Independents. Andrew Faulds was an actor. Hugh Jenkins was a former Assistant General Secretary of Actors' Equity, and, like Norman St John-Stevas, a future Minister for the Arts.

The Committee first met on 26 July and George Strauss, the senior member of the Commons team and who was later to introduce the Theatres Bill for the abolition of stage censorship, was appointed Chairman. Because of the parliamentary recess their next meeting was not until 15 November and thereafter they met fourteen times, the last occasion being on 6 June 1967. During six meetings they examined nine witnesses and received written evidence from twenty-four sources (including the Lord Chamberlain's Office). At the remaining meetings it is recorded that 'The Committee deliberate', i.e., the committee members deliberated among themselves.

The first memorandum which the Joint Committee considered was submitted by the League of Dramatists. The League is a branch of the Society of Authors, founded in 1931 to protect the rights and interests of playwrights, and all the most prominent of dramatists were members. Their basic contention was, as the memorandum stated it:

> A novelist or historian or poet or critic is simply subject to the criminal law: no government official is there to prevent him freely expressing his opinion . . . It is only in the last two decades when the 'New Drama' has found things to say about contemporary life, that there has been acute conflict between dramatists and the Lord Chamberlain . . . We see no reason why we should not be allowed to use the language of Shakespeare and Ben Jonson; who are free of the Lord Chamberlain's blue pencil . . .
>
> Aside from all legal considerations, dramatists feel that this is a profound moral issue and are deeply resentful of the way in which they have been treated, and by their arbitrary regulation by a Court official. We feel that our public is the best judge of what is good for them; and although we realise that our position may be, for the time being, more difficult if we are exposed to the criminal law, this is a risk we are prepared to take. We only wish to be subject to the same controls as our fellow writers and fellow citizens.

The Executive Committee of the League of Dramatists

passed a resolution which was submitted as an annex to this memorandum. It was punchy and obviously carried weight with members of the Joint Committee:

> The present system (of theatre censorship) has remained virtually unchanged for over 200 years and is vested in one man, the Lord Chamberlain. Dramatists have no right of appeal against his decisions and he is not bound to give any reason for a refusal to license a play or for any changes or deletions for which he may ask (though in practice an explanation will sometimes be given). We feel this to be wrong in principle and unfair in practice.

John Mortimer, a QC and a playwright himself, was the first witness. He was questioned principally about the memorandum submitted by the League of Dramatists of which he was a member. A week later John Osborne was examined. He was all for abolishing the censorship. Although he agreed that the Lord Chamberlain conducted matters fairly and in a civilised fashion, he contended that that was 'utterly irrelevant, and I think it is high time that both the office at St James's Palace and members of the House of Lords should stop congratulating themselves on this fact'. He was questioned in particular about his plays *A Patriot for Me*, *Inadmissible Evidence* and *Look Back in Anger*.

At the same meeting Benn Levy, the playwright and former MP who had tried to get his private Bill through Parliament in 1949, was called in and examined. Soon after this, a comment appeared in the 'As it Happens' column of *The Times*:

> A situation, not without its comic side, has arisen over the proceedings of the Joint Committee on Censorship of the Theatre. Its eight peers and eight commoners sit both in private and in public. Normally such committees meet in private. The censorship proceedings began with two meetings of the members in camera. Then they heard, at what were, by all accounts, lively sessions, witnesses including Mr John Mortimer, Mr John Osborne and Mr Benn Levy. These gentlemen were closely cross-examined – in open session – on the subjects which the Lord Chamberlain

insists are taboo. But the reporters of parliament were not alerted. So a wail is being heard in the corridors. The views of the angry young or not so young men of the stage will, the complaint goes up, get less prominence than those of Lord Cobbold, the Lord Chamberlain, and his Assistant Comptroller, Lieutenant-Colonel J. Johnston, who are to be witnesses tomorrow. A notice about the proceedings being open to the public and press was posted in the Press Gallery on Friday. So a full covey of reporters is expected.

We suggest an easy way out of the difficulty. Let the evidence of the playwrights be handed to the press today. Then the stage will be given a fair share before the 'censors' put their case.

Lord Cobbold, accompanied by Ronald Hill (Assistant Secretary, Lord Chamberlain's Office) and myself duly appeared before the Committee the next day, 6 December. I do not recall 'a covey of reporters', but I do recall that I was not, in the event, required to give evidence.

Lord Cobbold had written a personal letter to the Home Secretary (Roy Jenkins) a few months previously in which he expressed the hope that the Joint Committee would go along with the general feeling prevailing in the House of Lords debate and give the whole question of theatre censorship a good airing. Whatever other recommendations the Committee came up with, he hoped one would be to separate any future censorship from the Lord Chamberlain. He went on:

I have been toying in my mind with an idea that, pending legislation, a little experimentation might be a good idea. I should in principle be willing, if the Joint Committee, endorsed by some form of motion of both Houses, so recommended, to consider delegating my powers to an appropriate body for an interim period, reserving a right of veto only in cases which involved the Monarchy or Heads of State.

This suggestion was never followed up, however, nor, as far as I know, was it even debated.

In advance of his giving evidence the Committee had been

given a copy of Lord Cobbold's speech in the House of Lords debate, as well as a comprehensive memorandum prepared by the Lord Chamberlain's Office. The purpose of this was to explain how the Lord Chamberlain's Office was administering the 1843 Act and the principles on which stage plays were licensed.

In his evidence Lord Cobbold repeated his view that the present arrangement was no longer appropriate but he argued for some form of pre-censorship: 'I believe there must be some body with general supervisory powers over the theatre. To my mind the obvious body to which to entrust these powers is the Arts Council. They are independent, with Government backing. They already carry out considerable responsibilities in the theatre and have the confidence of the theatre and the Government.' Lord Goodman replied that it would be quite inappropriate for the Arts Council to take on such a task.

Lord Cobbold was less worried about obscenity than he was about violence, blasphemy and the offensive treatment of persons. On this he was closely questioned by the Chairman, and was given quite a grilling by Michael Foot on how he carried out the censorship and the guidelines he set; he was further questioned by Lord Norwich, Lord Scarbrough, Norman St John-Stevas (who shared his concern about members of the Royal Family) and Andrew Faulds who, as an actor, concentrated on language cuts. The heat was then taken off Lord Cobbold as Faulds, Annan and St John-Stevas started to argue amongst themselves as to whether words and phrases quoted by Faulds should be allowed, but the Chairman called a halt to this. He concluded by thanking Lord Cobbold: 'I think this brings your ordeal to an end and I am sure you will not have objected to the probing questions . . . You have been extremely helpful to all of us.'

The Committee was sent a memorandum, prepared by the Law Officers, which stated that, if pre-censorship *was* abolished, there would be protection for the public through the common law. When the Solicitor-General, Sir Dingle Foot, was examined on 13 December, he was questioned on the 1843 Act and on what he thought the legal position would be if there were no censorship.

Another memorandum was submitted in January 1967 by the Royal Shakespeare Company and was included in the report immediately prior to the evidence of Peter Hall, Director of the Company, who felt strongly about political censorship: '. . . not being able to deal with contemporary subjects in an open way is terribly dangerous'. He was followed by Kenneth Tynan, who spoke of his experiences as Literary Manager at the National Theatre and the difficulties of mounting some productions because of the Lord Chamberlain's requirements. Both he and Hall were unequivocal abolitionists.

A week later Emile Littler (President of the Society of West End Theatre Managers) and Peter Saunders (also a member of the Society) were examined together. The Society had submitted a short memorandum confirming a 1965 resolution, 'namely that the office of the Lord Chamberlain for censoring stage plays works satisfactorily and should be continued'. The Society proposed the addition of 'A' and 'U' certificates on the lines of current film censorship, and Littler and Saunders were questioned on what certificates they might give certain plays, e.g. *Mrs Warren's Profession* (Littler said he would give it a 'U' as it was a classic); Orton's *Loot* (Saunders thought an 'A'); and *The Staircase* by Charles Dyer (Saunders suggested 'A' and Littler 'X'); while of the productions of the Royal Shakespeare Company Littler said, 'Some of their plays have not been to my taste and would probably come under the "X" certificate'.

This completed the evidence of the nine witnesses who were called. The Committee also received written evidence from the following, amongst others:

(a) the Home Office, on the history and working of stage censorship and details of theatre censorship abroad;

(b) the BBC and the ITA, on the manner in which they exercised control over their programmes;

(c) the British Board of Film Censors;

(d) the Arts Council, which stated that 'The case against the Lord Chamberlain is not that he does the job worse than the next man, but that the job imposed upon him cannot and should not be done . . . Even recent Lord Chamberlains have not been able to escape legitimate ridicule, though they and their staff have admittedly been enlightened, conscientious and sympathetic men . . . The fault is in the office, not (at least lately) in its officers';

(e) the Church of England, the Roman Catholic Church and the Free Church Federal Council;

(f) the Association of Municipal Corporations and the Greater London Council;

(g) the Bow Group which stated: 'We believe that playwrights and theatre managers should have exactly the same liberty (and thus responsibility) in their own field as authors and publishers do in theirs.'

The Committee's report, which runs to over two hundred pages, including transcripts of the examination of witnesses and the written evidence, ends by considering the choices of recommendation that were open to them: there were four: (a) the continuation of the Lord Chamberlain; (b) the continuation of compulsory pre-censorship; (c) voluntary pre-censorship; and (d) the abolition of pre-censorship.

'The continuation of the Lord Chamberlain' was only favoured by the Society of West End Theatre Managers and the Association of Municipal Corporations:

> The main arguments adduced in its favour are that it is quick, simple and cheap: that the Lord Chamberlain by virtue of his office possesses a unique authority which no other censorship body could have: that the licence of the Lord Chamberlain affords adequate and necessary protection to theatre managers: that recent Lord Chamberlains have been increasingly tolerant: and that any change might lead to a greater rigidity and restriction.

However, as Lord Cobbold had said, it was time for the Lord Chamberlain to be freed from the responsibility of licensing plays:

> The Committee are convinced that the case for removing the powers of the Lord Chamberlain is compelling and outweighs the administrative convenience of the present arrangements. Accordingly they recommend that the powers should be abolished as soon as possible.

Lord Cobbold had expressed concern that if there were no censorship there would be no protection for the Sovereign and the Royal Family. The Committee did not advocate any legislative protection in this matter which

> should be left to the judgement and good taste of managements and playwrights and, above all, to public opinion, which would not be likely to tolerate personal offensive references to the Sovereign or her family in plays any more than in a book or newspaper.

The second possible recommendation, 'the continuation of compulsory pre-censorship', was supported by Lord Cobbold himself. He had said in the House of Lords that, at any rate for the immediate future, some form of theatre censorship should be maintained. In his evidence to the Committee he suggested the censorship should be entrusted to the Arts Council but Lord Goodman, as its Chairman, would not agree to this. The Committee decided it would be wrong to replace the Lord Chamberlain with another pre-censorship authority.

The third choice, 'voluntary pre-censorship', had been a recommendation of the 1909 Committee. The only supporter of this option was the Greater London Council, while the Arts Council strongly opposed it. The best reason in its favour was that it gave protection to theatre managers. It might also cover one of the objections voiced by the playwrights since they would not *have* to submit their plays, but in the Committee's view it was a system that would offer the worst of both worlds.

The Committee plumped for the fourth alternative, 'the abolition of pre-censorship'. The views of its members are contained in Paragraph 39 of the report:

> The ending of pre-censorship in its present form will not necessarily mean that henceforth there will be a complete free-for-all. Censorship in the widest sense of the word will inevitably continue and by various means control will be exercised over what appears on the stage. Managements will continue to refuse to put on plays whenever they think

fit. Theatre critics will continue to describe plays as they wish. The public will be free to refuse to attend plays or to walk out if they do not like them. Finally the Courts will have the task of ensuring that those responsible for presenting plays which transgress the law of the land will receive appropriate punishment.

The report did not finish there, for the Committee felt it was necessary to draw attention to 'The Operation of the Law in the Future'. First, legislation would be required to repeal the 1843 Act and to exclude the revival of the Royal Prerogative. The Committee considered too whether stage plays in the future might require any special safeguards, e.g., the protection of children, but they decided this was not necessary. They recognised, however, the need for amending various Acts to include stage plays, in particular the Public Order, Race Relations and Obscene Publications Acts. The Committee therefore suggested that legislation should 'have regard to the following considerations':

(a) The prevention of frivolous prosecutions;
(b) The right of trial by jury;
(c) The admissibility of expert evidence;
(d) The effective treatment of obscene plays;
(e) The uniform application of the law.

The report concluded:

The effect of the recommendations of the Committee will be to allow freedom of speech in the theatre subject to the overriding requirements of the criminal law which generally speaking applies to other forms of art in this country. The anachronistic powers of the Lord Chamberlain will be abolished and will not be replaced by any other form of pre-censorship, national or local.

Many people, including myself, thought that the report was an excellent one and that the members of the Committee deserved praise. I recently asked most of them still living for their recollections, which, not surprisingly perhaps after twenty years, were few. Lord Lloyd of Hampstead wrote, 'Off the cuff, the only episode I can particularly recall was when Lord Cobbold gave evidence, and the immediate horror expressed by Lord Goodman that he, as (then) Chairman of the Arts Council, should assume the Lord Chamberlain's role as theatrical censor.'

Lord Annan preferred to recall the Lords debate in which he had made what he hoped was a moderate speech:

> I am afraid I did not please John Osborne who was in the gallery. He had suffered at the hands of the Lord Chamberlain and was snorting with indignation. I thought the best line to take was not to abuse the censors but to suggest that the censorship was an anachronism . . . I was very glad that no brickbats were hurled at the officers who served on the Lord Chamberlain's staff: in my own view theirs was a disagreeable task – I won't say impossible because they did it, but certainly controversial.

Lord Goodman wrote:

> . . . My own contribution was to suggest that – although totally supportive of the abolition of the Lord Chamberlain's role – it might be wise to have a voluntary system whereby theatrical managers could obtain a clearance in cases of doubt. This proposal aroused outrage on the part of certain witnesses, particularly Benn Levy and Kenneth Tynan. In the end since it was clear that it had small support from the Committee, who were anxious to remove the Lord Chamberlain root and branch, I withdrew the proposal. I particularly remember a speech from Benn Levy denouncing me for the suggestion and conveying the firm impression that all my ancestors had been illegitimate.

Hugh Jenkins (now Lord Jenkins of Putney) wrote briefly about the Joint Committee in his book *The Culture Gap*. In his letter he recalled: 'There may have been other committees where membership was drawn from so wide a spectrum, whose views were so unanimous and where recommendations were so promptly put into effect but I don't know of them.'

William Wilson's 'overall impression from the very first meeting of the Committee was that the powers of the Lord Chamberlain were on their way out and the witnesses were being taken through the motions to enable the Committee to justify its ultimate conclusion. Most probably, or so it seems to me,' he went on, 'the majority of the members of the Committee had already reached their conclusion before they started their deliberations.'

The report was published in the autumn of 1967, although its findings were made known earlier. Lord Cobbold meanwhile had continued to press his own views on the Home Secretary (Roy Jenkins) while other Ministers also urged speedy legislation. Lord Cobbold summed up his reaction to the report in the Note which he wrote to his own family:

> I personally thought some reserve censorship powers should be maintained. I was mainly worried about two things, violence (already, in my view, dangerous on television) and abusive criticism of people recently dead where there was no protection under libel laws for their widows or families. I was not particularly worried about 'sex' censorship, as I thought things would find their own level. I suggested that thought should be given to some more sensible 'reserve censorship powers' to cover all the art forms, theatre censorship and the media. This idea made no progress, but I still think that the theatre has suffered by its failure.

Previously, on 21 June 1967, at the time the Committee's findings were made public, the Lord Chamberlain's Office had issued a press release as follows:

> As Lord Cobbold stated in the House of Lords last year, and again in evidence to the Committee, he feels that it is not appropriate in present conditions that the Lord Chamberlain should have this duty (i.e. theatre censorship) imposed on him by Parliament. Lord Cobbold therefore welcomes the recommendations of the Committee in this respect. He cannot make any further comment until he has had an opportunity of considering the general implications of the Report and discussing them with others concerned.

So there it was – a clear-cut recommendation to do without the Lord Chamberlain or censorship of any kind. Everyone was delighted – including the censor himself, despite his reservations – and only the theatre managers, who had so long enjoyed the 'protection' of the Lord Chamberlain's writ, were hesitant; but they were later to become reconciled to the outcome.

Chapter Nineteen

Curtain Down on the Censorship

On 22 June 1967 *The Times* ran a leading article entitled 'Last of the Blue Pencils'. Referring to the conclusions of the Joint Committee and the wish of Lord Cobbold to be rid of his licensing authority it made a rather unfashionable comment:

> Moreover the censor pants along fairly actively in the wake of progressive playwrights. He is never right up in front, but then nor are the great majority of the theatre-going public, which has some reason to be grateful for his jurisdiction. He cannot convincingly be represented as a stifling influence on English drama. Most of the excisions and changes he demands concern the trivia of indecency, which are not the stuff of intellectual and artistic freedom.

On 27 June the Lord Chamberlain wrote to the Home Secretary, Roy Jenkins, saying that, whilst it was his duty to continue to administer the 1843 Act until a new Act was passed, he felt he should keep an eye on the recommendations of the Joint Committee and therefore he proposed to:

(a) discontinue censorship of obscenity and indecency;
(b) discontinue censorship of violence and irreverence, although carefully watching the reaction of public opinion;
(c) discontinue withholding a licence of a play 'calculated to impair friendly relations with a foreign power';
(d) continue to protect living persons and those recently dead, including members of the Royal Family;
(e) include with the play licence a warning that observance of the law would lie wholly with managements.

He asked for the Home Secretary's agreement to this and sought advice on how he should make a public statement on these lines.

The Home Secretary replied on 25 July to the effect that the Lord Chamberlain must carry on *as before* until new legislation was enacted; however he would announce in the House that the Government had accepted the report and intended to bring in new legislation. Thus no changes were made for another fifteen months to the way the Act was administered.

In September the Home Office began to draft a Bill and I attended two meetings, on 20 and 21 September, to give what help I could by answering questions on procedure.

On 19 October Lord Cobbold again wrote to the Home Secretary, asking how things stood and urging speedy legislation: 'We all agree it is difficult to maintain proper respect for a law which is . . . under sentence of death. Any long delay would inevitably tend to bring the law into disrepute. Continuing uncertainty is likely to be damaging to the Theatre.'

On 1 November *The Times* reported that the Government had dropped the Bill it had intended to introduce in that session of Parliament because the Home Office had so much legislation to get through and because also of drafting difficulties.

On 29 November the Lord Chamberlain went to see the Prime Minister, Harold Wilson, who told him that the general feeling of Ministers was to let *everything* go free, but he himself wanted protection for the living and those recently dead. Lord Cobbold followed this up in a letter underlining that he, too, felt strongly on this point:

> I remain greatly concerned about questions of libel and slander . . . I must re-emphasise my conviction that there would be strong and widespread criticism of any new arrangements which failed to give adequate protection to those who cannot in practice take advantage of the ordinary laws of libel and slander or to the families of persons recently dead.

That same day some Private Members' Bills, including George Strauss' Theatres Bill, were formally introduced and read for the first time. They were set down for a Second Reading on 23 February 1968.

Also on 29 November James Callaghan replaced Roy

Jenkins as Home Secretary. Lord Cobbold went to see him on 14 December and discussed the various points he had made to his predecessor, voicing particularly his concern over the living and recently dead, for whom George Strauss had made it clear that in his Bill there would be no protection. Callaghan said he would let Strauss get on with his Bill but that he was prepared to raise the matter in Cabinet. He did not, however, want to risk a delay if such an amendment to the Bill was not acceptable to Strauss and his supporters.

In January 1968 the Queen was asked about two matters concerning the new Bill. The first was that, unless specific mention was made in the Bill of the Royal Prerogative, it could be revived if the 1843 Act was repealed. The second was that, unless provision was made, there would be some doubt as to the authority of the Letters Patent for Covent Garden and Drury Lane. These Letters, which are of great historical interest, link the modern theatre to the days when the actors were the Sovereign's servants. Her Majesty approved that the Royal Prerogative should not be revived and that the Letters Patent should be retained with the proviso that the two managements should comply with any safety or suchlike requirements of the Greater London Council.

On 26 January the first draft of the new Bill appeared and other drafts appeared soon after.

On 9 February the Home Secretary wrote to the Lord Chamberlain confirming that the government had agreed in principle last summer to the recommendations of the Joint Committee and that the new Bill gave effect to them. He added, 'Your main anxieties spring from the Joint Committee's recommendations rather than the way in which the Bill gives expression to them.' Callaghan said the government was holding its hand about the representation of living persons until after the Second Reading.

On 14 February Lord Cobbold replied, referring to the draft Bill, 'I realise that these Clauses aim to put the Theatre on the same basis as Literature . . . although on a different basis to TV, broadcasting and films . . . watching a play is very different from reading a book . . . it is surely arguable that treatment of the Theatre in this respect should be closer to treatment of TV than to that of literature.'

On 23 February the Bill received a Second Reading in the Commons without a division. A month later the Prime Minister wrote to the Lord Chamberlain saying he was not too hopeful of the Bill completing all the stages during that session. Lord Cobbold replied, 'I would stress once again the difficulties of carrying on for much longer an administration which is, so to speak, under public sentence of death.'

The Queen raised the matter with the Prime Minister at his next weekly audience on 26 March. Perhaps as a result the Prime Minister was able to give the Lord Chamberlain on 11 April rather more encouraging news about the passage of the Bill.

The following month saw the Committee stage of the Bill. Only one amendment was put to the vote, a proposal by Norman St John-Stevas to give protection to living persons, including the Royal Family. This was negatived on the grounds that the law applying to the stage should not be more restrictive than the law applying to literature and art.

On 28 May, in the House of Lords, Lord Stow Hill (the former Home Secretary as Sir Frank Soskice) moved the Bill be read a second time and he outlined its main provisions. Lord Cobbold then took the opportunity to repeat his concern about certain matters, i.e. living persons, violence, and religious questions, and he spoke of his regret at the ending of a relationship between the Lord Chamberlain and the Theatre – 'and indeed between the Crown and the Theatre, which has existed for several centuries'.

Lord Norwich said that the Bill would have the effect of abolishing all forms of official pre-censorship for the theatre, thus putting it on the same basis as the written word. The Earl of Scarbrough, in a moving speech supporting the Bill, expressed his sadness too that the link between the stage and the Lord Chamberlain was coming to an end. Shakespeare, he said, for nine years was one of the Lord Chamberlain's Players and one of his first folios was dedicated to the Lord Chamberlain. He hoped that 'the long and honourable relationship between the stage and the Lord Chamberlain will not be entirely lost and that some way of continuing it will be found'.

The Viscount Furness, a theatre manager, supported the

Bill even though his Society had submitted written evidence to the Joint Committee calling for the retention of the Lord Chamberlain as the censor. He reckoned the Bill would free the theatre from specific censorship and with the passing of it the 'theatre will have grown up'.

Lord Stonham, a Home Office Minister who had helped draft the Bill, wound up the debate in support of the government:

> Let us be trusted to act responsibly, and let the law step in when any of us does serious harm to someone else. That is why in the Bill the criteria for obscenity are drawn in terms of the tendency to deprave and corrupt . . . a line must be drawn where stage performances may be conducive to a breach of the peace or incitement to racial hatred; and the Bill does this too. That, in the view of the Government, is as far as we need to go.

The Bill was thus given its Second Reading 'and committed to a Committee of the Whole House'.

The Bill was read a third time on 19 July and the Royal Assent was given on 26 July. Lord Cobbold asked that the usual three months wait between the Royal Assent and a Bill becoming law be reduced to one month. In the event, two months was decided on. Thus the 1968 Theatres Act had the force of law from 26 September onwards.

Between the Second Reading in the House of Commons in February and the Bill becoming an Act Lord Cobbold had attempted, without success, to secure three amendments:

(a) to protect living persons and in particular such persons as the Royal Family, the Archbishop of Canterbury and the Pope who, whatever their rights, cannot usually go to court for reasons of policy;
(b) to give near relatives the right to sue for slander in respect of recently dead persons who *would* have had redress had they been alive;
(c) to prevent reference on the stage to living persons in a way calculated to offend public feeling.

The Theatres Act 1968, compared to some Acts, is quite short. It has only twenty sections. Its preamble describes it as 'An Act to abolish censorship of the theatre and to amend the law in respect of theatres and theatrical performances'.

It begins by repealing the 1843 Act and removing the powers of the Lord Chamberlain by, or on behalf of, the Sovereign by virtue of the Royal Prerogative. The licensing of theatres was transferred to the local authority. Provision was made for criminal proceedings for performances of a play which are obscene. It amended the law of defamation so that publication by performance of a play should be treated as publication in permanent form for the purposes of the law of libel and slander. It made it a criminal offence to present a play with intent to – or that was likely to – stir up racial hatred or to provoke a breach of the peace. It decreed that the Attorney-General's consent must be given before any proceedings were to be taken for these offences.

The provisions of the Act do not apply to performances in a private house on a domestic occasion, nor to rehearsals, nor to plays performed for the purpose of making a record, broadcast or film. This also meant that club performances are not excepted.

The Act extends to England, Wales and Scotland but not to Northern Ireland.

In an article published in the *Solicitors' Journal* on 16 August, there was this comment:

> This Act is open to criticism, like so many other measures, in so far as it amends other branches of the law which would better have been dealt with by amending Acts relating to the particular statutes . . . Whereas in the past the Lord Chamberlain has provided an umbrella against penal proceedings for obscenity, sedition, criminal libel, and to some extent indirectly against potential actions for slander, the burden of responsibility for guarding against all these risks now falls upon the theatre manager, producer and director. This is what the theatre wanted, but they will surely have to lean more heavily in the future on their legal advisers.

On 8 August Lord Cobbold wrote to all theatre managers who received licences from him, extending their existing licences to 25 March 1969 and pointing out that, in accordance with the Act, the Greater London Council would be responsible for theatre licences after 25 September. He added:

> I should like to express to you and those associated with you my own thanks, and the thanks of the staff of this Office for the ready co-operation which we have always had from the Theatre Licensees.

He received in reply many letters thanking him (and us), for example,

> . . . for a quite exceptional degree of co-operation and understanding.
>
> National Theatre

> I have received nothing but help and courtesy from your department since I have been a licensee of theatres from Lord Cromer, Lord Clarendon, Lord Scarbrough and now yourself. Personally I shall feel sad at the end of next month.
>
> Prince Littler

> I am sure that I am not alone among theatre licensees to view the outcome of the Theatres Act with something like dismay. Over thirty years I have always regarded my dealings with your office as one of the pleasantest parts of my job. To know that one will always be met with unfailing courtesy . . . and a personal interest in one's problems is a rare and precious experience in these days of rubber stamps, computers and automata.
>
> John Counsell, Theatre Royal, Windsor

> I myself have been in the theatre too long not to be sad that the old order is changing and feel that the London theatre is losing much.
>
> J. A. Gatti, Vaudeville Theatre

> We shall now no longer have your advice and guidance . . . When my husband became a Licensee I remember him

telling me how shy he felt and how Lord Cromer helped and encouraged him; and when I had to take over you were so very kind and helpful and I am *most* grateful to you.

Mrs Sylvia Stuart Watson, Theatre Royal, Haymarket

Once it was clear that new legislation would take away the Lord Chamberlain's censorship powers, there was concern over what would happen to the manuscripts of new plays, as copies of all plays licensed by the Lord Chamberlain since 1900 were held in the Lord Chamberlain's Office. As early as September 1967 the Society for Theatre Research wrote to Lord Cobbold expressing a desire for the preservation of the MSS of new plays in some way for the future. The Society was told that this was a matter for the Home Office to decide. Peter Saunders raised the question of ownership of scripts again in May 1968. At the Second Reading of the Bill in the House of Lords, Lords Norwich and Farrington expressed the hope that some plan would be made to preserve the MSS of new plays somewhere, to which Lord Annan replied that the Trustees of the British Museum would like thc British Library (the Museum's own library) to be sent a copy of all new plays, as it was of all new books. Lord Stonham was unable to give this assurance, but in the event the Act did provide that a copy of each new play should be sent to the British Library within one month of its first performance. So a copy of each new play is being preserved.

In addition, the British Library now possesses the scripts of all plays licensed between 1900 and 1968, and in due course it will also receive from the Lord Chamberlain's Office all the correspondence, including the Examiners' reports, relating to these plays.

Although Lord Cobbold had not succeeded in obtaining the safeguards he sought, a new Act had been passed and this would not have been the case if successive governments had not been nudged and cajoled by the last two Chamberlains. Some of the credit must go to Lords Scarbrough and Cobbold (the reluctant censors) for bringing it about. On the government side the most helpful Minister was probably Roy Jenkins, Home Secretary during those crucial years of 1966 and

STAGE PLAY SUBMITTED FOR LICENCE.

Title: AS LONG AS I LIVE

No. of Scenes or Acts: One Act

Place of Production: The David Lewis Epileptic Colony, Great Warford, Cheshire

Date of Production: 20.9.68

Author: J.C.F.Grey

Submitted by:

LORD CHAMBERLAIN'S OFFICE,
ST. JAMES'S PALACE, S.W.1.

READERS' REPORT.

17 SEP '68

13.9.68

The period is 1900. The rich business man's daughter has eloped with an ineligible young man and the heavy father has brought them back. There is a fine family row and the couple are being forced to promise to wait for five years. Then the family physician arrives with the news that the daughter has only three years to live and that her slightest whim must be obeyed. The reluctant father has to change his mind about the marriage. The young people are suspicious of a trap and, since he dare not tell the truth, he says that his own health is in danger. But his daughter has ceased to respect him or trust his statements and the couple go off - to Australia - leaving the parents in despair.

RECOMMENDED FOR LICENCE

permit 17/9

C.D.Heriot

LICENCE NO.
2506

(E5327) G63 500 11/67 H & S Ltd. Gp. 937

The Examiner's report on the last play to be licensed by the Lord Chamberlain, 1968

1967. Lord Jenkins, in his memoirs, relates that Lord Cobbold held him to have been responsible for the new Act and told him how grateful he was to be relieved of the censor's role; and he continued to refer to the matter in later years right up to his death in 1987.

However the Act did require the Lord Chamberlain to continue as the censor for two months after the Royal Assent was given on 26 July. During this time about fifty new plays were submitted, dealt with by the readers and given licences. It was almost 'business as usual' except that, for obvious reasons, there were no 'difficult' plays on which to pass judgement. The very last play to be given a Lord Chamberlain's licence was *As Long As I Live*, a one-acter by J. C. F. Gray for production at the David Lewis Epileptic Colony in Great Warford, Cheshire. This last Examiner's report is reproduced on the previous page.

So, on 25 September 1968, Lord Cobbold, with a sigh of relief, put away his blue pencil. To borrow a cricketing analogy, it had been a long innings for the team of censors, lasting over four hundred years. Some Lord Chamberlains had come up against hostile bowling. The likes of Ibsen and Shaw gave them a few bruises and, later in the innings, Osborne, Tynan and Bond were effective change bowlers, not easy to play. Between them, however, their Lordships had made a lot of runs (in terms of the number of plays licensed), and I like to think that Lord Cobbold, who ran himself out, was given a standing ovation as he walked back to the pavilion.

Whether, of course, the job was one that *should* have been done will always be a matter of controversy.

CHAPTER TWENTY

Aftermath

On 28 November 1968 Lords Scarbrough and Cobbold gave a reception in the Lord Chamberlain's Apartment in St James's Palace for the licensees and general managers of the theatres licensed by the Lord Chamberlain. This was at the time of year when, but for the 1968 Theatres Act, the Lord Chamberlain would have been renewing their licences. Past and present members of the Lord Chamberlain's Office were invited.

It was a rather jolly wake. I remember Peter Saunders, who was then President of the Society of West End Theatre Managers, making a charming speech; and Bernard Miles asking all present to sign what would have been his theatre licence for the Mermaid Theatre for the ensuing year. This he had framed and almost exactly twenty years later, when he and his wife came to lunch with us, he generously gave it to me (see overleaf).

Lord Cobbold received some very pleasing letters. Peter Saunders wrote:

> I would like to thank you and the Earl of Scarbrough most sincerely for your hospitality yesterday evening. It was a delightful gesture, though a sad occasion, and I do hope that in some way my Society will find the opportunity to maintain the friendly link between your Office and our Members.

Perhaps a fitting conclusion to this story is to quote from the letter of Michael Hallifax, Executive Manager of the National Theatre:

> I would like to thank you and Lord Scarbrough so very much for inviting me to your apartment on Thursday last

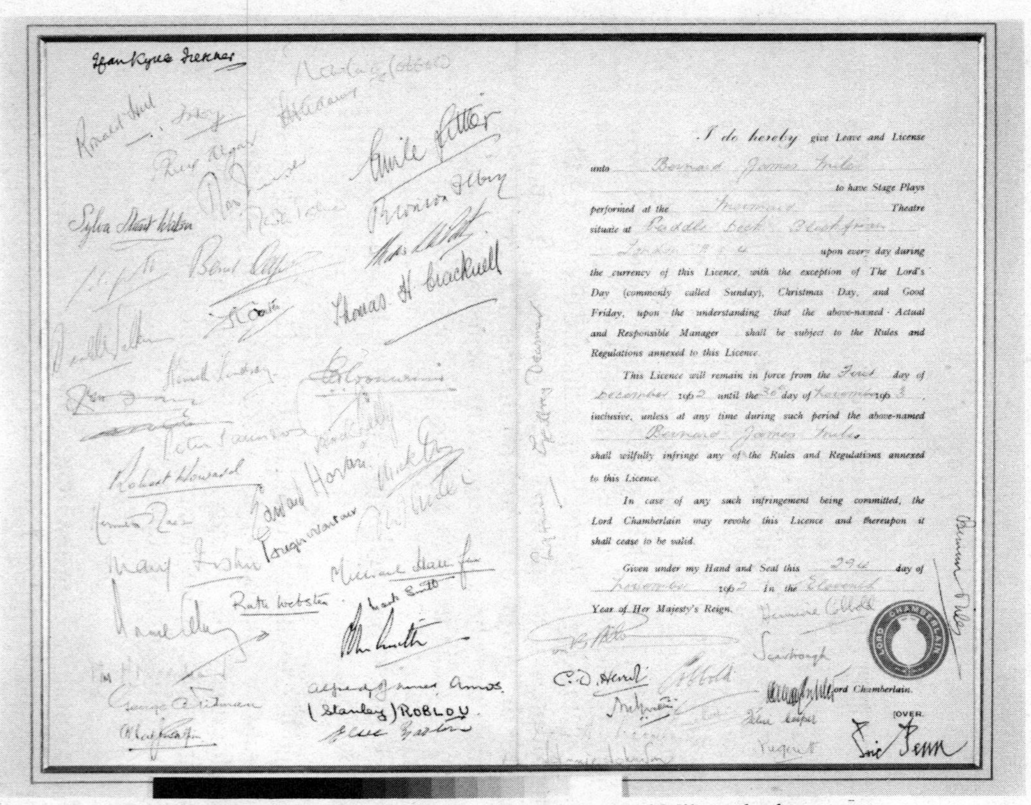

I do hereby give Leave and License unto Bernard James Miles to have Stage Plays performed at the Mermaid Theatre situate at Puddle Dock Blackfriars London E.C.4 upon every day during the currency of this Licence, with the exception of The Lord's Day (commonly called Sunday), Christmas Day, and Good Friday, upon the understanding that the above-named Actual and Responsible Manager shall be subject to the Rules and Regulations annexed to this Licence.

This Licence will remain in force from the First day of December 1962 until the 30th day of November 1963, inclusive, unless at any time during such period the above-named Bernard James Miles shall wilfully infringe any of the Rules and Regulations annexed to this Licence.

In case of any such infringement being committed, the Lord Chamberlain may revoke this Licence and thereupon it shall cease to be valid.

Given under my Hand and Seal this 29th day of November 1962 in the Eleventh Year of Her Majesty's Reign.

Lord Chamberlain.

LORD CHAMBERLAIN

[OVER.

At the celebrations of the ending of the 'censorship' Bernard Miles asked everyone present to endorse his Mermaid Theatre licence for the following year and for making it such a very pleasant, friendly and warm farewell to one of your departments.

It was good to meet old friends from your Office and also good to meet Miss Mary Fisher for the first time. We have only ever been telephone voices to each other and it was splendid to meet at last that voice which used to telephone so often and say 'The Lord Chamberlain disallows the following . . .' followed by a string of expletives!

Except for these theatre managers there was, generally, a sense of relief in the theatre world that there was no longer any censorship of the stage.

Some people, who had cheered the demise of the censorship, may have looked back on the Lord Chamberlain as *Private Eye* described him in 1965 'in all his prudish glory: a heraldic figure in gold-embroidered regalia, wielding the blue pencil, with the face of the toothily beaming Lord Cobbold, and the mind of a sex-mad hypocritical maiden aunt.'

Others may have agreed with the *Guardian Journal* (Nottingham) in the same year. After reporting a speech in which George Devine claimed that the censorship was a puerile system which should be changed with the new status of theatre in society, the writer commented:

> This suggests the Lord Chamberlain is oppressive in his censorship, that he is an old humbug who is behind the times. But the evidence does not support this at all. Rather does he serve as a bulwark between the public and the over-enthusiasm of the theatre.

The objective of the Theatres Act 1968 was, of course, to replace the pre-censorship of the Lord Chamberlain with post-censorship by the courts. William Gaskill had told me that, to him, the passing of the Act was a great relief. People in the theatre, he said, were united as to what they were fighting for, namely freedom of expression. Michael Codron too welcomed the end of the censorship however much he missed the cut and thrust of taking on the Lord Chamberlain. John Arden, for his part, wrote:

> I suppose my small recollections amount to one overall recollection of comparative irrelevance, minor inconvenience, and a general sense of incongruity. I was always aware, that with some other playwrights the Lord Chamberlain's restrictions could on occasions prove quite devastating, and all-in-all I was glad that his role as censor of the theatre was eventually abolished. Without him, however, and since his time, there have always been more than enough people about to interfere in various unacceptable ways with a dramatist's scripts, ideas and intentions . . .

Plus ça change! But Geoffrey Dearmer, referring to those plays which were refused a licence, wrote, 'The fact that now, some twenty years after the passing of the censor, few, if any, have been thought of sufficient merit to be given a public performance, argues strongly, surely, that no harm was ever done to the Theatre.'

Similarly, I believe that very few new plays of note in London during the last twenty years would have given the Lord Chamberlain much cause for concern with, perhaps, the notable exception of *Oh! Calcutta!* As the *Oxford Companion to the Theatre* (1988 edition) records, 'The heady sense of freedom that followed [the 1968 Act] generated a brief wave of plays in the early 1970s that sought to test public reaction to verbal obscenity and physical nudity and eventually to prove that playwrights, actors and managers between them could be trusted to know where artistic necessity ended and pornography began.'

The Lord Chamberlain himself, and members of his Office, received many requests for interviews or to lecture, both before and after 1968. These, with the exception of the *Sunday Times* interview of Lord Cobbold in 1965, were turned down as a matter of policy. In reply to one such request from the British Council in 1969, I explained:

> It has always been the Lord Chamberlain's policy, during the time he was responsible for administering the Theatres Act (1843), not to discuss the methods whereby he administered the Act. Although there is now a new Theatres Act,

> and the Lord Chamberlain is no longer responsible for theatre censorship, nevertheless both the Home Office and ourselves feel that we should continue our policy of not granting interviews.

That same year Lord Cobbold was invited to give an address to undergraduates at Cambridge University and he replied:

> I am afraid that it would not be possible to accept your kind invitation. I have already said what I have to say in the House of Lords debate, and if I once started talking about censorship now I should never be able to stop.

The new Act stipulates that a charge against any production may only be brought with the consent of the Attorney-General. This has only been obtained once, in 1971, when a prosecution was brought at Manchester Crown Court under Section 2(2) of the Act in respect of a revue called *DeeJay* at Brownson Brothers Revue Bar in Manchester, against six defendants, five of whom were convicted and given prison sentences ranging from fifteen to eight months. The show had been advertised in the *Manchester Evening News* as 'the most turned-on and savage musical of the decade'. It opened with six naked women dancing round a man in bed. It was reported in the press that the show's jokes were 'obscene even by lavatory-wall standards'. Performers undressed each other and danced naked on the stage; and there was also a masturbation scene. The show ended with the performers inviting the audience to tell their friends how filthy it was.

There has been the occasional private prosecution, the best known being that brought in 1982 by Mrs Mary Whitehouse against the National Theatre over Howard Brenton's play *The Romans in Britain*. Mrs Whitehouse had not been to see the play but, at her request, her solicitor (Graham Ross-Cornes) did so. He complained to the Attorney-General, Sir Michael Havers, who refused to allow a prosecution under the 1968 Theatres Act and proceedings were initiated instead under the Sexual Offences Act 1956.

Michael Bogdanov, the play's director, stood trial at the

Old Bailey in March, accused of staging a simulated act of homosexual rape by a Roman soldier on a Celt. He pleaded not guilty. The case attracted considerable publicity and was expected to last two weeks. This was not to be, however, for after Ross-Cornes gave evidence and Mr Justice Staughton had ruled that there was a case to answer, the prosecuting counsel (Ian Kennedy, QC) withdrew the prosecution and asked defending counsel (Lord Hutchinson, QC) to inform Bogdanov. This left the judge no alternative but to issue a writ of *nolle prosequi*; thus the case was withdrawn before any point of law could be established. Bogdanov said he was ambivalent about the outcome: happy that it was over, but disappointed at not being able to defend himself in the witness box. The champagne flowed in the National Theatre but Mrs Whitehouse had no cause for celebration.

Perhaps surprisingly, Kenneth Tynan's *Oh! Calcutta!* had not been proceeded against. This controversial revue, described as 'an evening of elegant erotica', opened in New York in 1969 and came to London a year later.

The Law Officers' Department, on 31 July 1970, issued the following press statement:

> The Attorney-General has considered, in consultation with the Director of Public Prosecutions, whether he should authorise criminal proceedings, in respect of the production *Oh! Calcutta!* The only provision under which proceedings could be brought is section 2 of the Theatres Act, 1968, which makes it an offence to present or direct an obscene performance of a play. Section 2(1) provides that a performance of a play shall be deemed to be obscene if, taken as a whole, its effect was such as to tend to deprave and corrupt persons who were likely, having regard to all the relevant circumstances, to attend it. On the evidence which has been placed before him concerning this production as it is now presented, the Attorney-General has formed the opinion that there is no reasonable likelihood that a prosecution under section 2 would be successful. Accordingly, he has decided that no proceedings should be taken.

The production was a success and most critics, though not all, gave it good notices:

> If as seems likely following to-day's revue no action follows then the public and the whole of show business will ensure that *Oh! Calcutta!* standards are a yardstick for the future.
>
> *Evening News*

> If you think masturbation, rape, sexual frustration and homosexuality are screamingly funny then this revue may be for intellectually you.
>
> *Daily Mirror*

> The intention is not to appeal to the belted raincoat trade, but to bring people together by means of the last surviving natural link in urban culture and if this is pornography, then pornography is no bad thing.
>
> *The Times*

> Since it dares and challenges every established concept of what may or may not be sexually permissible I can well understand and even appreciate why complaints and protests have flourished in its wake, and will continue to do so . . . In my opinion little in this bizarre little revue is as unpleasant as the tone of some of the vigilantes calling for its suppression.
>
> *Daily Express*

> Labour MP George Strauss, who sponsored the 1968 Theatres Act, said 'I am quite sure that there is nothing in it that would corrupt or pervert anyone.' Actor Laurence Harvey said 'I advise anyone coming to bring their children. They will love it.'
>
> *The Sun*

There were a number of complaints in various quarters, a few of which reached us in the Lord Chamberlain's Office, including one from a titled lady who sent Lord Cobbold a copy of a formal complaint – running to six pages – which she had lodged with the police. She provided a synopsis of the fourteen scenes which included stripping, bondage, simulated copulation, simulated masturbation and plenty of 'foul' language. Perhaps it was not surprising, then, that one critic, that of the *Daily Telegraph*, wrote:

> For the time being, many will feel that the Lord Chamberlain's role in the world of theatre was abolished at precisely the wrong moment.

Epilogue

With the passing of the Theatres Act in 1968, some people believed the Lord Chamberlain would no longer have anything to do – *and* that the Lord Chamberlain's Office would be closing down! Happily this was not the case. Both the Lord Chamberlain and the Lord Chamberlain's Office, now at Buckingham Palace, continue to carry out their royal duties, which up until 1968 accounted for eighty per cent of their work but brought them far less publicity than their theatre censorship role.

For myself, I missed the theatre work, certainly to begin with. It had been a most interesting four years. I had come to know a number of theatre managers, producers and playwrights; and I am glad still to be associated with the theatrical profession through, for example, the Theatre Royal, Windsor.

Yet it does not surprise me that there have been so many opponents of the censorship. Lord Chesterfield is possibly the most memorable, for that stirring speech in which he tried to prevent Walpole pushing through Parliament his Licensing Act of 1737. Later, in 1899, Bernard Shaw made quite clear what he thought should be done: 'Abolish it, root and branch, throwing the whole legal responsibility for plays on the author and manager, precisely as the legal responsibility for a book is thrown on the author, the printer and publisher.' This is what did more or less happen, but not until sixty-nine years later.

After reading early drafts of the chapters on Lord Cromer's and Lord Clarendon's administration of the Lord Chamberlain's Office, Geoffrey Dearmer remarked how these demonstrated that the censorship, even then, was dying and that the media and public opinion were, and are, the better judge.

Lord Willis, in the House of Lords' debate on theatre

David Langdon's cartoon marking the closing of the 'censorship'

censorship in 1966, echoed the views of Shaw, saying: 'I want it to be subject to the same checks and controls in law as any other form of art or literature'; and the Bow Group and the League of Dramatists said much the same in their written evidence.

On the other hand, many tributes were paid to the Lord Chamberlain, for example that of the Earl of Dundee at the Second Reading of the Theatres Bill in the Lords on 28 May 1968:

> I think that successive Lord Chamberlains have carried out their unpopular duty – which Parliament imposed upon them and which they never asked for – with understanding, with tolerance and with a great and devoted care in the interests of the public and the theatre. I think that this should be stated and a tribute paid to the Lord Chamberlain's Office for the way they have carried out this very unacceptable duty.

Remember, however, John Arden's word of caution when referring to the end of the Lord Chamberlain's censoring duties: 'Without him and since his time, there have always been more than enough people about to interfere in various unacceptable ways with a dramatist's script.'

Raymond Massey made a valid point about the Lord Chamberlain's Office when he wrote in his autobiography:

> The office was outside politics and had a dignity which no bureaucrats could have. Of course, whether the system would work really depended on the man himself, who was the Lord Chamberlain.

The ending of the censorship, however, was really the only sensible solution. In the present century, with popular demand for free speech and for freedom from autocratic authority, the need for playwrights to obtain a licence for a new play was anomalous in theory and anachronistic in practice. Even though, by and large, the system had been operated humanely and worked quite well in practice, this was little consolation for authors like Shaw who had to wait over twenty-five years for a licence for *Mrs Warren's Profession*; or for other writers like Laurence Housman or Marc Connelly (author of *The Green Pastures*) or John Osborne whose legitimate self-expression and consequently their earnings could be 'censored' without appeal, and without intellectual justification.

Since 1968 the theatre has enjoyed an unparalleled period of freedom. Instead of pre-censorship we now have self-censorship practised by writers, producers and directors who assess the current level of public tolerance. Even the resulting plethora of four-letter words is probably being regretted. Is the Prince of Wales the only person who is appealing for a higher quality of language?

Bernard Miles, in a letter in 1988 after I told him about this book, counselled me:

> My humble advice is that you should steer (more or less) free from solemnity and officialdom and make it a funny book. After all, most of the case histories are backed up with the ridiculous which the Lord Chamberlain had of necessity to treat in a serious way.

Perhaps the best expression of this comes in a humorous ode written by Geoffrey Dearmer who, as an Examiner of Plays, was always sensitive to the effect which the views and opinions of himself and his colleagues, of the censorship indeed, might have:

'Those poor damned plays'
A plea to the Lord Chamberlain by one of his Examiners

I often think of those poor plays
some long ago submitted
but now to death committed
'all silent and all damned'
and all together crammed,
sorry for themselves
where no-one delves
in dark and dusty shelves.
O shame, my lord!

EPILOGUE

Can you not hear them mutiny
  for lack of further scrutiny
  in these enlightened days?
And will you not now, even now,
  turn the key softly
  oiled with the oil of hope
  (that sweet Beatitude)
  and set them free,
  give them their liberty,
  and feel their gratitude?
You would not hawk them on a tray –
  they are not penny toys,
  nor can they fly away
  they haven't wings, poor things.
But works of art, my lord,
  aren't lifeless things.
O Censor of our plays
  from the beginning to the end,
  you of the loyal heart,
  the theatre's faithful friend,
  who always waited with sparkling eyes
  to see the curtain rise.

Appendixes

Appendix A

Lord Chamberlains 1724–1968

Where there is more than one set of dates opposite a Lord Chamberlain's name, this indicates different terms of office. Until the appointment of the Earl of Cromer in 1922, the office of Lord Chamberlain was a political post which changed with changes of government.

Charles, Duke of GRAFTON	1727–1757
William, Duke of DEVONSHIRE	1757–1762
George, Duke of MARLBOROUGH	1762–1763
Granville Leveson, Earl GOWER	1763–1765
William Henry Cavendish, Duke of PORTLAND	1765–1766
Francis Seymour, Marquess of HERTFORD	1766–1782
	1783
George, Duke of MANCHESTER	1782–1783
James, Earl of SALISBURY	1783–1804
George, Earl of DARTMOUTH	1804–1812
Francis, Marquess of HERTFORD	1812–1821
James, Duke of MONTROSE	1821–1827
	1828–1830
William Spencer, Duke of DEVONSHIRE	1827–1828
	1830–1834
George Child Villiers, Earl of JERSEY	1830
	1834–1835
Richard, Marquess WELLESLEY	1835
Francis Nathaniel, Marquess CONYNGHAM	1835–1839
Henry, Earl of UXBRIDGE	1839–1841
George, Earl DE LA WARR	1841–1846
	1858–1859
Frederick, Earl SPENCER	1846–1848
John, Marquess of BREADALBANE	1848–1852
	1853–1858
Brownlow, Marquess of EXETER	1852–1853

John, Viscount SIDNEY	1859–1866
	1868–1874
Orlando, Earl of BRADFORD	1866–1868
Francis, Marquess of HERTFORD	1874–1879
William, Earl of MOUNT EDGCUMBE	1879–1880
Valentine, Earl of KENMARE	1880–1883
	1886
Edward, Earl of LATHOM	1883–1886
	1886–1892
	1895–1898
Charles, Lord CARRINGTON	1892–1895
John, Earl of HOPETOUN	1898–1900
Edward, Earl of CLARENDON	1900–1905
Charles, Viscount ALTHORP (later Earl SPENCER)	1905–1912
William, Lord SANDHURST (later Viscount SANDHURST)	1912–1921
John, Duke of ATHOLL	1921–1922
Rowland, Earl of CROMER	1922–1938
George, Earl of CLARENDON	1938–1952
Roger, Earl of SCARBROUGH	1952–1963
Cameron, Lord COBBOLD*	1963–1968

*Lord Cobbold continued in office until 1971. He was succeeded by Charles, Lord Maclean. The present Lord Chamberlain since 1984 is David, Earl of Airlie.

Appendix B

Examiners of Plays 1737–1968

Between 1738 and 1968 twenty-one Examiners of Plays were employed. The longest serving were John Larpent (46 years), William Chetwynd (40 years), Rev. A. E. Jones (37 years) and Charles Heriot (31 years).

CHETWYND, William	1738–1778
ODELL, Thomas (Deputy Examiner)	1738–1749
CAPELL, Edward (Deputy Examiner)	1749–1781
LARPENT, John	1778–1824
COLMAN, George ('Colman the Younger')	1824–1836
KEMBLE, Charles	1836–1840
KEMBLE, John	1840–1857
DONNE, William Bodham	1857–1874
PIGOTT, E. F. S.	1874–1895
REDFORD, G. A.	1895–1911
BROOKFIELD, Charles	1911–1913
BENDALL, Ernest	1913–1920
STREET, George	1914–1936 (Senior Examiner 1920)
GAME, Henry	1930–1953 (Senior Examiner 1936)
DEARMER, Geoffrey	1936–1958 (Senior Examiner 1953)
HERIOT, Charles	1937–1968 (Senior Examiner 1958)
TROUBRIDGE, Lt-Col. Sir St Vincent (Assistant Examiner)	1952–1963
COLES, Maurice (Assistant Examiner)	1958–1965
KYRLE FLETCHER, I. (Assistant Examiner)	1964–1968
HARWARD, Timothy (Assistant Examiner)	1965–1968

JONES, Rev. Albert Evans (Welsh Reader) 1931–1968

Appendix C

Memorandum and Letter to G. A. Redford, Examiner of Plays

COPY of a MEMORANDUM dated 13th March, 1895, which was given by the Lord Chamberlain to Mr Redford for his guidance as Examiner of Plays.

Lord Chamberlain's Office,
St. James's Palace, S.W.

The Examiner of Plays is an Officer appointed to examine all Theatrical Entertainments on the Part of the Lord Chamberlain who is responsible to Parliament, and generally to advise with him, and the Officers of his Department, upon all matters relating to the Stage.

With regard to the reading of Plays, the Examiner is solely responsible to the Lord Chamberlain for the pieces which he recommends for Licence.

The Manuscripts pass through the Examiner's hands alone, excepting in cases of doubt, when he is bound to consult the Lord Chamberlain, who in all other cases has been in the habit of accepting without question the recommendations of the Examiner.

As a matter of convenience the Licences for Pieces pass through the Office to be registered, and the manuscripts and correspondence are retained for reference with other records of the Department.

The Examiner is further expected to visit the Theatres constantly to see that the rules of the Lord Chamberlain are carried out with regard to the Pieces licensed by him.

In all other Theatrical matters the Examiner is an Officer of the Department, and as such is expected to attend at the Office and to co-operate with his colleagues there. It is his duty to keep himself informed, and to report to the Lord Chamberlain anything that may come to his knowledge through the Press or any other channel with regard to the conduct of Theatres generally, and be present at the annual inspection, and to assist the officers of the Lord Chamberlain in all matters relating to Theatres, whether in licensing or any other question which may arise.

He is expected to appear at subpœnas in Law Cases, more especially those having reference to the Licensing of Plays, and it is his duty also to examine the Play Bills with reference to the performance of unlicensed Pieces at the Theatres, and to see that they are sent regularly to the Lord Chamberlain's Office for this purpose.

COPY of a LETTER from the Comptroller of the Lord Chamberlain's Department to Mr. Redford, stating the Lord Chamberlain's wishes with regard to the Examination of Plays.

Lord Chamberlain's Office,
St. James's Palace, S.W.
28th June, 1909.

Dear Mr. Redford,

In confirmation of the explanation I gave you verbally, when I saw you on Saturday last, of the Lord Chamberlain's wishes regarding your treatment in future of plays about which you are in doubt, I write to inform you as follows:–

The Lord Chamberlain wishes you, whenever matter of any nature, contravening his regulations, appears in a play submitted for your examination, to interview the Manager of the Theatre concerned, and thus, if possible, ensure that the objectionable matter is eliminated without friction or further discussion.

In submitting a play which has been thus dealt with, the Lord Chamberlain would like always to be told of what has passed on the subject, previous to the alterations, which, in your opinion, have rendered the play eligible for licence.

Should your personal interview with the Manager prove abortive; in other words, should the objection you see to the play be likely to produce a deadlock in the negotiations, the Lord Chamberlain wishes you at once to inform him so that the play under discussion can be thoroughly examined here before a final decision is come to.

Yours very truly,
(Sd.) *Douglas Dawson.*

P.S. – The Lord Chamberlain wishes me to thank you very much for your letter of the 27th instant, which he has been unable through stress of work to answer himself.

Appendix D

Memorandum dated 16 December 1924 from the Lord Chamberlain to the Home Secretary (see Chapter 6)

The Licensing of Theatres and the Censorship of Stage Plays by the Lord Chamberlain.

CONFIDENTIAL

The Office of Lord Chamberlain having now assumed a non-political character, a question of policy and expediency arises as to whether it is advisable or not for the existing control over Theatres and Stage Plays to remain vested in the Lord Chamberlain.

Any statutory change in the present legal position would of course entail either amendment of the Theatres Act of 1843, or its repeal and the passing of a new Act of Parliament.

1. With regard to the Licensing of Theatres, the present system works well and satisfactorily on the whole, owing largely to the co-operation of the London County Council in the matter of periodical inspections.

Theatre Managers would mostly oppose any change likely to result in their interests being handed over to direct supervision by the London County Council, whose policy as regards restrictive Regulations is liable to periodical changes, which might adversely affect the interests of the Lessees and Managers of Theatres.

2. It is, therefore, in the matter of the censorship of Stage Plays that the policy of the future calls for early examination and decision.

From the outset it may be accepted that no system for regulating the performance of Stage Plays will ever be considered as ideal by the general public as a whole.

The present system has hitherto worked satisfactorily to the minds of most people, as is evident from the fact that there has been no public outcry for any drastic reform.

On the other hand, there are many people who do not consider the present system satisfactory and who would welcome alteration.

This section of the community may be divided into two classes who view the matter from diametrically opposite points of view.

First there are the people – authors, free-thinkers and others – who object to any censorship whatever, and who would like to see its complete abolition.

Secondly, there are the Clergy and many serious-minded people who deplore the tendencies of modern thought, and who would urge a far stricter censorship of Stage Plays.

To satisfy these two opposing schools of thought being an impossibility, the problem that will always confront any Government in this country is how best to reconcile these contending factions in the best interests of the community as a whole, and with the least possible disturbance to the machinery of Government, and to the interests of those whose lives and fortunes are dependant upon Theatrical work and enterprise.

Censorship of the Stage exists in some form or another in all civilized countries, but in many it devolves upon the Police Authorities.

That a similar system of Police supervision only should be adopted in this country would be most undesirable, and would probably meet with wide-spread disapproval. It may, therefore, be assumed that the majority of the public are in favour of some form of censorship being maintained.

The question at issue, therefore, is what is the best form of machinery for regulating the Censorship of the Stage?

The answer to this question is doubtless capable of assuming various forms, but in this Memorandum it may be confined to the four following alternatives:–

1. Censorship by the Lord Chamberlain with such improvements in the constitution of his Advisory Board as may be considered desirable in the public interests.

2. Censorship by the Home Office, for which the Home Secretary is directly responsible to Parliament.

3. Censorship by local County and Borough Councils. For the London Area by the Theatres Committee of the London County Council.

4. Censorship by a specially created Board of Authority nominated by the Government for a term of years on the advice of the Home Secretary.

All these methods are open to objection and criticism, as well as having their attendant difficulties in practice.

As to (1), it may be urged that although it maintains tradition and the link with the Crown, which is highly valued and appreciated by the Theatrical Profession, the Lord Chamberlain being now a non-political officer and no longer a member of H.M. Government, is capable by misguided policy of involving the Crown, H.M. Government and the Office he holds in serious embarrassment.

On the other hand, no Lord Chamberlain is likely to act without taking advice from responsible and best qualified quarters. In practice, the Lord Chamberlain would therefore generally assure himself of support from H.M. Government before any serious questions arise in Parliament.

Being a Member of the House of Lords, the Lord Chamberlain should always be able to state and defend his case in that Chamber, while in the House of Commons the Home Secretary would reply for the Government, subject to having previously approved the line of action taken by the Lord Chamberlain, upon whatever point of criticism arises. Thus responsibility to Parliament is unimpaired.

As to (2), no Government would be anxious to assume direct responsibility for the duties of Censorship, which are inseparable from continual and ill-informed criticism liable to reflect adversely upon the political interests of the Government in Office.

This alternative would be opposed by the Theatrical Managers and that section of the public which objects to the extension of Bureaucratic control by Government Departments.

The alternative (3) would be very cumbersome and vexatious to all Theatrical interests, and would be opposed on the grounds of expense, delay and continual changes and variations of policy.

Very careful thought would be required as to (4) as whatever the constitution of this Board, it would meet with much opposition and criticism. Still it is capable of creation, although it would be confronted with far greater difficulties than those with which the Board of Film Censors has to contend.

Mention must here be made that alternatives 2, 3, and 4 entail a break with tradition and constitutional practice involving the Prerogative of the Crown through the medium of the Lord Chamberlain.

Any departure from (1) would therefore necessarily entail obtaining The King's assent.

The whole question of Stage Plays Censorship was investigated by a Joint Select Committee of Parliament in 1909 when certain recommendations were made, but the Theatres Act of 1843 remained unchanged.

It remains then for the Home Secretary to consider the various aspects of the Censorship question, and to tender such advice to His

Majesty as he and the Cabinet may deem most expedient in the public interests of the Community as a whole.

(signed) CROMER

16th December 1924

Appendix E

The Censorship

The Lord Chamberlain, Lord Cobbold, discusses the controversial issues surrounding his office in an interview with J. W. Lambert (printed in the Sunday Times, *11 April 1965, and reprinted by agreement with Times Newspapers Ltd)*

Supposing it is accepted that such a function as yours should be carried out, is it really a good idea that the job should be so closely associated with the Crown?

That is a matter for Parliament to decide. If one were starting from scratch in 1965 I don't think one would invent this particular set-up.

Apart from any possible embarrassment to the Crown, the idea of the censor being an officer of the Court lays the job open to a certain amount of derision. Some people take it for granted that he will be an entrenched member of the Establishment. Do you think that this makes it more difficult for you to do the censor's job effectively?

Some people do have an image of the Lord Chamberlain sitting in a cocked hat wielding a large blue pencil. To this extent it does make the job more difficult. On the other hand, I think quite a lot of people like to know that the job is right outside politics. As a matter of fact most people, if they think about it at all, have a pretty clear distinction in their minds, which is a quite correct distinction, between the Lord Chamberlain in his theatrical capacity and the Lord Chamberlain in his Court functions. And after all whoever does the censorship job is obviously going to be a natural target for criticism and ridicule, a natural Aunt Sally.

You would hardly have accepted the post of Lord Chamberlain if you personally objected in principle to the censorship of plays?

No, not if I had had any strong convictions of principle against it. I think I had rather an open mind on the subject.

What is your personal view of the censor's function? Is it to maintain a norm of generally acceptable freedom?

Norm is the operative word. If I may go a bit ahead of your question, we always think of ourselves as a licensing authority rather than as a censoring authority. The bias is always to give a licence unless there is very strong ground for objection. My personal objective is to try to assess the norm of educated, adult opinion and if possible to keep just a touch ahead of it. I find I have to make a positive effort to keep my own personal tastes, likes and dislikes right out of the picture. They are obviously irrelevant for censorship purposes. Of course, one must make some allowance for selectivity; people don't have to go to the theatre; they choose what they want to see and if they want to they can quite easily find out something about the play before they go.

Would you then regard yourself as existing primarily to control extremists rather than to protect the public?

I think more the latter really, though I suppose the two things fuse to some extent. The vast majority of people feel that a line has to be drawn somewhere on some subjects – sex, religion, and so on. For proof of that one only needs to listen to the reaction when television oversteps the mark a bit. The question is where should the line be drawn: on which, obviously, everyone has his own ideas.

Do you think this line-drawing is more necessary in the case of the theatre than in the case of the other media, where there isn't in fact pre-censorship or licensing of an official kind?

Are you not putting too much emphasis on the word official? There is a pre-censorship of various kinds; there is a board of film censors and BBC and ITA themselves all have responsibilities in their own fields. The media are of course different and different considerations apply in each case. But in each one *somebody* is concerned to draw a line. I would agree that the whole question of censorship has entered a new phase with the growth of drama on radio and television. It might well be that in due course it would be a good thing to have a comprehensive new look at censorship in all these media. But I feel myself that that might perhaps be more productive in a few years' time, when there has been longer experience on the television side. Literature, of course, is another problem. I doubt whether people feel too happy about the present arrangements in that field, but I don't think that comes into our discussion.

If you require something to be altered or cut, and the people concerned want some reconsideration or to talk the matter over, how is that handled?

Most of the managements have been in touch with the people in my office for years and are on very good terms with them. They write in, and they come in, and explain and ask for reconsideration; and of course one is always ready to look at any arguments that are put up. There is a bit of gamesmanship in all this. Some managements, not all, put in a number of four-letter words and other things that they know perfectly well will be cut out, possibly in the hope that we will cut them out and leave one or two border-line things in. And of course there is some advertising value in 'banned by the censor.' So there's a good deal of give and take on this. And very often we arrive at an arrangement which is perfectly proper and suits everyone concerned. I should like to emphasise one point. When we ask for a phrase to be altered we never, as is often alleged, ourselves suggest an alternative text.

You say that you yourself, in difficult cases, will consult outside your own Office. Are the managements submitting to scripts entitled, as it were, to produce witnesses for the defence? I seem to remember that when the question of 'Hang Down Your Head And Die' came up Lord Gardiner and one or two others came to discuss it with your office. Was that at your suggestion, or the management's?

The management's, and their 'witnesses' were very helpful.

Would you say that most difficulties arise over words and phrases rather than situations or basic ideas?

In quantitative terms, certainly over words and phrases. You'd be surprised to see the number of four-letter words, and I think I can say obscenities, that are sometimes included in scripts by the most reputable people. I can't help feeling that in most cases even if they didn't know that we were going to cut them out they would cut them out themselves before they got on to the stage. Words and phrases rarely cause a lot of difficulty. There are some that we always cut. There is sometimes an appeal because a word is used in a particular context. We normally cut certain expletives, for example, 'Christ' and 'Jesus', which are admittedly used in common parlance and are not put forward in any irreverent spirit, I think, but still do give offence to a great number of people. But in terms of quality, it is of course the situations and the basic ideas that give one the headaches.

I believe that once a play has been licensed – including its stage directions – it is available for production anywhere. This could open up alarming possibilities, which I suppose you have to bear in mind?

Yes, indeed, very much so. I believe I could actually have power to reverse a decision in extreme cases. But it is obviously difficult and in fact I've never done it. But there is a great problem because we are dealing with highly reputable managements, highly competent producers, who come to us and say, quite properly and quite accurately, that they can put on a certain scene without giving the slightest offence to anybody. I accept that as absolutely true; but the same scene as produced by a less competent management with a quite different production might result in something very undesirable indeed.

Do you in fact keep tabs on performances at all?

Occasionally, if we've been doubtful about business, I get somebody to have a look and see if the stage directions we've authorised are also being carried out accurately. Also, if we get two or three complaints I usually send somebody to have a look at it. And I might add that we get more complaints about what we pass than about what we don't pass.

I suppose sex, religion and politics are the basic subjects most likely to run into difficulties. Which is first in the field?

I would think in these days sex. In terms of the most controversial cases that we get, quantitatively those are the most troublesome. I have personally found the religious ones most difficult of all. I would say that the single play that has given me the most preoccupation was 'The Representative'.

You felt that for our audiences it needed alteration?

In the end, not a great deal. We did ask for one or two references to Pope Pius to be modified.

If you were confronted with a play which deliberately set out to be a savagely satirical attack on Christianity, what sort of considerations would you have in mind?

Well, I should have to look at the actual play and judge it on its merits. But I would start with a bias against it.

In the case of sex, I suppose as far as subject matter is concerned you wouldn't necessarily bar anything so long as it was acceptably handled at its own level? A serious play, or a farce, about an illegitimate child might be inoffensive, for example, and so might a serious play about venereal disease, but hardly a farce about venereal disease?

I think that's about right. If I may say so, I think that I should have no great difficulty in the particular instances you give. The ones which have really given me difficulties are the ones which go a little further along the line – abortion on the stage, farces about artificial insemination, physical contact between homosexuals and such like.

Would you in fact, would your Office, take a different view of physical contact between homosexuals and physical contact between a man and woman?

To some extent a different view.

Homosexuality came up pretty prominently a few years ago, and led to the formation of a lot of club theatres. At the end of the 1920s and again at the end of the 1950s, this business of forming a theatre into a club became a popular way of evading censorship or the necessity of licensing. At the moment there is talk of one well-known London theatre doing this so that it can put on one particular play. Do you regard this as an acceptable procedure?

So long as they are genuine clubs for a genuine purpose I am very much in favour of theatre clubs. They give selective and interested audiences a chance to see experimental work and I think they are very useful to the theatre. Whether or not they could strictly be brought under the Lord Chamberlain's jurisdiction – which has never actually been tested in the courts – my predecessors and I have never wished to interfere with genuine theatre clubs. Where a management uses them for a different purpose, e.g., to put on for a long run a play part of which has been refused a licence, I think rather a different position arises. The arrangement is then really being used more as an attempt to evade the law. That has come to a head once or twice before, actually. I can think of circumstances in which the Lord Chamberlain as custodian of the Theatres Act would feel it his duty to challenge the arrangement and to test the law in the courts. I very much hope myself that managements will have the good sense not to force the issue to this point, which might well involve difficulties for all theatre clubs and which would, in my view, be harmful to the general interests of the theatre.

I take it you would agree, and I think the managements would agree, that this job is one that must be done ultimately by one man; nobody would welcome censorship by committee; so that it then all depends on the man who holds the office. It must be very difficult, with the best will in the world, to find an ideal candidate for the wide-ranging post that you are holding at the moment.

You say it all depends on the man who holds the office. Of course, the Lord Chamberlain has the final responsibility but, as I think I've said, there's a wealth of experience and technical advice available to him. There are some disadvantages in the connection with the Royal Household, but there's not much point in saying that unless one's got a constructive alternative. Who would one suggest? A politician – surely not. A judge – I scarcely think so. A top civil servant – possibly, but would the image be very much improved?

No. But I think that the objection that a lot of the progressives feel about the present situation is that they have, because of this association with the Crown Office, the image of a very upper-class character, an image of the bowler hat, the rolled umbrella, and an extremely limited knowledge of or feel for moods in the contemporary world. Setting the job up on quite a different basis might at least clear away this image from their minds, even if it's an unjust image. You've mentioned some possible alternatives – there's another: could it be a man who's been closely involved in the theatre?

I think it is a great advantage to have an interest in the theatre, and I would say even to enjoy going to plays, because that keeps one in touch with the current theatre. I don't find it easy to keep entirely in touch merely by reading the scripts alone. But I would not think anybody with professional theatre contacts would be a good candidate.

Coming back to the other line of your question – you're really asking me whether I'm the right sort of person to do this job? If you want my opinion as objectively as I can give it, it's this. As I've said, there's plenty of technical advice and long experience about theatrical censorship available. I would personally have thought that the main qualities required for the person at the top were wide experience, a knowledge of what is going on in the contemporary world, and the habit of sifting advice, reaching decisions and taking responsibility. If a person is appointed to be Lord Chamberlain, quite apart from his theatrical responsibilities, he must surely be presumed to have these qualifications.

Appendix F

Stage Plays Submitted for Licence

between January 1990 and September 1968

Years	*Lord Chamberlain*	*Total*	*Licensed*	*'Waiting Box'*	*Refused a Licence*
1900–05	Earl of Clarendon	3,028	3,015	–	13
1905–12	Viscount Althorp (afterwards Earl Spencer)	3,450	3,423	–	27
1912–21	Lord Sandhurst (afterwards Viscount Sandhurst)	7,912	7,861	11	40
1921–22	Duke of Atholl	669	653	1	15
1922–38	Earl of Cromer	12,885	12,609	80	196
1938–52	Earl of Clarendon	13,589	13,376	134	79
1952–63	Earl of Scarbrough	10,219	10,110	79	30
1963–68	Lord Cobbold	4,405	4,347	47	11
	TOTALS	56,157	55,394	352	411

Notes

1. No details of 'Waiting Box' plays before 1913
2. Over the period of sixty-nine years the annual average was:
   Licensed 800
   Refused a licence 6
3. The greatest number of plays licensed in one year was 1,314 in 1950.

Index

Italicised numbers represent illustrations. The abbreviation LC = Lord Chamberlain

INDEX

Index

Index